W9-BZG-292

The Scope of History

The Scope of History explains how the Alfonsine histories became well-fashioned and independent works of literature, having begun as simple compilations of preexisting texts. The author seeks to point out that the editors of the Alfonsine histories amplify and alter their sources, rejoin them with artistic skill, and generally arrange the elements into an ordered system. In so doing, Fraker explains, the final text speaks uniquely, giving voice to themes alien to the original texts. Fraker also aims to illustrate the scope of the editorial labor that sets Alfonso's *General estoria* and his *Estoria de Espanna* apart from their contemporary histories.

The Scope of History is a collection of eight essays written by Charles F. Fraker between 1974 and 1991. To these works he has added four new pieces: a general introduction and three prefaces to accompany the essays as he has grouped them. This collection reflects the durable nature of Fraker's work, which has been characterized as vitally important to the field of Castilian history, focusing on the historiography of Alfonso X of Castile.

The author dedicates his introduction to addressing the place of Alfonso's works in their own time, giving the reader a notion of what other works in the genre were like and how they differ. The first and second of the essays are partly about a lost epic song prosified in Alfonso's history of Spain, and they include a *cantar* very much like the story of King Lear and a passage on the rivalry between Pompey and Julius Caesar. The next group also deals with Roman themes, but two of the essays also address questions of literary influence, and all three touch on Alfonso's views on statecraft and policy. The final three essays in the collection are on the Hermetic component in Alfonso's histories and, in particular, on the large role assigned to astronomy and astrology in the Alfonsine view of the world.

The Scope of History

Studies in the Historiography of
Alfonso el Sabio

Charles F. Fraker

Ann Arbor

THE UNIVERSITY OF MICHIGAN PRESS

Copyright © by the University of Michigan 1996
All rights reserved
Published in the United States of America by
The University of Michigan Press
Manufactured in the United States of America
⊗ Printed on acid-free paper

1999 1998 1997 1996   4 3 2 1

No part of this publication may be reproduced, stored in a retrieval
system, or transmitted in any form or by any means, electronic,
mechanical, or otherwise without the written permission of the
publisher.

A CIP catalog record for this book is available from the British Library.

Library of Congress Cataloging-in-Publication Data

Fraker, Charles F.
   The scope of history : studies in the historiography of Alfonso el
Sabio / Charles F. Fraker.
         p.   cm.
   "This book is primarily a collection of my essays published
between 1974 and 1991 on the historiography of Alfonso the Learned
of Castile"—Introd.
   Includes bibliographical references (p.   ) and index.
   ISBN 0-472-10669-4 (hardcover : alk. paper)
   1. Alfonso X, King of Castile and Leon, 1221–1284. Primera
crónica general. 2. Alfonso X, King of Castile and Leon,
1221–1284. General estoria. 3. Spain—Historiography. 4. World
history. 5. Historiography. I. Title.
DP64.F73 1996
907'.2046—dc20   96-10298
                                                              CIP

Preface

This volume contains my essays published between 1974 and 1991 on the two historical compilations of Alfonso X of Castile and on related matters. I have added translations of the material in Spanish, Italian, and Old French and have made a few small changes that I hope will make the old articles more at home in their new setting; in no case do these alterations affect the substance of those writings. I am including also four completely new pieces, designed to guide the less specialized reader through my older essays. The translations are mine; they are more free than literal, and they aim at clarity, comprehensibility, and fidelity to the spirit, if not to the letter.

I wish to express my thanks to Professor Sabine MacCormack, whose idea this collection was, and who has encouraged me greatly in this project. Thanks are also due to the members of the staff at the University of Michigan Press who had a hand in preparing this book, not only for their efficiency but for their courtesy and kindness. I must express special gratitude to my wife, Doris, my personal copyeditor and one of the most rigorous proofreaders I have ever met.

Acknowledgments

Grateful acknowledgment is made to the following publishers and journals for permission to reprint previously published materials written by Charles F. Fraker.

Department of Romance Languages and Literatures, Harvard University for "Abraham in the *General estoria*." *Alfonso X of Castile, the Learned King (1221–1284): An International Symposium,* edited by Francisco Márquez Villanueva and Carlos Alberto Vega, 17–29. Harvard University, 17 November, 1984.

Bulletin of Hispanic Studies for "Alfonso X, the Empire and the *Primera crónica.*" *Bulletin of Hispanic Studies* 55 (1978): 95–102.

La Corónica for "The Beginning of the *Cantar de Sancho.*" *La Corónica* 19 (1990): 5–21.

Dispositio for "Scipio, and the Origins of Culture: The Question of Alfonso's Sources." *Dispositio* 10 (1987): 15–27.

Exemplaria Hispanica for "The *General estoria:* Material Culture and Hermeticism." *Exemplaria Hispanica* 1 (1991–92): 38–57.

Hispanic Review for "The *Fet des romains* and the *Primera crónica general.*" *Hispanic Review* 46 (1978): 199–220.

Franz Steiner Verlag for "A Hermetic Theme in the *General estoria.*" In *Homenaje a Hans Flasche: Festschrift zum 80. Geburtstag am 25. November 1991,* edited by Karl-Hermann Körner and Günther Zimmermann. 257–68. Franz Steiner, 1991.

Romania for "Sancho II: Epic and Chronicle." *Romania* 95 (1974): 467–507.

Every effort has been made to trace the ownership of all copyrighted materials in this book and to obtain permission for their use.

Contents

Introduction

This book is primarily a collection of my essays published between 1974 and 1991 on the historiography of Alfonso the Learned of Castile. One article presented here may seem to be completely out of place; it is not on Alfonso but on epic poetry, on a group of medieval chansons de geste. I felt it necessary to include this piece because of what seemed to me to be an inaccuracy in my first essay, part of which happens to be on questions of epic. The three essays following this pair are mainly on Alfonso's treatment of Roman themes. One deals with his presentation of Scipio Africanus; the other two have to do in one way or another with Alfonso's concept of empire. The last group of three papers all center their arguments on an astonishing set piece, a notoriously unmedieval history of religion, which is included in the first part of Alfonso's universal chronicle.

Learned articles submitted to journals, Festschriften, and the like, even at their best, surely belong to a flawed species. They are by their very nature limited and local, and they do not often look beyond their own narrow provinces. What is more, such pieces are essentially timely and occasional; they speak to issues that are alive and interesting for one season only. The essays assembled here are not exceptions to either rule. It is useless to pretend that by themselves a collection of such pieces makes up very much of a book. I have therefore added some material that, I hope, will salvage these *disiecta membra* of mine and give this volume a tidier look. Aside from this present general introduction, I have written three shorter pieces, each of which will preface one group of the articles. All of these are intended to guide the reader to and from the remote areas covered by the essays themselves. My wish in particular is that these new pages will make nonspecialists and non-Hispanists feel at their ease. Alfonso's historical texts are valuable and interesting in absolute terms, but my essays about them, which were addressed to a narrow audience, are not especially tactful to outsiders. I offer the new pages as a remedy for this shortcoming. I would guess that at the least a few lines of commentary would do no harm either to my readers or to my writings.

In this general introduction I will begin by describing in broad terms Alfonso's two great historical works,[1] and I will continue by trying to formulate a poetics of the medieval historical compilation as a whole and of Alfonso's historiography in particular. As we know, the Learned King of Castile presided over the composition of two remarkable texts, the *Estoria de Espanna,* a history of Spain, and the *General estoria,* a universal history. Both these works are compilations; that is to say, they are cut-and-paste jobs, mosaics of existing texts. What is more, both histories are made up largely of translations. Alfonso's language is Castilian, but his sources are nearly all in other languages, principally in Latin. Readers may wonder from the first why writings like these, which are in no obvious way original, deserve much attention of any sort, even on the part of specialists. The essays that follow are in effect a response to this challenge; each in its way tries to show how the Alfonsine editors shaped and manipulated their material to make it yield the themes that interested them. But even in general terms it is not difficult to say what is remarkable about Alfonso's work, or, more narrowly, what exactly it is that rescues it from mediocrity. The compilers' art, in a word, is not contemptible: it is powerful and subtle. The editor confronted by his sources and *auctores* need not feel at a loss. One should emphasize strongly, however, that these, his authorities, are more or less a given; he does not ordinarily choose them, and only occasionally may he shape his product by preferring one *auctor* over another. The compilers' ideal, indeed, is not selection but inclusion; compilers would like to put into their text everything they have available. But they have many other

---

1. In these pages I do not plan to survey in any breadth or detail the acres of writings about Alfonso X and his two histories or to consider any great number of the standing problems they pose to the scholar. My argument will be limited, and my aims are more than anything else practical. Readers unfamiliar with things Alfonsine could profitably look at Rico 1972 and Márquez Villanueva 1994. The best account of the two Alfonsine histories, their sources and their structure, is Fernández-Ordóñez 1992. Indispensable for an understanding of the history of the composition of the *Estoria de Espanna* and its branches and continuations is Catalán 1962, 17–203.

areas of freedom. They may, for example, combine their *auctores* and splice them together as they like. Many of the liveliest and most striking narratives in Alfonso's histories are actually artful combinations and permutations of preexisting bits. The possibilities the Alfonsines actually exploit are very broad. Translation, for example, is a powerful tool. More than once, a compiler's version of a Latin source specifies only a little more than does its original, and yet, that new small element will carry the text to regions undreamed of by the first author. Finally, there is the original part, the editors' own words, transitional sentences, introductory phrases, short explanations and expansions, and, indeed, occasional extended texts. These are perhaps the most decisive of all in the construction of the Alfonsine histories; the editors' own words are powerful in setting the context, such that the inherited matter that surrounds them can take on the meanings the compilers wish them to have.

The two Alfonsine histories are fully independent texts (Fernández Ordoñez 1992, 71–158); their differences go far beyond the fact that they have different subject matters. It is important to stress these differences, because of the texts' obvious similarities. It was their fate to be similar. The two were composed in the same place and at roughly the same time, and one can only guess that the members of the teams that produced each were known to each other, if, indeed, they were different in person. In any case, traces of their interaction are everywhere. The *Estoria de Espanna* and the *General estoria* were, of course, years in the making, and there is plain evidence that, as the work progressed, in leapfrog fashion, on the two, each lent material to the other. Translations were shared by the two projects; there is even good reason to believe that certain source texts in languages other than Castilian were turned into Alfonso's vernacular entire, to be available to the composers of either text. These are strong links. But despite all of that, the *Estoria de Espanna* and the *General estoria* are quite unlike, both in large outline and in detail. The fundamental differences are legion. The Spanish history is largely annalistic, while the universal one measures time with dates more widely scattered. The actual order of events in each is different with respect to chronology; in the narrative of the *General estoria* there are more leaps in time backward and forward than in its companion. The translations in the Spanish history are freer and more adventuresome than in the universal. The piece of evidence above all that tells us that the two histories are intentionally different is that some of the historical events recounted in both are narrated in the two in totally different ways, as though each body of editors had forgotten the existence of the other. The most notorious case in point is the treatment the two histories make of the Roman Civil War, the conflict between Pompey and Julius Caesar. The *General estoria* gives us Lucan's *Pharsalia* whole in a virtually complete translation, whereas the *Estoria de Espanna* has an independent narrative, a well-constructed composite of several sources. The focus and emphasis of the two passages are not at all alike.

Neither of the two histories is complete. The *General estoria* covers the period from the Creation to shortly before the birth of Christ; one could have expected it to continue into more modern times. Even as it stands the work is far from being a polished whole; it has its gaps, and there are passages that are fragmentary and that show every sign of being little more than drafts and sketches. The *Estoria de Espanna* for its part is complete to a time shortly after the Moorish conquest, but there also exist extensive drafts and reworkings covering later periods. The text edited by Menéndez Pidal with the title *Primera crónica general de España* (First general chronicle of Spain) includes all of the extant *Estoria de Espanna* and a large portion of the provisional material. The *General estoria* is, as we have seen, a universal chronicle. It is laid out according to Augustine's scheme of world history, divided into six ages. The large text is best described as a heavily amplified biblical history. The skeleton narrative is that of the Bible supported by elements out of Josephus's *Antiquities of the Jews* and of the twelfth-century biblical summa, Petrus Comestor's *Historia scholastica*. The long histories of the Gentile nations are fitted into the biblical framework as chronology demands.

The *General estoria* is a secular history. Obviously, a historical text that draws much of its material from the Bible must admit narratives and narrative motifs that refer to supernatural events, miracles, visions, and the like. But in the *General estoria* most of these elements belong to sacred history proper, and even these are momentary and local. Generally speaking, happenings in the narrative are moved along not by the hand of Providence but by natural, this-worldly causes. We may dramatize this nondivine character of the narration in the *General estoria* by focusing on the role within it of an institution close to the heart of Alfonso X of Castile, the empire. In his mind and that of his contemporaries the empire was a living reality: the royal line represented by the seated German emperor went back to Augustus or, as some thought, to

Julius Caesar, and it included Tiberius, Caligula, and the rest. What is more, Alfonso was, in his own mind and that of many others, the legitimate ruling emperor (O'Callaghan 1975, 371–75). In the ordinary sense, of course, he was the heir of Julius Caesar, but in the extraordinary account of the *General estoria* the Learned King had a still more remote predecessor, the "mighty hunter before the Lord," the biblical Nimrod (Gen. 10:8–9). This personage is for the compilers of the *General estoria* a major actor in history. Medievals, following Josephus's *Antiquities,* believed him to be the builder of the Tower of Babel.[2] The Alfonsines turned him into something equally important; he is for them the first world ruler, in effect the first emperor. One must explain. The imperial theme appears in the two histories in the form of the great myth of the *translatio imperii,* the passage in time of universal power from one people to another. In the *General estoria* this *translatio* is traced explicitly from Jupiter, King of Thebes, to Alfonso's predecessor on the imperial throne, Frederick II: the line runs from Jupiter through Alexander the Great and the Caesars down to the two Fredericks (Alfonso 1930, 200–201). But Jupiter's predecessor Nimrod himself is also explicitly linked to the idea of empire. And here is the surprise. The connection made in the passage tells us how very earthbound the Alfonsine notion of history really is. How is Nimrod catapulted into greatness? What force or forces thrust him into such an important time and place in history? The Alfonsines' answer is astonishing. It is not God but the stars. Nimrod, set on acquiring power, consults the all-wise astrologer Yonitho (in Spanish, Yonito). The latter, drawing on his knowledge of the heavens, tells him what they had disposed: that, of the four parts of the world, the Western—that is, Europe—was the noblest; that it would in time conquer the other three; and that it would establish a world order that would last forever (Alfonso 1930, 72). Medievals of course believed that the Roman Empire—that is, the German—would never die, and so the allusion to empire in this text is absolutely clear. In the view expressed in this passage it is not God acting directly but his ministers, the stars, that determine and shape the existence of empire. Now surely, a historical vision that attributes to nature, that is, to the stars, the continuous being of such an important institution, a view that in the short run at least denies God a direct role in its formation, is not in the ordinary sense of

---

2. Josephus, bk. 1, chap. 4; Petrus Comestor 1855, cols. 1088–89; Alfonso 1930, 42.

the word providentialist. We may generalize. With a few notable exceptions the Alfonsine editors do not attribute the great events on earth to
the hand of God. The role of Nimrod in the text is symptomatic.

Much of the material recounted in the *General estoria* is by our standards legendary, and the editors make absolutely no distinction between
what for moderns might be history and what fable. For the Alfonsines
Hercules is just as historical as Julius Caesar. The story of the Trojan
War forms a large subsection of the second part and is one of the most
important portions of the history. The account of Alexander the Great, a
fine mixture of what is for us sober history with the purest fiction, figures
large in part 4. The Alfonsines' tolerance for myth and legend for its part
runs parallel to their choice of sources. Many of the authorities they cite
are by our standards not history at all. Poetry makes a large contribution: Lucan's *Pharsalia* is a major source, and even vernacular poetic
texts like the Spanish *Libro de Alexandre*[3] and the French prose version
of the poetic *Roman de Thèbes* (Kiddle 1936, 1938) have their place in
the makeup of the history and keep company with more sober writings
more generally regarded as historical. But even here we must be cautious. Earlier historians are as hospitable to legendary matter as are the
Alfonsines, and many of the most fantastic motifs and narratives in the
General estoria come to it from works that are anything but poetic.

The most notorious case of both an unlikely source and what, by
modern standards, is unquestionably nonhistory is Ovid, a major con-
tributor to the Alfonsine *General estoria*. The *Heroides* are drawn on
regularly in the *General estoria* as the narrative demands. Direct discourse is not alien to the two histories, and the translations from Ovid
are among the most effective cases in point. Vastly more dramatic than
the editors' exploitation of the *Heroides,* however, is their use of the
Metamorphoses; a very large proportion of the myth narratives in that
work are translated whole in the *General estoria.* One should understand
that, on the one hand, history for medievals is assuredly not what it is for
us, and that, on the other, Ovid in the Middle Ages was in fact read in
ways that seem to us very strange. But there are limits: no one before
the Alfonsines ever regarded the *Metamorphoses* as a legitimate historical text. The inclusion of Ovidian narratives in the *General estoria* is thus

---

3. The *Libro de Alexandre*'s version of the judgment of Paris (stanzas 362–87) is the
source of the *Estoria*'s account (Alfonso 1957–61, 2:106–9); the observation was made by
Milagros Villar Rubio in her anthology of the *Estoria* (Alfonso 1984a, 301).

an extraordinary move, one that makes that work unique among medieval historical compilations. Every source in the Alfonsine text is of course an authority; that is what earns Orosius, Isidore, and the rest their place in the history. But the *Metamorphoses,* the *Libro mayor* in Alfonsine language, is set apart; it has among the *auctores* a special status. The compilers call it "la Biblia de los gentiles" [the Bible of the Gentiles] (Alfonso 1930, 162–63). It is for them a source of information about Gentile heroes analogous to the Bible for figures in sacred history. This special status should not mislead us.

The first point that has to be made about Ovid's inclusion in the *General estoria* is that he brings to the text not fantasy or fine phrases but information. In this sense his function in the history is identical to that of every other Alfonsine source. This includes the Bible; the term *Biblia de los gentiles* and the explicit analogy between Ovid and Scripture means simply that the Bible and the *Metamorphoses* are both large and authoritative encyclopedias, prestigious compendia of facts about certain individuals and peoples. That is the beginning and end of the matter. The last thing we should imagine is that with the two great texts aboard with all their weight of authority, the standards of history are somehow lowered to admit prodigies and wonders on every page. History is a sober business, and the Alfonsines know a fact when they see one. The editors of the *General estoria* have a very clear conception of the verisimilar, that is, of what is factual. Their notion is assuredly not ours: in the biblical passages, the compilers allow for occasional interventions of the divine; in the nonbiblical stretches, they assume the efficacy of magic, and the text in fact explains many of the fantastic or anomalous motifs in their sources by an allusion to this art. But generally speaking, the storytelling in the *General estoria* is sober, plausible, well motivated, believable, and, to our eyes, nonfantastic. This sobriety in the biblical passages is traceable to the editors' deep respect for the literal sense of Scripture. The mythical matter in Alfonso is for its part subject to all sorts of modifications and reworkings; the treatment of the stories from the *Metamorphoses* represents one special case among these possibilities.

The editors' procedure with Ovid is uniform. They begin by presenting the Ovidian passage in a fairly accurate translation. Alfonsine versions of Latin texts tend to be rather free, but in the case of Ovid we can say that the narrative is largely unaltered and that the fantastic elements are left in place. Ovid plain is then followed by a detailed euhemeristic commentary. Euhemerism is the practice of interpreting and reducing myths to make them refer to purely human events; more particularly it consists of recasting legends about gods into stories about mortal men and women. Ovid says that the king of the gods was able to carry off Europa by taking on the appearance of a bull. The *General estoria* tells us the real truth. A purely human and mortal Jupiter carried away Europa on a ship that was named the *Bull,* or, possibly, one that had a bull represented on its figurehead (Alfonso 1957–61, 1:54–56, 58–59). This is the pattern: an Ovidian sandwich, with one layer of genuine Ovid and another of prose and plausibility. In this remarkable way, therefore, the most unlikely and intractable source used by the Alfonsine editors is brought into line and is made to yield what was to their mind genuine history. There is no need in a summary like this one to identify every source in the *General estoria.* Suffice it to say that the text attributes its euhemeristic Ovid commentaries alternately to "el frayre" [the friar] and to "Johan el ingles" [John the Englishman]. As matters stand now, we cannot say exactly what text the editors were using that cited these authorities. "Johan el ingles" is most probably John of Garland, but the poor "frayre" leaves us at a loss. The fact is that the euhemeristic glosses in Alfonso coincide almost completely with those of Arnulf of Orléans, who is almost certainly their real source. How exactly they came to be connected with the names in Alfonso is a question that need not concern us.[4]

We turn now to the *Estoria de Espanna.* Alfonso's Spanish history has a structure that is highly original. It is in effect a series of histories, one each devoted to the affairs of each of the peoples and successions that ruled Spain. The first of these is Hercules and his line. These are followed by the "almujuces," not really Vikings but a generic northern people as conceived by Arab historians (Fernández Ordóñez 1992, 198–200). Then come, in order, the Carthaginians, the Romans, a group of lesser Germanic peoples, and, finally, the Goths. The Roman section includes a virtually independent imperial history, one that, oddly enough, makes little mention of Spain or of things Spanish. The presence of this apparently alien material in the *Estoria de Espanna* is best explained by the Learned King's own interest in the empire and by his own claim to the

---

4. Arnulf's glosses are to be found in Ghisalberti 1932; the whole question of their attribution in Alfonso to "el frayre" and to "Johan el ingles" is treated in Ginzler 1971, 15–19.

imperial throne; as we recall, the German line and the Roman, that of the Caesars, are to the mind of medievals one and the same. This whole matter of Alfonso and the empire is the subject of two of the essays in this book. The Gothic section, as I have said, runs to the end of the extant *Estoria de Espanna,* and it is obvious from the fragments that remain of the rest of the work that the Gothic section was meant to extend to the end of the chronicle as projected, to the reign in Castile of Alfonso's father Ferdinand III and perhaps to that of the Learned King himself. To modern readers this will seem anomalous; one would have to conclude that in Alfonsine terms the Ferdinands, Ramiros, and Ordoños are Goths along with Recared and Tulga. But this is exactly the intention of the editors; there is a long-standing tradition in Spanish historiography, one that gives the same afterlife to the Gothic succession of the kings of post-Gothic Spain that Alfonso and many others give to the Roman Empire in Germany. On this premise Roderick is not the last Goth to rule Spain; he is succeeded by Pelagius (in Spanish, Pelayo), legendary hero of the Reconquest, and then in an unbroken line by all the Ramiros and Alfonsos down to the time of the kings of the historians' own day. Alfonso and his histories are entirely within the tradition, both by the editors' choice and because their sources preserve the pattern I describe. One of the strangest corollaries of the Gothic hypothesis as I describe it is that the Moorish invasion and the Islamization of the peninsula are simply episodes or incidents in the Gothic era. Historians are forced to admit that at one point the Gothic domain is nothing more than a tiny string of Christian kingdoms in the north of the peninsula, but this for them did not make that heritage less real; the Reconquest that followed that unhappy moment of Christendom was a splendid restoration of Gothic dignity and power.

The unique structure of the *Estoria de Espanna* as a series of histories is not really comprehensible unless we take into account one of its most important sources, the historical writings of Rodrigo Jiménez de Rada, known as Rodrigo Toledano, the archbishop of Toledo in the time of Ferdinand III. His corpus consists of a series of historical writings on Spanish subjects. The most extensive and most important of these is a global history of Spain. Significantly, the work's alternative titles are *De rebus Hispaniae* and *Historia gothica.* The work realizes the Gothic thesis fully. For Rodrigo the history of Spain begins with the rise of Gothic power in Europe and continues as the Goths establish themselves in Spain and rule the peninsula for centuries. The Moorish

invasion is of course presented as a genuine disaster but is in no way an
interruption of the Gothic succcession and its unfailing right to rule
Spain. The Reconquest vindicates this right, and Rodrigo has no hesitation in calling the first two Sanchos, Ferdinand the Great, and other
Spanish kings Goths with full title. Rodrigo's other writings are an-
cillae, as it were, to the *De rebus*. Each tells of the rule in Spain of a
non-Gothic people. The miniscule *Historia romana* is a history of Rome
in Spain; the longer *Historia arabum* likewise limits itself to Arab and
Muslim doings in the peninsula.[5] So it is with the other short treatises.
Now all of these texts are included in the *Estoria de Espanna* and its
continuations; very little of any of these works is left out. The *De rebus*,
by far the longest of these histories, forms the backbone of the Gothic
section of Alfonso's work, including the provisional material. There are
many chapters of the *Estoria de Espanna* that are little more than
translations of the Latin work. As a major source, then, Rodrigo's
writings cast a long shadow on Alfonso's great project. But more important, perhaps, the whole large plan of the *Estoria de Espanna* borrows
its design from Rodrigo; it is hard to imagine the Alfonsines forming
their large Spanish text as a series of shorter histories had they not had
before them the model of the *De rebus* and its satellites.

As we have seen, both the *General estoria* and the *Estoria de Espanna,*
along with its continuations, are compilations. This is where our study of
Alfonso's histories should begin; we must start with a description of the
historical compilation as a literary kind. Needless to say, Alfonso's two
historical texts are not the first works of this sort in the Middle Ages, nor
are they the last. Composite histories like Alfonso's were written over a
long period, from many years before his time to well into the sixteenth
century. Grammarians who are called on to produce such a work assemble
all the texts available to them on their subject and then sew the texts
together to form a more or less continuous narrative. Originality is not
ordinarily the grammarians' object. They leave long stretches of their text
in the words of others, and only exceptionally do they make any effort to
assemble their material in a distinctive way. Historical compilations tend
to resemble each other. This is especially true of the ones that happen to
be universal histories. It is not an exaggeration to say that works in this
large subgroup look and feel like variants of a single text, especially in

---

5. Rodrigo Toledano 1793 contains all of Rodrigo's histories; Rodrigo Toledano 1987 is
a critical edition of the *De rebus Hispaniae*.

their earlier portions. Other nonuniversal compilations, those that are primarily local histories—chronicles of a single kingdom or dynasty, for example—are of course a much less compact group, although it must be said that many of these begin as universal histories and narrow their scope only relatively late in their text. This, incidentally, cannot be said of the *Estoria de Espanna*, which is Spanish almost from the start; its universal section occupies only a very few pages in the text.

The literary source for the chronology in the universal history is always the same. It is the *Chronici canones* of the Greek Church historian Eusebius, turned into Latin and extended by St. Jerome (Eusebius 1923). The *Chronici canones* is not a continuous narrative and is therefore hardly a work of history in the ordinary sense. It is rather a sort of extended chart or table with parallel columns, one each for events in the history of various peoples; one column is given over to the Hebrews, another to the Assyrians, and so forth. The basic chronology is drawn from the Bible, and the dates of nonbiblical events are fitted into the biblical framework. If, for example, the Alfonsine *General estoria* tells us that the Greeks besieged Troy while Ibzan (in Alfonso, Esebon) was judge in Israel, we can be almost certain that the work's compilers are depending on Eusebius-Jerome.[6] One should add that the *Chronici canones* also often supplies the chronology for local histories; long sections of the *Estoria de Espanna,* for example, depend on Eusebius and his continuers.

We must understand that the sources of the compilation are *auctores,* at least in the broad sense, and that their *auctoritas,* individually and collectively, is the one and only guarantor of the truth of the stories they tell. There is no other, no appeal to "what really happened"; no document in an archive can be invoked to prove this *auctor* right and that one wrong. There is no sailing upstream from the words of Orosius or Josephus, once they are set down in a compiler's text. When a thirteenth- or fourteenth-century person picked up the *Estoria de Espanna,* or had it read to him or her, and was informed that Hercules was the first king of Spain, what assured such a one that this was indeed the case? The answer is simple: it was the authority of the chronicle's sources. There are, of course, cases in which the compilation's *auctores* are at odds with each other, and on these occasions the editor himself may wish to adjudicate

---

6. Eusebius 1923, 96–97; Alfonso 1957–61, 2:48. Both Eusebius-Jerome and Alfonso call Ibzan "Esebon"; the Vulgate calls him "Abesan" (Judges 12:8).

the differences. But practically never do compilers go behind their
sources to justify them; they do not try to verify the information that
comes to them from Orosius or Comestor. Authority is a yes or no affair.
The text that has it possesses it 100 percent. This means that all the
selections that make up a historical compilation function there in exactly
the same way. All are truthful, all equally valuable; all are on the same
level. This whole pattern produces for the modern reader anomalies of
the most extreme sort. Orosius is not the greatest of historians; he is not
Tacitus or Thucydides. But he does draw on unexceptionable sources,
and in broad terms the material he presents on events in the Greco-
Roman world is accurate. How, then, can the Alfonsine compilers grant
the same pride of place they concede to Orosius to, shall we say, the
chronologies of Eusebius-Jerome, in which Prometheus, Atlas, and
Ceres are presented as entirely historical beings, on a par with Julius
Caesar? And yet, this is exactly the system of the *General estoria* and the
Estoria de Espanna. The prejudice and the difficulty are ours.

The issue of authority is not simply the concern of chroniclers and
historians; it is basic to the literary practice of a whole age. The *auctores*
whose texts appear in chronicles are not the only ones who possess
auctoritas; all of them do, whichever list they are on, whatever literary
works they are cited in. Curtius spoke of all this years ago, of the
authority of authors, of their equality (that is, the fact that an Arator
had the same weight as a Virgil or a Cicero), of their timelessness, of the
fact that their authority was the basis for general knowledge and culture
(Curtius 1953, 49, 51, 52, 57–58). There is little mystery in all this; the
supporting evidence is everywhere. As I say, the authors who appear in
historical compilations have no monopoly on authority, but for a fact,
histories and chronicles do make the case very eloquently for the power
of *auctoritas.* Consider the makeup of the historical texts themselves.
Except in the most marginal of cases editors of compilations do not
intervene to qualify or evaluate their sources. None, for example, develops a case on Orosius, telling us how accurate he is or what his special
perspective might be. Neither do compilers tell us that Eutropius was a
zealous forager in archives (which he was not). The composers of the
history are completely silent about their authors, and this is because they
have nothing whatever to add to what the authors have to say. And on
the other hand, the very way the grammarians—that is to say, the teachers of literature—present their *auctores* tells us plainly all we need to

know about their self-sufficiency. The *accessus*[7] are, of course, the pro-
logues the *grammatici* attach to their authors. In many cases this is the
grammarian's first word of many: this composition is often the first item
in the master's commentary or set of glosses on the text. Now, the
accessus and its contents offer the modern reader a unique and privileged way to learn what medievals thought about their authors. In its
most characteristic and best-known form this conventional prologue is
built around a series of topics for the description of literary texts, title of
the work in question, the life of its author, its matter, intention, utility,
quality—something like literary genre—and, finally, the part of philosophy to which it belongs. Philosophy, as we should note, is made up of the
seven liberal arts, ethics, physics or medicine, and perhaps metaphysics
or theology. What to modern readers is most stiking about the *accessus*
themselves is their uniform optimism, the certainty they express that the
works they introduce are indeed useful, that they surely will instruct us
in astronomy, medicine, or grammar. "Philosophy" and its parts are the
same as knowledge simply, and the different areas of this totality are
easily specified. The *auctores,* therefore, are the transparent mediums
through which we may see and grasp the particular, fully specified part
of knowledge in which the *auctores* are supposed to specialize. On this
premise, as we can see, not only do the *auctores* possess *auctoritas;* that
is all the *auctores* possess. In other words, the *auctores* are identified
with that *auctoritas* and have no being outside it. The names of the
auctores authorize the information or doctrine the *auctores* convey, and
that is the *auctores'* whole function.

Accessus shed light in particular on the practice of historians and
historical compilers as we have described them. We may in this respect
ask two questions. First, what for the *grammatici* of the twelfth century
constitutes a historical fact? Second, which *auctores* are able to validate
such a fact? A partial answer to both questions can be found in the
accessus that accompany the narrative poets. Lucan, as we read, is not a
pure poet but part poet and part historian. He is thus in contrast to
Terence, who is pure comic, or with Juvenal, who is pure satirist (Arnulf
1958, 4). So runs one prologue. To modern eyes this makes sense, since
the *Pharsalia* deals with what for us are the real events of the Roman

---

7. Quinn 1945 and Hunt 1948 give us a fine account of the several species of the genus
accessus and how they succeed each other in time.

Civil War. It is significant that this *accessus* and one other on Lucan's poem both rehearse some of the main happenings of the conflict, including some that are not in the *Pharsalia* (Arnulf 1958, 4–5, Huygens 1970, 39–43). This confirms our impression that for the twelfth-century grammarian the war was quite real and that Lucan's poem was admirable, because it narrated in its way a fully real occurrence.

The term that contrasts with *historia* is *fictio*. An *accessus* to Horace's *Ars poetica* tells us that the true vocation of the poet is to invent *fictiones* (Huygens 1970, 51). The reason why Lucan is a *poeta mixtus* is that the *Pharsalia* contains elements of both history and fiction. But where do the grammarians draw the line between the two categories? The answer may surprise us. The supposed events of Achilles' youth—the fact that he was disguised as a girl and that his true sex and vocation were revealed only when he saw arms, the tools of war, for the first time—are as historical as Caesar crossing the Rubicon. This and nothing else is what is implied by an *accessus* to Statius's *Achilleid,* which states that the *utilitas* of the poem is precisely "cognicio gestorum Achillis" [knowledge of the deeds of Achilles] (Statius 1968, 21). Statius too must be a *poeta mixtus,* since the grammarian throughout his short text applies the word *ystoria* to the poem (Statius 1968, 22–23). In a word, history ranges wide. The heroes of the Trojan War or of the tragedy at Thebes, figures evoked by the poets in the twelfth-century canon, are fully "historical." Lest we imagine that these notions are the affair of a handful of obscure scholars, let us turn to an author as familiar—and, indeed, as late—as Dante. In the second book of the *Monarchia,* Dante develops the view that Rome occupied a unique place in the designs of Providence. Virgil's *Aeneid* is referred to and quoted many times in these pages, and there is no evidence whatever that Dante's attitude toward the poet and his work was in any way different from that of our grammarian with regard to Statius and his *Achilleid.* The events in the *Aeneid* are simply true. Dante, to be sure, shows great interest in the material in book 6, in which Anchises foretells the greatness of Rome—in other words, reviews Roman history up to and including the reign of Augustus. But the later poet's faith in the earlier is not restricted to these elements. For Dante, most of the events recounted in all twelve books are genuinely historical. Anchises himself is real, as are all the events of the Trojan War and of Aeneas's founding of Rome.

In a word, the welcome the authors of compilations afford Prometheus, Hercules, or Saturn is not a fluke; the total respect these editors show Eusebius and the others who purvey information about these figures is in no way whatever peculiar to them. The reverence for *auctores* and their *auctoritas* was simply universal.

I have insisted from the first that the two Alfonsine histories are distinctive, that they are unique within the genre. I have argued in particular that what set the two histories apart was the total independence of the editors before their *auctores,* the fact that the compilers, so to speak, bent their material to make it serve their own interests and intentions. There are other features that separate the two *Estorias* from their fellows. For one thing, the two works are exceptionally long, and the repertory of sources of each is unusually large. Most notably, perhaps, both works draw on Arabic materials, the *General estoria* extensively (Fernández-Ordóñez 1992, 173–203). But the differences in general between the Alfonsine histories and the others should not be exaggerated. The description I have made of the compilation as a genre fits the two *Estorias* very adequately. The *Chronici canones* sets the time scheme for both; the same mix of Orosius, Eutropius, and the rest carries the burden of the narrative over long stretches of the text. Some episodes in Alfonso are told in much the same way as they are in other histories. The Alfonsines' independence and freedom notwithstanding, authority has the same force in their work as it does in that of other compilers; the very layout of the material in the two Spanish histories makes it clear that the editors regard their *auctores* as the *fons et origo* of historical truth.

On the other hand, the non-Alfonsine compilations are far from identical, common elements notwithstanding. I have suggested that universal chronicles tend to become more unalike as the narrative moves closer to the editors' own times. Lucas of Tuy's *Chronicon mundi* (ca. 1230; see Linehan 1993, 357), surely a universal chronicle over much of its text, becomes in its later pages a genuine history of Spain, particularly a chronicle of the Leonese monarchy. The Frutolf-Ekkehard chronicle, composed in the early twelfth century (Thompson 1942, 191–92), also surveys new territory in its later pages. Frutolf is the first editor, Ekkehard his successor. Both write about the investiture controversy, but from opposite points of view; Frutolf is favorable to Henry IV, Ekkehard to Hildebrand. In Ekkehard the great events of the day are recounted in his own words; there pass in review the investiture affair, the Crusades, and happenings in France, England, and Italy. Otto of Freising for his part incorporates much of Frutolf and Ekkehard into his own work; he is in this respect a compiler like any other. But his

Chronicon also goes its own way. Otto, the uncle of Frederick Barbarossa, is a privileged witness to the events of his day and is an eloquent commentator on the civil and religious dramas that unfolded before him. As his twofold status as churchman and person of royal blood would suggest, his view of investiture is complex; at some points he favors the imperial cause, and at others the papal. Otto ranges far. His new material is not restricted to the last books of his history. Indeed, the texts he is most famous for, the ones that expound his theology of history, are scattered throughout the work. He interrupts his narrative from time to time and introduces chapters that comment on and interpret the events retold in his preceding pages. These nonnarrative passages taken together set forth his unique view of the role of Providence in human affairs, an Augustinian rehearsal of the character of the Two Cities, in which the City of God is boldly identified with determinate events and institutions on earth.

Otto's work is perhaps the best known and the most provocative of what could be called the enhanced chronicles. The *Pantheon,* composed by Godfrey of Viterbo in about 1200 (Thompson 1942, 204), in the earlier sections gives us the usual Josephus, Orosius, and Isidore, but it includes a set of very characteristic narrative pieces of the author's own making, some of them in verse. The all-important sequence in the *General estoria* about Jupiter, king of Thebes and civilizing hero, is, for example, an amplified version of one of these pieces.[8] The omnipresent *Historia scholastica* of Petrus Comestor presents a very different picture. It too has the apparatus of the historical compilation: Eusebius, biblical material from Josephus, secular history from Orosius and Isidore—all according to the standard pattern. But the core and center of this extraordinary work is a very different project from that of most compilers. The *Historia scholastica* is first and foremost a running commentary on the narrative books of the Bible in their literal sense; the conventional elements of universal history are attached to this core. This biblical summa, as we could call it, is one of the most frequently copied books in the Middle Ages, one that is incorporated in turn in numberless other compilations, in large portions and small. The *Speculum historiale* of the Dominican Vincent of Beauvais, completed sometime after 1250, is perhaps the most normal of historical compilations, the one closest to the

---

8. See Godfrey 1726, 77–78; Alfonso 1930, 193–200.

ideal type. James Westfall Thompson points out the large proportion of nonnarrative matter in the *Speculum*—texts on the religions of ancient peoples, for example, or what could be called "cultural history" (Thompson 1942, 270). One could add that Vincent's work includes extensive material on Church history. As modern readers consume page after page, they are struck by the awkward leaps and gaps in the narrative between one excerpt and the next, even when these are on one subject. But this is, of course, the norm in works of this kind; they are designed as miscellanies, as collections of historical information, bound together only by chronology. The *Speculum* is in any case a splendid monument, a text that was read and studied well into the Renaissance and that enjoyed its last printing in the seventeenth century.

As we have seen, the art and practice of historical compilation was remarkably uniform throughout Europe. In this sense it seems hardly necessary to say how the pattern came to the Castile of Alfonso and his contemporaries. One could point out that the art of the Alfonsines was a subtle one, and that this fact by itself argued for the broad familiarity of its editors with the work of other compilers. But positive evidence is not lacking. Compilations were composed in Spain—not a few, but many. As I will show later in this volume, histories of Spain up to the thirteenth century were cumulative, each including material from its immediate predecessor. Lucas of Tuy's *Chronicon mundi,* a major source for both of Alfonso's histories, is the latest member of the series. It is also, of course, a normal and orthodox universal history, well within the law. One can hardly say that the Alfonsines were unfamiliar with such compositions. The two *Estorias* included them. Lucas's *Chronicon* is an obvious case in point; it is the Alfonsines' source for both Spanish history and ancient. Comestor's *Historia scholastica* is quoted rarely in the *Estoria de Espanna* but is central to the *General estoria.* Vincent's *Speculum historiale* carries the burden of the narrative over large portions of the Spanish history's imperial section (the one that rehearses the history of the empire, from its beginning in the time of Julius Caesar on, over more than 250 chapters). The splendor of this early portion of the section is, surely, the portraits of the emperors translated from Suetonius. But the editors do know Suetonius firsthand; he comes to them from Vincent (Donald 1943).

Alfonso's two histories are composed in a vernacular, Castilian. Many historical compilations are in Latin, but the two *Estorias* belong to a group of fair size that includes two Old French compilations that circulated widely, the *Orose en français,* a world history (not simply a translation of Orosius), and the *Fet des romains,* a life of Julius Caesar made up largely of Sallust, Lucan, Suetonius, and Caesar himself—the *Commentaries on the Gallic War.*[9] In many ways these vernacular compilations are similar to their Latin fellows, but in others they are quite different. The very fact that most of their source material is translated separates them from Latin compilations in ways other than the obvious. *Traduttore traditore;* translations always betray. One could say that the translator of a text has a program and an agenda unlike that of the author of his text, and that this difference inevitably shows. Motivations are always complex and hard to fathom, but on one level the program of the Alfonsine translators is hardly obscure: their aim is to make their end product as clear and as self-sufficient as possible. Ambiguities, ellipses, and anomalies are eliminated, complicated periphrases unraveled, and rhetorical tropes reduced to their plain sense, or at least identified. Causes must be specified: in cases in which the source text fails to tell us why something happens, the editor must fill the gap and give us the actor's motive for his or her deed or the circumstances that made the occurrence possible.

Here is a fair sample of Alfonsine editing. The original is in this case Orosius. Homer sometimes nods, as we know too well, and in this case so also does our Latin author. In this account Orgetorix, the Gallic chieftain, is about to meet Julius Caesar in a major encounter. So that the Gauls may not think of retreat, the great general orders them to burn their villages. But at the end of two battles it is Caesar who is the victor, and as our historian tells us, he sends the Gauls back to their lands. There the episode ends; Orosius seems to have forgotten that the defeated have nowhere to go (Orosius 6.7). The Alfonsine editors step into the breach. In their version Caesar sends his defeated enemies home to rebuild their villages and orders them to submit to the power of Rome (Alfonso 1955, 62). The absurdity in Orosius disappears; in the new version Caesar's charge to the Gauls makes full sense. In the bargain the text sounds two themes that are very pertinent to the large scheme of the *Estoria de Espanna.* The Roman sees to the population of desert places and so fulfills one of the duties of the medieval prince, and he augments Rome's territory and power—we must emphasize that the

---

9. *Li fet des romains* 1935. There is no modern edition of the *Orose en français;* see Meyer 1885. Meyer calls the *Orose* "Histoire ancienne jusquà César."

Estoria de Espanna is within limits quite as much a Roman history as it is a Spanish one.

So much for clarity and logic. But for Alfonso's text to be intelligible to a lay and Latinless audience it had to be not only clear but self-explanatory; it could assume no prior knowledge on their part. Difficult terms and concepts had to be defined, and historical, geographical, and mythical allusions had to be explained. We are told what a legion is (Alfonso 1955, 55); the triumph (in the Roman sense) is defined (57). We are informed that Memphis is a city in Egypt (78), and that Linus is of the lineage of Belus—"de linnage de Belo ell antigo" (Alfonso 1957–61, 1:141; the expression translates "Belide" in Ovid's *Heroides* 14.73). These expansions may be no more than a phrase, or they may fill a whole chapter. They are in any case omnipresent and, as a practical matter, leave the Alfonsine audience few obscurities to cope with.

Many medieval translations are like that, loaded down with explanation and supporting information. They are translations and something more; they preserve much of the substance of the original but take further steps to place the matter at hand within the reach of the unculti-vated reader/listener. The addendum could be described as a sort of a gloss, carrying the audience over the rough spots of the original. I must clarify that I do not speak of glosses lightly. Earlier on we considered the role of commentary, when we saw how the stories in the *Metamorphoses* were fitted into their new setting in the *General estoria*. We should understand, however, that in this case we are not dealing, as we were before, with double entries—the story as Ovid tells it and the event as it really happened—but with the explanatory phrase or paragraph, the small clarification, matter that in one way or another supports the text and makes it more accessible. This is, of course, precisely the scope of much late antique and medieval commentary or gloss. It has been pointed out that large portions of the *General estoria* are organized like a grammarian's *lectio,* in which the text of the poet being explicated alter-nates with the master's commentary (Rico 1972, 167–88). This is a very important generalization. It should be pointed out that it applies as much to the *Estoria de Espanna* as it does to the *General estoria*. Indeed, other medieval vernacular histories fit the pattern nicely, eminently the all-important *Fet des romains.*

It is important to realize that many details in Alfonso's two histories are actually glosses in the full and literal sense. Solalinde years ago pointed out that in the passages in the *Estoria de Espanna* that are based on Lucan there are many details that coincide with known commentaries on the *Pharsalia*. The identification of "Menphis de Egipto" is a case in point: Lucan has the place name, but the "de Egipto" is the word of the glossator.[10] I can cite a parallel instance, the Orpheus and Eurydice episode in the second part of the *General estoria* (Alfonso 1957–61, 1:320–24). The passage is a translation of the Orpheus episode in the *Metamorphoses* and is by Alfonsine standards a fairly close version of Ovid. We must emphasize that the Alfonsine editors go to some lengths to give their text uniformity of style—to disguise, as it were, the fact that their material comes from very dissimilar sources. This does not mean that their Lucan or Suetonius has wandered very far from the sense of the originals; the compilers reconcile these two interests, fidelity and uniformity, very well. In the case of the Orpheus passage we can say that, while it is true to the letter of Ovid, the style is in no significant way different from that of the surrounding matter, from other translations of Ovid in the *General estoria,* or from Alfonsine versions of other authors. The small modifications the original undergoes in the Spanish text are of the sort that we have been considering and are in any case absolutely normal for Alfonso. Within four of the six chapters of part 2 of the *General estoria,* I count no less than eighteen instances in which these innocent and inconspicuous additions coincide with some well-known glosses on the Orpheus story in the *Metamorphoses*. These come from an important medieval Ovid commentary known as the *Vulgate* (*Vulgate* 1991, 116–45). One should point out that in the first chapter of the series in the Spanish text a commentary is actually mentioned: "departe la glosa" [the gloss says] introduces an explanation of the curious phrase "pueblos liuianos" [light people] used to refer to the shades in the underworld. This plain reference to commentary, one of many in Alfonso, should leave us in no doubt that preexisting glosses like this one form part of the corpus of Alfonsine sources. It so happens that this gloss does not belong to the *Vulgate*. This fact, however, does not make my allusion to this commentary less significant. Late antique and medieval commentaries on canonical texts are generally not distinctive. They often copy

---

10. García Solalinde 1941, 239; see also Alfonso 1955, Pidal's index of sources, 2:lxxxiv. "Memphis" appears in Lucan 3.222, and Arnulf's commentary identifies Memphis as "a city in Egypt" (Arnulf 1958, 175). The *Fet des romains* makes the same expansion of Lucan (the prevailing source at this point) as do the Alfonsines, and in a note the editors cite a gloss as its source.

each other or, more properly, are cumulative, each borrowing glosses from its predecessor. The *Vulgate* is such a text and so also, almost certainly, is the one used by the compilers. The two, therefore, need not have been wholly unlike. And in any case, commentaries on a certain level—those on narrative poetry certainly—always tend to gloss the same kinds of details in their authors. As I have suggested, they explain mythological and historical allusions; earlier passages in the text are recalled; ellipses are filled in; paraphrases, simple and complex, are reduced; other rhetorical figures are pointed out and explicated; and causes and motives are proposed for actions in the story, when these seem to be required.

It is not far off the mark to assert that the aims of the Alfonsine translator and the commentator or glossator are one and the same. What, in the first place, is the grammarian's real function? It is to make a difficult text accessible to the student. The grammarian's commentary, if it is worth anything at all, has got to be clear and explicit. The poetry, the art, the complexity, and the erudition are all in the text, but it is the grammarian's calling to be prosaic and plain and to reduce the poem to terms the student can understand. Any reader who compares the material in the two *Estorias* with their sources should be easily convinced that their compilers were about more or less the same business as a good commentator. A modern student of Alfonso has said, in effect, that when compilers, independent of any source, expand on Comestor or add a phrase to Josephus, they are genuine glossators in their own right (Rico 1972, 167–88). It is certain that the editor's own productions along this line are scarcely different from the material taken from preexisting commentaries. Except for those cases in which the text speaks openly of the glosses being cited, the two species are exactly alike; the uninformed reader has no way of distinguishing between them. One can therefore only conclude that the genuine gloss, known to the compilers and actually incorporated into their text, was also for them an effective model to be exploited elsewhere in their work. The rapid alternation of narrative and comment that is universal in both histories is thus not a pattern of style hit on spontaneously but a conscious imitation of the ways of the grammarian.

In considering the glosses, genuine and simulated, in the two *Estorias,* I have not focused especially on the ones attached to any single kind of text as opposed to another; I have treated all glosses and commentaries alike, whether they accompanied poetic texts or historical or some other.

But obviously, we must distinguish. It should be emphasized first that in their role as glossators the compilers were in large part forced to be original. Ancient and medieval grammarians did not comment in black and white on every piece of writing that lay about, much less did they happen to add glosses to the very material the Alfonsine editors claimed for their histories. Given the plain intentions behind the two texts, therefore, the compilers were obliged to amplify and explain most of their texts on their own. When they did turn to existing commentary, their choices were by no means unlimited. Biblical commentary aside, their nonoriginal glosses, the ones the editors did not make up, belonged mostly to one species; they were largely the ones on ancient poetry, mainly on Ovid, Lucan, and Statius. But with regard to the *General estoria,* the Bible itself poses serious problems. How is Scripture treated in that work? How is the biblical text expanded and explained to make it suitable for the Alfonsine audience? Scripture and scriptural material make up a very large part of the *General estoria.* What are their fortunes? Do the editors graft existing biblical commentaries into their text? Do they invent some of their own? These questions are not frivolous. Biblical commentary has been a major industry in Christendom throughout its history, before and after Alfonso and his collaborators; we therefore can hardly avoid trying to gauge how and in what form this formidable tradition affected him and them.

In one sense biblical material is treated in Alfonso in much the same way as nonbiblical. Bible narratives come to the *General estoria* largely from three sources, the Bible itself and two sets of biblical paraphrases, the ones in Josephus's *Antiquities of the Jews* and those of Petrus Comestor's *Historia scholastica.* The Alfonsines do not treat any of these sources differently from the way they do Orosius or Lucas of Tuy. A dozen lines in Comestor turn into a whole chapter in the *General estoria.* Every virtuality in the original is realized, everything unexplained is explained, and nothing is left to the reader's imagination. In other words, the editors gloss their text heavily, and the glosses are their own. But homegrown commentary is not the only sort found in the *General estoria.* Existing biblical commentaries are named and cited frequently in the text—among others, those of Rabanus Maurus, Remigius of Auxerre, and Walafrid Strabo. Most often these texts are called on to explain difficult terms or to give the etymology of biblical names.

The first part of the *General estoria* offers us at one point an exposition of the name *Noema;* according to "the gloss," *Noema* means "will," and "will" in turn signifies "avarice" (Alfonso 1930, 15). The "glosa" cited here is the *Glossa ordinaria* of Walafrid Strabo (1879, column 101); the Alfonsines reproduce Strabo faithfully. This instance is significant. In Genesis 4 Noema, so called in the Vulgate (in Hebrew, Naamah), is the daughter of Lamech and the sister of Tubalcain. The *General estoria* adds that she is also Tubalcain's wife but goes on to say that in those days marriages between siblings were quite sinless. Why, then, make the point that the name signifies something vicious? The *General estoria* explains: "Mas esto dezimos nos que non es estoria si non esponimientos que fazen y los sanctos; *e* por ende dixiemos que segund la estoria que era este casamiento sin peccado" [But we say that this is not history but the commentaries the saints make about it, and that is why we say that according to history this marriage was without sin] (Alfonso 1930, 15). These lines follow a strictly narrative piece out of Comestor. The whole package, story and gloss, is interesting in two senses. First, we may see here the Alfonsine editors actually adjudicating a difference between two conflicting sources; modern readers must wonder what compilers did when their authorities were at odds. Second, we find the text drawing a sharp line between history and gloss and stressing the complete autonomy and dignity of the former: the commentary, no matter how prestigious, must not be allowed to detract from the plain logic of the events narrated. The issue is complicated, but I believe that the intention of this passage is to vindicate the full dignity of the literal sense of Scripture (as opposed to the spiritual or allegorical senses).

The lines just quoted tell us clearly that, as the editors think, the material that comes before the gloss is authentic history. But is the text from Comestor simply history? The plot thickens. In an obvious sense the three scriptural texts in the *General estoria*—Bible, Josephus, and Comestor—are all on one level, equally historical, even though each has its own versions of the events narrated. But there is a catch: the Bible tells the stories plain, while the other two do a good deal of shading, explaining, and gap filling. Flavius Josephus is addressing a Greek-speaking audience, one completely ignorant of anything Jewish or biblical. To suit these readers, he decorates his narrative generously with material largely missing from the Bible: reasons and motivations. This is what we would expect; narratives in Greek historical texts are rational and fully explanatory, and they abhor causal vacuums. Genesis does not tell us why God accepted Abel's sacrifice but rejected Cain's. Josephus does: Cain invented farming, and this was held against him, for his motive was greed. Cain, of course, offered God the fruits of the earth, but Abel offered milk and the first fruit of his flock. God was more pleased by the gift of things that grew naturally, by themselves, than by the inventions of a greedy man (Josephus 1.2). We are on familiar ground. However much Josephus's literary practice differs from the Alfonsines', he is with them in this one respect: he in effect glosses the narrative material he inherits by adding reasons and specifying causes. Transplanted into the *General estoria,* his text functions, practically speaking, in much the same way as do some of the glosses on Ovid; just as these make explicit what is virtual or elliptical in the poet's lines, so does Josephus elucidate the bare scriptural text, giving it a plenitude of explanation it does not possess in its own right. One should add that genuine commentaries on the Bible, including some that are known to the Alfonsines, do not hesitate to draw on Josephus in their glosses on the Sacred Page.[11] Scholars and writers whose first and primary intention is to elucidate Scripture bring Josephus into their explanations as a matter of routine. It is therefore in no way remarkable that Josephus's role in the *General estoria* should be what it is, that of a virtual glossator on Scripture.

Comestor, Alfonso's other biblical source, also sets out to make the Bible story more intelligible. Not least, he quotes from Josephus extensively; as it stands, the *Historia scholastica,* part compilation, is rich in Josephan etiologies. But left to his own devices, in his own text, Comestor works very differently from Josephus. Petrus makes the biblical narrative more logical, not simply by adding reasons and explanations, but by bringing in narrative motifs of his own, some of them extensive, which give the whole text a coherence and a flow the biblical original does not have. We return to Lamech and his wives and children. Comestor inherits from Genesis 4 the information that Jabel was the inventor of tents and husbandry, Jubal of music and musical instruments, and Tubalcain of metallurgy. Does music seem to be out of place in this trio? Music is, after all, a liberal art; the other two are servile. Comestor seems to think that the discovery of music needs some special explanation. In his account Jubal invented music to make the shepherds'

---

11. In all this discussion I do not try to distinguish between commentary and gloss. Strictly speaking, a gloss is a short explanatory phrase, while a commentary is a long explication.

labor easier and more pleasant. What is more, the *Historia* also says that Jubal's invention owed everything to his acquaintance with Tubalcain and his craft. Jubal made his great discovery when he heard the sounds produced as his brother struck his bits of raw iron. The first musician was able to perceive that the pieces whose sizes were in simple numerical proportions gave out harmonious sounds. The Greeks erroneously attributed this discovery to Pythagoras, but its true author was none other than Jubal.

These bits of Comestorian invention are modest compared to his version of the life of Lamech himself. The matter is complicated. Genesis gives us a minimum. Lamech had two wives, in the Vulgate called Ada and Sella. Ada bore him two sons: Jabel, inventor of husbandry; and Jubal, inventor of music. Sella was the mother of the first smith, Tubalcain, and of Noema (4:19–22). At this point in the story, the compiler of Genesis adds, without any transition or explanation, a brief song:

> Lamech said to his wives Ada and Sella:
> Harken unto my voice, o wives of Lamech: listen to my harangue: because I killed a man who wounded me, and a young man out of spite,
> Cain shall be avenged sevenfold, and Lamech, indeed, seventysevenfold. (4:23–24; my translation from the Vulgate)

This is the last the Bible has to say about Lamech and his family. The "man" and the "young man" belong to parallel phrases and are of course one and the same person. The *Oxford Annotated Bible* (1962, 6) says that these verses were meant to express the spread of wickedness before the Flood. But by any standards, the connection of ideas between the verses and the preceding brief narrative is very loose. Comestor ties together the two passages in a most original and astonishing way. First of all, the murdered young man is split into two, Cain and one other person. Lamech, in his account, was a great archer who hunted both for sport and for utility. Antediluvians did not eat meat, but they did clothe themselves with animal skins; hence the need for hunting. Even in his old age Lamech pursued his hobby, or calling. But it was a risky business, because, with the years, he had become nearly blind. He was, however, assisted in his outings by a young man, who guided him and told him where to aim. Cain in those days was a perpetual wanderer; he was hirsute and unkempt, more brute than man. Lamech one day came upon him and heard him stirring behind a bush. The hunter, convinced that he had found legitimate game, loosed an arrow and shot Cain dead. But the young man, recognizing the all-important mark of Cain, was obliged to tell the older man of his tragic mistake, and Lamech, full of spite, beat the young man to death with his bow. This whole episode was the occasion of Lamech's strange address to his wives (Comestor 1855, column 1079). As we would expect, the *General estoria*'s Lamech narrative, which is long, draws heavily from Comestor and includes all the elements we have discussed: the circumstances surrounding the invention of music (Alfonso 1930, 13, 15) and the sad story of the death of Cain and the murder of the boy (16–17).

What are we to think of these narratives? What is their logic? Why does Comestor feel free to spin out his story so fine? First of all, we must understand that, Alfonso notwithstanding, these passages are genuine commentary. The very layout of the *Historia scholastica* tells us nothing else. The work is disposed exactly like any biblical commentary: a verse or two of Scripture is followed by several lines of explication, and the pattern is repeated until the whole text to be commented on is covered. The special profile of Comestor's glosses, the fact that they include extensive narrative, does not disguise their real status. The author of the *Historia* is in fact perfectly plain about what his biblical writings are; he refers to them in so many words as glosses. Much of the matter he presents is not his own, and as he says in his prologue, the very purpose of the work is to compose a book on sacred history that would be short and would collect in one place glosses that lay scattered in many other texts (Petrus Comestor 1855, column 1053). Some of these sources have been identified. Comestor owes a large portion of his glosses to his older contemporary Andrew of Saint Victor and to Peter the Chanter, who in turn borrows much of his material from Andrew (Smalley 1952, 179–80). Andrew represents a turning point in Christian biblical exegesis. He is a pioneer Hebraist, a reader of texts in Hebrew, and a personal friend and informal disciple of contemporary rabbis (Smalley 1952, 120–73). He is therefore able to pass on to his Christian contemporaries a wealth of ancient and medieval Jewish exegetical lore. His lifework belongs to his time. The interest in things Jewish in Christian Europe in those days coincided with a rising sense of the importance of biblical history and, consequently, with the revival of attention to the literal sense of Scripture. Christian exegesis had long concentrated on the spiritual sense of the biblical text, and to change direction, scholars had to turn to the Jews, who in the first place still possessed the Hebrew Scriptures, and who in the second place had traditions of commentary totally unlike the Christian. Literal commentary is indeed what we have in Petrus Comestor. It is important that we understand what exactly his exegetical project consists in.

As we have seen, Comestor is not concerned, as Josephus is, simply to add etiologies and explanations to the biblical story. Least of all does he work the way a modern commentator might, studying the text in its own terms, unraveling its literal sense, its syntax, its inner logic—all of this to make it yield some very limited and exact meaning. Comestor's procedure is different from either of these. First of all, his glosses address what appear to be genuine defects in his text. Let us recall the strange account Genesis gives us of Lamech and his family; the story jumps, without explanation, from a plain account of the patriarch's wives and children to an allusion to a murder, victim unspecified. Comestor's remedy, in this case as in others, is to envisage a coherent life situation or sequence of events that would include the troublesome biblical motifs and thus to reduce them to logic and good sense in their new setting. What might have been, or what must have been, is recounted to make the disconnected reports of the Bible more intelligible. This is not the place to expound the background of this strange procedure. Suffice it to say that Comestor himself did not invent it, and that practices that are very similar are followed by certain medieval Jewish exegetes and by some of the Christian scholars who were influenced by them (Smalley 1952, 179). It is significant, for example, that the essence of Comestor's Lamech narrative is attributed by one writer to a Jewish source; Walafrid Strabo knows a simple version of the story and introduces his text with the words "Aiunt Hebraei" (Walafrid Strabo 1879, column 101). The contribution of Comestor to the biblical narrative of the *General estoria* is very large indeed. As readers of the Alfonsine histories cannot fail to see as they go on page after page, logic, coherence, and verisimilitude are very basic goals for the compilers; whenever they expand, modify, or somehow manipulate their *auctores,* the resulting definitive text is generally more believable, natural, and intelligible. Comestor makes them a gift, a large fund of fully developed biblical narratives, a combination of scriptural text and literal gloss, which realizes all the narrative virtues they are striving for.

In dozens of different ways the Alfonsine editors elaborate on their sources with deliberation and skill. It is very important to realize that their reworking is always local; particular episodes may be shaped art-fully and given a distinctive focus and center, and on occasion one passage may echo the theme of another. But taken as a whole, the *Estoria de Espanna* and the *General estoria* are and remain miscellanies. Other than their chronologies, there is not a great deal that holds the bits together. It would be a serious mistake to suppose that the compilers, with all their arts, composed closely woven historical texts, comparable to those that might be written under other rules. But as I hope the essays in this book will show, the separate units can be quite ambitious and complex in their own right, and certain sequences were laid out with fine malice aforethought. To show in detail some of the resources the Alfonsine editors draw on when they are at their best and most artful, I conclude this introduction with a discussion of some passages in one of the finest narratives in the *Estoria de Espanna,* the set of chapters on the history of Scipio Africanus.[12] The whole episode is the subject of one of the essays in this book, but in that piece I call less attention to the formal and rhetorical aspects of the section than in the present short study.

In the *Estoria de Espanna,* Scipio, called Africanus, the hero of the Second Punic War, is the subject of a lengthy sequence of chapters. The main sources for this narrative are the familiar Orosius, Eutropius, and Paul the Deacon, along with Rodrigo of Toledo. Scipio, scion of a great family, a very young man, emerges as the savior of Rome at a dark hour. Roman security is threatened on no less than five fronts: by Philip of Macedon in Sicily, Sardinia, and Greece; by Hasdrubal in Spain; and by Hannibal in Italy itself. The generals draw lots to see which is to be sent to each of the five fronts. Scipio draws Macedonia. But, alas, lots or no, no one can be persuaded to take on Spain; Spain is such a formidable battleground that none of these leaders is willing to go there. None except Scipio, that is, who abandons his Macedonian charge and volunteers for this most difficult assignment (Alfonso 1955, 20–21). The focus of the episode is on two points: the resolve and gallantry of Scipio, obviously, and the special character of Spain, fearsome even to the greatest Romans. The *Estoria de Espanna* is, after all, a Spanish chronicle, and it in fact repeats this topic, the invincibility of Spain and of the Spaniards, several times. This whole narrative unit is virtually an inven-

___

12. The remainder of this introduction is based in part on an article of mine that does not appear in this collection, "How Original is the *Estoria de Espanna?* Problems of Translation and Others," *Romance Languages Annual* 2 (1990): 395–99.

tion of the compilers. It is put together out of bits of Orosius taken out of context and out of one passage in Rodrigo Toledano's *Historia romana*.[13] The five theaters of war is out of Rodrigo. Orosius, for his part, does speak of Scipio's emergence on the scene at a difficult moment, the drawing of lots, and of Scipio's assignment to Macedonia; but, alas, this story has to do with the wrong person: with Scipio, the hero of Numantia, not with the conqueror of Cartagena. The remark that Scipio was the only one brave enough to go to Spain is, in Orosius, also a reference to the later figure, not to the Scipio of our narrative. Neither is this particular power crisis in the peninsula the same one the *Estoria de Espanna* is speaking of.

Other parts of the Scipio story in Alfonso are nearly as independent of their sources as is this one. In Orosius's account the young man is the hero of the hour; when the war with the Carthaginians has taken a particularly bad turn, it is he who gives the demoralized Romans resolve and discipline. But for all of that, the person who looks after the practical details is not he but the dictator Decimus Junius. The latter is the one who drafts criminals into the army; supplies arms by collecting the weapons of aged veterans, as well as those that have become temple offerings; and appropriates the temple treasures generally to finance the war. The Alfonsine compilers remake this episode completely. In the *Estoria de Espanna*'s version we are carried back one step in time. At a certain moment there is a taking of accounts. Rome on that unhappy day is lacking three things: manpower, arms, and cash to pursue the war. Scipio is, of course, the man of the hour; he offers himself as a general remedy. He asks the crowd for their confidence, and it is granted. At that point in the story the *Estoria de Espanna* attributes to him everything Orosius had assigned to Decimus Junius—the drafting of criminals and the rest. (Orosius 4.16).

The first change in Orosius's story, the taking-of-accounts motif, is very typically Alfonsine. What is its function? It makes Scipio's emergence and his decisive actions look like a consequence: it is, as it were, plain that at that bad moment, arms, manpower, and money were lacking, and that it was Scipio who responded to these needs. The Alfonsine

---

13. The *Estoria de Espanna*'s account of Scipio in Rome is from Orosius 4.16; the drawing of lots and the later Scipio's Macedonian charge and his decision to go to Spain (others lacking) is from the beginning of Orosius 4.21. The five theaters of war is from Rodrigo's *Historia romana* (Rodrigo Toledano 1793, 218).

version brings antecedence and consequence to the text; its narrative is more logical and more verisimilar than that of its Latin original. The whole unit, for its part, is notable for two things. First, the transferring of Decimus Junius's deeds to Scipio enhances for us the latter's greatness. It simplifies the larger story; the number of agents is reduced, and the focus on the single heroic character is therefore greater. I would point out that this procedure is used more than once in the *Estoria de Espanna;* frequently when the source attributes great deeds to several persons, the Alfonsine version makes just one responsible. The literary effect is much the same as it is here: to make the hero more heroic. Second, this episode in the Scipio biography embodies what one could call the opposition principle: we are made to admire a character for the obstacles he confronts and overcomes. This is also the rationale for the drastic changes the editors make in the drawing-of-lots sequence: we can only think Scipio a great man, if he is indeed the only one to carry the war to Spain, admittedly the most difficult and dangerous theater. One need hardly add that in Alfonso's narrative, as in Orosius's and Livy's, Scipio is eventually the once-for-all conqueror of Spain.

The opposition principle is also brought to bear on the *Estoria de Espanna*'s account of Scipio's last battle on the peninsula (Alfonso 1955, 24). Once again, there is a notable gap between the editor's version of the event and that of the source, in this case not Orosius, but mainly Eutropius (Eutropius 3.17). The *Breviarium* gives us a scant four lines— a colorless account of the Roman's victory over a local prince, the victor's kindly treatment of his sometime enemy, and his refusal to take hostages from him. This bare sketch turns into a fair-sized chapter in Alfonso, nearly a column in Pidal's edition. It is not necessary to review the whole passage and its novelties. What is distinctive about the new story is that the prince is treated as a holdout. In some lines that are wholly original we are reminded that Scipio had pacified nearly all of Spain. This sets the stage for what follows: "Pero fincara un rey en la tierra, que non dize en ell estoria so nombre, y este non quiso obedecer a Cipion; antes saco grandes huestes e fue lidiar con el, e la batalla fue muy grand" [Nevertheless, there remained one king in that land whose name the history does not record, and this man refused to submit to Scipio; rather, he brought out his great host and fought with him, and the battle was very fierce] (Alfonso 1955, 24). This account of the heroic last stand of a courageous warrior is for all purposes an invention of the

Alfonsines. The prince's resolve and his ability to stand up to his Roman enemy are a testimony to his own greatness and, by implication, to that of Spain: it is surely no accident that Scipio's last military action there is, in this presentation, a difficult one. And by the same token the fact that Spain resisted Scipio to the very last makes the latter's valor and industry the more admirable. The opposition principle works here in two directions.

Scipio is greater than his circumstances. Hostile and fearsome as these may be, it is he that prevails. The Alfonsine editors make us, their audience, fully aware of this fact. But we are not the only witnesses. In one instance, one of the actors on the scene bears living testimony on his own to Scipio's excellence. Hannibal has just learned of the humiliation of Mago, of Hasdrubal's defeat, and of the loss of Spain to the Romans:

> Cuemo quier que muy poco auie aun que uenciera a Claudio Marcelo en batalla yl matara e destruyera toda la hueste de los romanos, e otrossi al consul Senpronio e a los otros dos consules Marcel e Crispino; mas con tod aquello, tan grand era el pesar que auie de so hermano Magon quel enuiaran catiuo a Roma e de Asdrubal que fincara en Espanna cuemo sennero e auie perdudo lo mas de la tierra, que toda la otra bien andança tenie por nada. (Alfonso 1955, 22–23)

> [Even though he had only recently overcome Claudius Marcellus in battle, had killed and destroyed the whole host of the Romans, and also had killed the consul Sempronius and the other two consuls Marcellus and Crispinus, for all of that, his sorrow was so great that his brother Mago had been sent captive to Rome, and that Hasdrubal, who was in Spain, was left all alone and had lost most of his lands, that he accounted all his good fortune as nothing.]

This passage has only the flimsiest basis in Orosius, who knows nothing of the general's sad reflections and tells only very hastily of the victory over Sempronius and the rest (Orosius 4.18). In Alfonso an important comparison between unequals is made by the Punic general himself; his glorious victories in Italy are nothing when weighed against the humiliation of Mago and, much more, against the loss of the greatest prize of all, Spain. The special character of that place and nation is emphasized once again, in Hannibal's view and in ours; and since, paradoxically, Carthaginian power is an issue here, Scipio and his Romans are the gainers, victors over such a fearsome enemy.

We have here still another application of the opposition principle, along with the tipped scale—the praise of something by comparison. We may now review some of the compilers' techniques over this whole episode. They are in great part reducible to two figures of rhetoric: *ratiocinatio* and *comparatio*. Both appear in Quintilian's list of figures of amplification in book 8 of the *Institutio*. What Quintilian means by *amplificatio* and what he says about it are entirely pertinent to the matter at hand. *Amplificatio* is the speaker's device that brings focus and drama to the person, thing, or event that he mentions in his text; *amplificatio* is emphasis. *Ratiocinatio,* which is one species of *amplificatio,* gives force to an account by indirection: instead, for example, of praising someone plainly, the orator plants evidence in his speech and lets the audience conclude on its own that the person is admirable. One of the varieties of *ratiocinatio* is precisely what I have called the opposition principle: praise a man implicitly by speaking of the obstacles he has faced and overcome. *Comparatio,* for its part, is the weighing of unequals: take a known large quantity and say that the subject of your discourse is larger. "The sufferings of widows and orphans are great, but they are nothing compared to those of George when his Ferrari was stolen"—this is a fair *comparatio*.

The mention of Quintilian is not meant to shock. The mutilated *Institutio* that circulated in the Middle Ages contains a great deal of his doctrine, and it in fact includes the treatise on amplification (see Butler's introduction in Quintilian 1920–22 1:xii). One must point out that the two figures I have mentioned do not appear in the other handbooks of rhetoric current in the Middle Ages; the all-important fourth book of the *Ad Herennium* knows nothing of either. To the objection that the compilers of the *Estoria de Espanna* did not need rhetoric or Quintilian to compose the Scipio text, that they could have hit on these devices on their own, one could answer as follows. The surgery they perform on Orosius and others is drastic; the liberties they take with these authors, their virtual reinventions of history, are, by modern standards at least, outrageous. But their practice seems a good deal less strange if we know that, in producing their texts, they had at hand a set of preexisting and consecrated procedures available to them, effective guidelines and precepts: the teachings of rhetoric. What should interest us about these lines on Scipio is not the editors' caprice but the new power they give their text, its new ability to convince, or, if one likes, the moral and political utility that comes to it anew. Needless to say, achieving all these things is what rhetoric is for. Rhetoric, to the compilers' mind, must have been well within the law, and so, only rhetoric could have given them the freedom to compose history in the bold and independent way they did.

The Scipio episode in the *Estoria de Espanna,* with its drastic remaking of its sources, its fresh rhetorical design, and its thematic focus and concentration, is a good example of what the Alfonsine enterprise was like and of what it could achieve. In one of the essays in this book, we will examine another fine narrative unit in Alfonso's history, the section of the *Estoria de Espanna* about the rivalry between Caesar and Pompey and the disastrous civil war that was the result. Let us for the moment observe that this passage, longer still than the Scipio episode, lives up to anyone's idea of a solidly conceived and well-executed narrative. There are no distracting digressions, the pace of events is well managed, the succession of cause and effect in the story is always clear, and the thematic focus is strong. I would not hesitate to call this unit one of the most successful pieces of history in medieval literature. As one might guess, the procedures the compilers used to put together this strong sequence are not at all unlike the ones that govern the composition of the Scipio chapters. The two passages are surely the fair flower of Alfonsine narrative art. They by no means represent all that is of value in the two *Estorias.* Indeed, the intention and design of the Alfonsine text is manifested in ways other than in the closely woven narrative episodes like these. It sometimes happens, for example, that theme and motives of widely separated chapters form coherent patterns and convey distinctive messages. Then, too, there are long stretches where the storytelling is quite loose and informal; these are not, on that account, devoid of art. But our two passages, on Scipio and on Caesar and Pompey, are the eminent cases. They are there to remind us that the Learned King and his collaborators were not routine compilers without discrimination but, in some decent sense of the word, composers of noble and genuine history.

PART 1

The first two essays in this collection form a pair related to each other rather like a father to his rebellious son. The first of the two is long and covers a good deal of ground. It begins by tracing the history of a remarkable epic song; the work itself is lost, but it is reconstructible from a series of chapters in the Alfonsine *Estoria de Espanna;* this history does include a prosified version of one of the poem's variants. The latter half of the first essay is about the parallels, both thematic and structural, between the song itself and other narratives preserved in the Alfonsine history that are not derived from popular poems. The latter passages, as one should point out, appear in both the completed portions of the *Estoria* and in the provisional parts. The contentious second article was written to correct a defect in the first, in the part that speaks directly and immediately about the epic song itself. This newer essay winds up being a sort of partial survey of Romance epic poetry—Castilian, Old French, and Provençal.

In this short introduction I should like to address an old problem, one that has been on the table for decades, the place of popular epic poetry in the Alfonsine *Estoria de Espanna.* I do not claim great originality here; some of my views on the matter are, however, distinctive and not entirely traditional. It is well known that in the provisional part of Alfonso's Spanish history there are a number of narrative segments that show clear signs of being prosified epic songs. With one exception the originals of these *cantares de gesta* have been lost. The exception is a fortunate one: two of the historical texts that are known to be related to the projected Alfonsine history of Spain preserve long portions of the *Poema de mio Cid.*[1] One of these chronicles includes most of the poem; the other breaks off so as to leave us no more than approximately the

---

1. See Menéndez Pidal 1951, introd., esp. xlix–lx; *Poema de mio Cid* 1976.

first third of the work (Catalán 1963a). Students of Alfonso can only rejoice at the survival of the *Cid,* and not only because of that work's absolute value as high literature. The independent *Poema* allows them to judge with fair accuracy how the editors of the *Estoria* went about adapting the Castilian epic songs to their new chronistic setting, what motifs the compilers tended to omit, what narrative and other elements they were likely to add, and how, generally, the style of the prosified poem was made uniform with that of the surrounding material.

But what do we know about the lost poems themselves? How can we be sure they even existed, and more modestly, how do we know that certain portions of the Alfonsine narrative actually have a poetic origin? There are four reasons for believing that the editors of the *Estoria* are including material from the epic songs. First, they tell us so. There is a formula that confronts us repeatedly in the *Estoria:* the words "as the minstrels tell us in their songs" or other words to the same effect. Second, we are alerted that nonchronistic sources might be involved, when we notice in our reading that the matter and the focus of the narrative has changed or that the style of presentation becomes different. If, for example, the narrative abandons kings and their wars, laws, marriages, and kin and moves over to episodes about family rivalries and personal vengeance, we may suspect that the jongleur/*juglar* is lurking in the wings. Likewise, if the story suddenly begins to offer an unwonted richness of detail and becomes, as it were, more realistic, we may also guess that there is a vernacular poem in the background. Third, versification plays a large part of the argument. As we know, Romance epic verses have a strong caesura approximately halfway through, and blocks of verses, for their part, are bound together in indeterminate numbers by vowel rhyme, or assonance. There are passages in the Alfonsine history that show traces of these patterns. We can sometimes even see the guilty hand of the redactor trying to erase these features of epic verse— displacing or disguising the caesura or destroying the rhyme. The very ease with which one can undo their labors is itself telling evidence. It has been shown many times that recasting certain pieces of Alfonsine prose into verse is no superhuman project.[2] Fourth, the ballads are independent witnesses to the existence of the lost songs. Spanish balladry over several centuries recovers many of the themes of the supposed epics;

---

2. A classic example of such a restoration is Menéndez Pidal's reconstituted *Cantar de los siete infantes de Salas* (Menéndez Pidal 1951, 199–239).

often the very narrative layout of the short popular poems is very similar to that of the hypothetical poem. In a few cases, to be sure, the ballad in question can be traced directly to a historical text, but this is exceptional; in most cases such a relationship is implausible, and it is vastly easier to suppose that the ballad is a trace or an heir or somehow a survival of the lost epic poem (Menéndez Pidal 1953, 1:173–243).

The incorporation of heroic narrative songs into chronicles and histories is not an exclusively Castilian practice. Catalonian chroniclers, for example, are acquainted with it; the early portions of Desclot's *Libre dels feyts* in particular show plain signs of being based on poetic and jongleuresque sources (Riquer 1964, 1:430–31). It is also well known that some French chansons de geste, including the most famous, find their way into historical material of all sorts (Riquer 1968, 288–92). In Alfonso's history one pair of epic songs offers a strange paradox. Each indeed adds its bit to the thematic substance of the *Estoria,* but each does so in an opposite sense. The subject in question is Charlemagne; one *cantar* treats him favorably, the other hardly so. The favorable one is a recension of the *Mainet,* the song about the youthful exploits of the great future king.[3] The negative piece is the *Song of Bernardo del Carpio,* a narrative we now know to be fictional, about the great Spanish warrior who defeated the Frankish king.[4] The plain intention of the singer of the poem was to attack the consecrated notion that it was Charlemagne who recovered Spain from the Moors.

These two insertions into the *Estoria* tell us little about the very special logic underlying most of the poetic ingraftings. First and foremost, the Alfonsine editors borrowed the epic songs for their text when they believed that something was missing from their strictly historical sources. In most cases the missing element was nothing other than Castile itself, a part of the world at one time neglected by formal histories and chronicles. The whole problem of the prosified songs in the *Estoria* is partly literary, partly historical. The literary part rests on a near tautology. A large portion of historical texts in the Middle Ages are royal chronicles, and royal chronicles have to do with kings. The latter proposition is not

---

3. The Alfonsine prosification is in Alfonso 1955, 2:340–43; Pidal's identification of the piece is in his index of sources in the same volume, p. cxliii.

4. The prosification is in chapters 617, 619, 621, 623, 649, 651–52, and 654–55 of vol. 2 of Menéndez Pidal 1955; this source is indicated in Pidal's index of sources, pp. cxlv, cxlvi, and cl of the same volume.

as trivial as it seems. One should point out that not only in Castile, not only in Spain, but in Europe at large, royal histories concentrate on the public lives of kings, their lineages, their marriages and offspring, the wars they wage, the lands they acquire, the public works they execute, and the laws they promulgate. This territory of the historian may seem broad enough, but its biggest limitation is that it is, strictly speaking, the king's world precisely; the historical narrative must present events from his point of view. In point of fact, when secondary themes are introduced into these texts—events abroad, for example, or the deeds of the king's vassals—they tend to appear in the historical text either in function of the royal interest or randomly, without system.[5]

The main problem this literary pattern poses for the historian in the service of a Castilian king is that, given the facts on the ground, it largely excludes Castile. These facts are easily summarized. The kingdom of León is the successor to the kingdom of Oviedo, which was founded in the tiny strip of Christendom left in Spain after the Moorish invasion. Castile, for its part, is a county originally dependent on León but progressively more independent.[6] We may be certain that a Leonese chronicler will ordinarily mention Castile only when its count does something that engages the king in some fundamental way, when the two are allied against the Moors, when there is hostility between them, or when dynastic marriages are being arranged. The structure of chronicles aside, León and its monarchy in any case occupies an eminent place on the Spanish scene. In my introduction to this book, I spoke of the Gothic hypothesis, the proposition that the kings of Spain are the successors of the Goths, and that they form a single line: in other words, that Ferdinand I of León or Alfonso VI are as Gothic as Receswinth or Recared. A whole succession of chronicles consecrates this theme.

The first literary text to articulate the Gothic thesis is the *Chronicle of Alfonso III,* written in the early tenth century.[7] This work, in its two major recensions, tells us that Pelagius (in Spanish, Pelayo), the legendary first hero and king of the Reconquest, was a Goth and thus the immediate successor of Roderick, by our reckoning the last Visigothic

---

5. These observations are my own. A wise and judicious account of the royal history is that of Brandt 1966, 43–80.

6. For information about medieval Spain any good history of the place and period will do. I have at hand O'Callaghan 1975.

7. Prelog 1980 has the text of four recensions of the *Chronicle of Alfonso III;* my date for its composition is out of Linehan 1993, 130.

king (Prelog 1980, 18–19). The chronicle conveys a further weighty bit of information. It tells us that Alfonso II established his capital in Oviedo and that he built extensively there, endowing his new churches with a splendid treasury of relics (Prelog 1980, 46–49). The nearly contemporary *Chronicle of Albelda* conveys to us the full significance of Alfonso's move: "onmemque [sic] gotorum ordinem sicuti Toleto fuerat, tam in eclesia quam palatio in Obeto cuncta statuit" [He (Alfonso) established in Oviedo the full Gothic order, in church and palace alike, just as it had been in Toledo] (*Crónica albeldense* 1932, 602). The symbolic power of the building of Oviedo as a new Toledo as seen by the chronicler is obvious; it is hard to imagine a better highlighting of the solidarity of the post-Pelayo Christian Spain with the great Gothic world than to equate Oviedo with Toledo. Toledo of course had been the capital of western Gothia. But for our purposes the link between Oviedo and the Gothic seat of monarchy is meaningful in a narrower sense. Oviedo becomes one step in a *translatio regni* that ends in the imperial city of León. In 914, only a few decades after the building of Oviedo, Ordoño II moves the seat of the kingdom south to the city that is to be its permanent site (*Historia silensis* 1959, 155).

The Gothic thesis generally, the special status of Oviedo, and the transfer of the seat of monarchy from Oviedo to León are all recovered in a very influential chronicle of the mid–twelfth century, the *Historia silensis* (in Spanish, *silense*). The *Silensis*'s lines on Ordoño II are especially impressive. At one point the chronicler states, without comment, that Ordoño settled on León as the seat of his kingdom, but this information is buried in a long sentence about the king's accession. Exceptionally for the *Silensis,* and indeed for other Spanish chronicles up to the thirteenth century, the chronicle in this line tells of the crowning and unction of the monarch, performed in this case in the presence of all the great men of Christian Spain, clerical and lay alike. This is surely a capital letter in the alphabet of the historian: the crowning and anointing of kings in Spain was uncommon in the earlier Middle Ages, and whether or not the text is being truthful here, it is clear that its author expects us to see Ordoño at the beginning of his reign as a very important person.[8] In a word, León, as the seat of an anointed king, is not an

---

8. Linehan (1993) points out the significance of royal crowning and anointing as these are mentioned in the chronicles; both rites are rarely practiced in earlier medieval Spain. He refers to the coronation and anointing of Ordoño (pp.122–23).

insignificant place. In this chronicle, then, Oviedo and León both figure large, and the suggestion is clear that in time León becomes the latter-day Toledo, just as Oviedo had been. As the lines on Ordoño make plain, the *Historia silensis* is in every sense a Leonese chronicle.

This work is important to our story because the two great Spanish histories known to Alfonso and his collaborators, Lucas of Tuy's *Chronicon mundi* and Rodrigo Toledano's *De rebus Hispaniae,* both inherit many elements of the *Silensis*'s narrative. The *Chronicon* actually incorporates some of its wording, while Rodrigo's very independent and original history borrows much of its material from Lucas. One must add that Rodrigo modifies heavily the matter he borrows from his great source. In its Spanish section the *Chronicon mundi* is decidedly a Leonese history, whereas Rodrigo is intent on giving a large place in his argument to Castile and in particular to Toledo, seat of the Visigothic monarchy and of the archdiocese that he rules, and by this time safely included in Christendom. How exactly Rodrigo works this transformation need not concern us; suffice it to say that to do so he must recast Lucas heavily and indeed turn to other sources (Linehan 1993, 350–412).

Given the whole bias and intention of the *Chronicon mundi,* which was his starting point, Rodrigo's task must not have been easy. We may well pose a general hypothetical question: given the character of the royal chronicle as a genre and the Leonese bias of the tradition, how does a Spanish historian living during the Castilian kingdom's formative years write Castilian history? The short answer is "with difficulty." Castile, one might say, demands a seat at the table. The land of the Cid and of Fernán González becomes a kingdom once for all in 1157 and enters into a union with León in 1230 on equal terms. But the composition of Castilian history is no easy matter. The Leonese tilt in the historiography is not the only obstacle. It is also the case that materials for such a history are in great part simply not there. We must remember that chronicles tend to focus on kings. But kings are precisely what Castile lacks. Castile first becomes a kingdom only in 1037, when Fernando I receives it from his father, Sancho the Great. The period between that date and the moment at which a Castilian history might be written is a paltry stretch of time, especially if we compare it with that of the Leonese line, traceable first to the kings of Oviedo, then to Pelayo himself, and beyond that, far back into the Gothic era. What is more, between 1037 and 1157 Castile's independence is anything but continuous. In fact, it hardly exists at all. Fernando I accedes to the throne of León a bare two years after his accession in Castile, and his son Sancho remains ruler of that kingdom alone for less than seven years, between 1065 and 1071. Fernando I, as we know, divided his lands among his children, the eldest son, Sancho, inheriting Castile. But, scarcely on the throne, Sancho resolved to reunite the lands his father had divided. When Sancho finally drives his brother Alfonso from the throne of León in 1072, independent Castile once again disappears from the scene, not to return until 1157.

Given the two factors, the character of royal chronicles generally and the Leonese bias of those written in western Spain, and given also the near nonexistence of Castile during most of the twelfth century, how can the Castilian historian write anything at all, much less give his subject dignity and standing? One recourse is to turn to texts on Castilian subjects that are not in the obvious sense historical or chronistic at all. The anonymous chronicler of Nájera (*Crónica najerense*), who draws on *Silensis* for much of his material on Fernando and his children, does at one point enhance considerably the role of Sancho of Castile by drawing on alien material: he incorporates into his text a prosification of a fine poem in Latin hexameters about the murder of that king (Entwistle 1928). The editors of the *Estoria de Espanna* follow a similar path; they ingraft into their text a prose version of the flower of Castilian vernacular epic, the *Cantar de Sancho*. The stormy career of that monarch has in itself the makings of high drama, and indeed, the Alfonsine narrative about him, which depends in large part on the poem, reads like a prose version of an Elizabethan tragedy.[9] This whole section of the *Estoria* is the subject of the essay that follows.

The composer of Nájera shifts attention to Castile in other parts of his history. As we observed, one reason why the historian of Castile might find his subject difficult is that, as a kingdom, this important part of the world has no past. But, as a county, it does, and here is where the compiler of Nájera makes his all-important move. The eminent witnesses to early Castilian history are not its chroniclers, who practically do not exist, but its very gifted epic singers, who know very well the doings of the counts of Castile and their subjects. The compiler of Nájera, then, gives Castile an illustrious past in a single moment by

---

9. Pieces of the *Cantar de Sancho* are scattered over the stretch of text in the *Primera crónica general* made up of chapters 813–45 (Alfonso 1955, Pidal's introduction, 2:clxvii–clxxii). The song Pidal calls the *Cantar de Fernando* is to my mind part of the *Cantar de Sancho,* as I try to show in the essay immediately following. The *Crónica de veinte reyes* has a longer, and on balance more accurate, version of the *Fernando* (Menéndez Pidal 1951, 240–56).

having his text include paraphrases of the extraordinary songs of its minstrels, which are the region's local treasure (R. Menéndez Pidal 1951, xxxviii–xliii). But as one should emphasize, the impulse to include them is not aesthetic or cultural; the editors' only purpose is to exploit the information they contain. The compilers of the *Estoria de Espanna* surpass the one of Nájera: they give us prosified versions of the poems entire or nearly so. They begin with the poetic account of the first count of Castile, Fernán González. In this case they happen to possess the popular epic only secondhand; the text they prosify is a learned recasting in the vernacular of the original poem. But this version preserves what must have been its original's most important theme, the definitive liberation of Castile from the rule and domination of León.[10]

We must understand. The two great Latin chronicles used by the Alfonsines, those of Lucas and Rodrigo, do not wholly neglect Castile over the crucial period between the time of Fernán González and that of the accession of Fernando I as the first Castilian king. But neither historian gives us a fully independent and internal account of Castile and its rulers for those years. The editors of the *Estoria de Espanna* do, precisely by incorporating into their text three more epic songs: *The Treacherous Countess, The Seven Infantes of Salas,* and *The Song of the Infante García.*[11] The splendid *Seven Infantes* recounts a bloody episode in the time of Fernán González's son and successor, García Fernández; the *Countess* tells of further events in García's reign and carries the story into the time of Sancho, his rebellious son and successor. Finally, the *García* tells how the last count of Castile was cut down young, at the hand of his family's enemies.

The most splendid moment in the history of Castile before the union of the two kingdoms is dominated by a person who is neither a count nor a king but a lowly *infanzón*, a lesser nobleman. This person is, of course, Rodrigo Díaz del Vivar, known as the Cid. Lucas de Tuy gives short shrift to the eminent Castilian hero: he tells of his capture of the king of Aragon and his conquest of Valencia in three sentences (Lucas of Tuy

10. The prosified *Poema de Fernán González* is spread out over the *Primera crónica general* in fragments between chapters 684 and 720 inclusive (Alfonso 1955, Pidal's introduction, 2:cliv–clvii).

11. The *Countess* is in two segments of the *Primera crónica general,* in chapters 729–32 and 763–64 (Alfonso 1955, Pidal's introduction, 2:clviii and clxi–clxii). The *Seven Infantes* is in chapters 736–43 and 751 (Alfonso 1955, Pidal's introduction, 2:clix–clx). The *Infante García* is in chapters 787–89 (Alfonso 1955, Pidal's introduction, 2:clxiii–clxiv).

1608, 101). Rodrigo Toledano for his part devotes a short paragraph to him; to Lucas's information he adds a word about the first bishop of Valencia, about the fall of the city after the Cid's death, and about the hero's burial at Cardeña (Rodrigo Toledano 1987, 212–213). By contrast, the editors of the *Estoria de Espanna* outdo themselves on the subject of Rodrigo Díaz. The Cid becomes a major figure in the narrative; over long stretches of the text he is actually given more space than his sovereign lord Alfonso VI of León. The account of the Cid in the *Estoria* is long, detailed, and rich in supporting information. The narrative itself is woven out of three strands, three major sources: the anonymous Latin memoir of the hero, known as the *Historia Roderici;* the *History of Valencia* by Ben Alcama; and, eminently, the *Poema de mio Cid,* which in one chronistic text closely related to the *Estoria de Espanna* is prosified entire.[12] The prosified *Cid* represents by far the largest contribution made by vernacular epic to the Alfonsine history. The epic song itself in its canonical form is more than 3,700 verses long; this probably makes it the longest in the Alfonsine repertory—longer, surely, than the *Cantar de Sancho,* and certainly longer than the *Poema de Fernán González.* As far as one can judge from the chaotic state of the provisional versions of the *Estoria,* the *Cid* was actually meant to occupy more space than any other prosified song. The bulk is clearly commensurate with the importance of the theme. The very fact that the compilers chose to support the poetic narrative with that of two unique historical texts, and thus to give their hero and his activities an unparalleled amount of space in their chronicle, shows clearly that they meant to draw their audience's attention away from the homeland of Lucas and his predecessors, toward what was, for him, the periphery and, for later generations, the center. The incorporation of the *Poema de mio Cid* into the *Estoria de Espanna* is, therefore, an eminent case; very nearly the whole function of vernacular epic in Alfonso's history is to give to Castile the place that historiography in Spain had until then denied it, and the Cid narrative, including the crucial *Poema,* is plainly the capstone of this whole project.

---

12. The question of the Cid narrative and what the editors of the *Estoria de Espanna* intended is complicated. It is virtually certain that the most authentic Alfonsine version of his story is the one preserved not in the so-called *Primera crónica general* but in the text known as the *Crónica de veinte reyes.* The full account of the whole matter is in Catalán 1963a, 207–15.

Sancho II: Epic and Chronicle

As we know, Menéndez Pidal treats Castile as a parenthesis in Spain. Castile for him is different from the rest of the peninsula in her language, in her laws, and in the fact that she possesses a popular epic. Now, the last two of these *differentiae* bear upon each other in a special way. Castilian legal customs, Germanic, traditional, unwritten, are at sharp odds, in content as well as in form, with the provisions of the Romanized *Forum iudiciorum,* in force in the rest of Christian Spain. But one of the best testimonies to the prevalence of Germanic custom in Castile, according to Menéndez Pidal, is precisely her epic, where these laws are reflected faithfully, where, indeed, they play a fundamental role.[1] In a sense the later *Cantar de Sancho II,*[2] the one that survives in the *Primera crónica general,* is a perfect instance of this witness. Germanic customs figure large in its plot. It tells of a judicial combat; it represents a whole city as accountable for the crime of one man; a fugitive is shown seeking sanctuary under the mantle of his lady. But it is also remarkable that not one of these details is quite in order; none of them works entirely according to the traditional pattern. Take the case of the challenge the Castilian Diego Ordóñez lays down to the city of Zamora after Sancho's murder. It is very traditional and full enough of apparent nonsense to look that way. It runs:

---

1. These ideas are found in several places in Menéndez Pidal's writings; one such is in Menéndez Pidal 1955, 12 ff.

2. It is begging the question to speak of a "later" *cantar.* Some have expressed doubts that there was an early one. Professor A. Deyermond, for example, feels there is not enough evidence to affirm that there was a *Cantar de Sancho* in existence when the Nájera chronicle was written. The present study will try to argue precisely this point: that there might have been at least two distinct versions of the poem, one older than the other.

Los castellanos han perdudo su sennor; et matol el traydor Vellid
Adolffo seyendo su uassallo, et despues que fizo esta traycion, uos
cogiestesle en Çamora. Et digo por ende que es traydor el, et
traydor el qui lo tiene consigo, si el sabie dantes de la traycion o
gela consintio o si uedargela pudo. Et riepto a los çambranos
tanbien al grand como al pequenno, et al muerto tanbien como al
biuo, et al que es por nascer como al que es naçudo, et a las aguas
que beuieren, et a los pannos que uistieren, et aun a las piedras del
muro. Et si tal a en Çamora que diga de non, lidiargelo e; et si
Dios quisiere que yo uenzca, fincaredes uos tales como yo digo.[3]

[The Castilians have lost their lord, and the traitor Vellido Adolfo
killed him while he was his vassal, and after he committed the
treacherous act, you (and yours) harbored him in Zamora. And I
therefore say that he is a traitor, and that that man is a traitor who
is protecting him, if he knew beforehand of the treason, if he
consented to it, or if he could have prevented it. And I challenge
the people of Zamora, both the grown man and the child, the one
yet to be born and the one already born; I challenge the waters
they drink, the clothes they wear, and even the stones in the city
wall. And if anyone in Zamora say to me nay, I will fight with him,
and if God wills that I win, you will prove to be all the things I say.]

As the poem proceeds, however, at least some of the traditional substance of the challenge is held up to judgment. In his answer to the
challenge Arias Gonzalo pours contempt on the absurdities in the
speech, the challenge to ancestors, to the stones of the walls:

Si yo tal so como tu dizes, non ouiera yo a nascer ; mas en quanto tu
dizes en todo as mentido, et dezirte quiero como: en lo que los
grandes fazen non an culpa los pequennos que non son aun en edad,
nin los muertos otrossi non an culpa de lo que non uieron nin sopieron. Mas saca ende los muertos et los ninnos et las otras cosas que
non an razon nin entendimiento, et por todo lo al te digo que mien-
tes, et lidiartelo e o dare quien te lo lidie. Et sepas una cosa: que tod
aquel que riepta a conceio, que deue lidiar con cinco uno en pos

---

3. Alfonso 1955, 513b (in vol. 2, but pagination is successive). All page references to
the *Primera crónica* henceforth will be to this edition.

otro; et si el uenciere a aquellos cinco, deue salir por uerdadero; et si
alguno de aquellos cinco le uenciere, deue el fincar por mintroso.

[If I were all the things you say, it would have been better for me
not to have been born, but in everything you have said you have
lied, and I will tell you why, for the children are not to blame for
what the grown men do, and the dead are not to blame for what
they neither saw nor knew about. So leave out the children and the
dead and all those (nonliving) objects that have neither reason nor
understanding. And as for everything else, I say that you lie, and I
will fight with you or provide someone to fight with you. And let
me tell you one thing, that he who challenges a group should fight
with five, one after another (that is, there should be five on each
side), and the one who prevails over the five should come out
(stand vindicated as) the truthful one, and if any of the five overcomes him, he is proved a liar.]

Be it noted that this attenuation of the traditional is not a piece of
tampering by the editors of the *Primera crónica.* It really belongs to the
Cantar. Thus Arias's speech survives, independently of the *Crónica,* in
an old traditional ballad derived from our poem, so there can be little
doubt about its authenticity.[4] The later poet plainly wished to make a
breach in the seamless garment of Castilian tradition. His *Cantar* is not
quite a typical Castilian epic song.

Other details in the later *Sancho* show that it has gotten well off the
traditional track. There is the matter of the right of sanctuary as customary law saw it. When the regicide Vellido Adolfo asks refuge under the
mantle of the infanta Doña Urraca, he is dragged away and brought to
justice, the sanctuary violated. We must point out that the poem treats
this act as entirely praiseworthy. Another still more dramatic weakening
of the Germanic and traditional substance of the *Cantar* is the way it
presents the judicial combat itself. This legal pattern is among other
things, of course, supposed to be a way of finding the culprit. But by
traditional norms the scene in the *Sancho* is pure confusion. As we
recall, the Castilian challenge is taken up, and all parties agree to a

---

4. Smith affirms that "Ya cabalga Diego Ordóñez" is a traditional ballad (Smith 1964,
95). The fact that this *romance* appears in the Antwerp *Cancionero de romances* of 1550 is
fair evidence to this effect.

combat of twelve against twelve in pairs. The issue is the guilt or innocence of Zamora in the murder of King Sancho. Now, Arias Gonzalo,
the elder statesman, is fully convinced that God will show his hand in the
contest; he is certain the right side will win, whichever that is. He therefore zealously examines the people of his town to assure himself that
none of them conspired in the death of Sancho. If one of them has, the
conflict will end disastrously.

What is more, the audience knows that the only guilty one is Vellido
Adolfo. Urraca's innocence is insisted upon particularly. There is strong
evidence that the later poet has gone to great lengths to dissociate her
from Adolfo's crime. He appears, in fact, to have made over completely
a text that was very hostile to her. The tradition, if we may speak of such
a thing, is, up to the time of the *Primera crónica,* uniformly severe with
Urraca. In the Sancho narrative of the Nájera chronicle, which is in all
probability based ultimately on an older *Cantar,*[5] Urraca simply offers
her person and her wealth to the man who breaks the siege. The one to
answer the call is, of course, Vellido Adolfo, who is in love with her, "qui
eam super omnia . . . affectabat."[6] But in the later *Sancho* Adolfo is not
a potential lover at all but is seeking only wealth, *algo,* in return for his
service as vassal. It is, therefore, in no way incriminating to Urraca when
she answers that she would do anything for the man who freed her city.
Her words are strong, but they contain no hint of a love match: "non a
ome en el mundo que mio hermano tolliesse de sobre Çamora et me la
fiziesse descercar que yo non le diesse quequier que me demandasse"
[there is not a man in the world who might take my brother away from
before Zamora and who might lift the siege for whom I would not do
anything he asked of me] (510). This is a significant change. But there is
more. Most of the surviving earlier texts on Urraca actually accuse her of
complicity in her brother's murder. Sancho's epitaph at Oña names her:

Sanctius, forma Paris, et ferox Hector in armis,
Clauditur hac tumba, iam factus pulvis et umbra.
Femina mente dira, soror, hunc vita expoliavit,
Iure, quidem, dempto, non flevit fratre perempto.[7]

---

5. See Menéndez Pidal, 1923, 349. Entwistle believes that there is a Latin poem
between the *Cantar* and the chronicle (Entwistle 1928, 205–19).

6. *Crónica najerense* 1966, 113.

7. Quoted in Menéndez Pidal 1969, 186.

[Sancho, a Paris in beauty, a ferocious Hector in arms, now dust
and shade, is enclosed in this tomb. A woman of cruel mind, his
sister, deprived him of life. Justice and law were set aside. She did
not weep for her brother, killed for a price.]

The *De preconiis civitatis numantine* of Fray Juan Gil de Zamora a
work that dates from perhaps the early 1280s, and that may in part be
based on traditional poetic material, also points the finger at Urraca:
"Byllidus . . . Zamoram veniens, de morte regis Sanctii cum Urracha
Fernandi tantum, omnibus civibus ignorantibus, pertractavit" [Vellido
having come to Zamora, planned the death of King Sancho with
Urraca Fernández, unbeknownst to the residents of the city].[8] In the
face of this coincidence the text of the *Primera crónica* is absolutely
distinctive. Urraca will take no responsibility for any crime Adolfo
might commit; she does not wish to see anything done wrong: "non te
mando yo que tu fagas nada del mal que has pensado" [I do not order
you to do any of the ill that you have planned] (510). There is no hint
of anything like this even in the Nájera text. The poet's effort to clear
Urraca is manifest.[9]

Now, in spite of the palpable innocence of all except Adolfo, and in
spite of the fact that Arias Gonzalo considers the judicial combat a valid
legal procedure, the contest goes badly: it is called off only after three of
Arias's sons have been killed. The meaning of this within the new poem
is perhaps not hard to grasp. It is likely that the later poet wishes to
present the judicial combat as irrational, antilegal, and inhuman. As we
will see, other aspects of the poem support this view. But once again, the
congruence of the episode within the poem does not disguise its oddity
within Spanish epic literature as a whole. Indeed even within the *Sancho*
there are problems. The poet could not alter history to the point of

---

8. F. Fita 1884, 159. Fita's essay includes an edition of the whole *De preconiis*. R.
Menéndez Pidal, in an essay, "Alfonso VI y su hermana la infanta doña Urraca," affirms
his belief that parts of this work of Fray Juan Gil are based on vernacular epic; the study is
in Menéndez Pidal 1952, 85–88. It is a fact that although much of this section of the *De
preconiis* is taken from the histories of Lucas of Tuy and Rodrigo of Toledo, our quotation
is not.

9. It should in fairness be pointed out that in the *Primera crónica* version Urraca does
once speak of killing her brother: "Yo mugier so, et bien sabe el que yo non lidiare con el,
mas yol fare matar a furto o a paladinas" (507b). I do not feel that this passage seriously
weakens my argument. Horrent (1961, 2:253) agrees with my view, but Menéndez Pidal
(1952, 86), says that the *Crónica* makes Urraca guilty.

making Philip II, for example, succeed Sancho, but why could he not have done what he liked in an episode like this? Yet in a poem whose narrative logic is impressive he lets stand a detail of plot that is very poorly motivated. If the Zamoranos are really innocent (as they are), why was the contest not fought to the end? But if, unlikely as it may be, the poet meant to cast doubt on the innocence of the Zamoranos, would not the suspension of the contest be an admission of guilt?

Anomalous details like these may be relics of an earlier state of the poem. Much of the intractable matter in the later *cantar* would fall into place if we could imagine it part of a simpler, more straightforward work, one in which the strictly traditional Germanic elements were allowed to stand without commentary, supposing total belief and acceptance on the part of the audience. It is not hard to make up a logical plot for this simpler *cantar*. Sancho, having invaded the territories of his brothers García and Alfonso, lays siege to Zamora, which by rights belongs to Urraca. She in vengeance arranges to have her brother killed. At that point the Castilians challenge the people of Zamora to a judicial combat, which the Castilians win, partly or wholly, since right is on their side. Urraca and her subjects would be the collective villains, and so the violation of sanctuary would make them seem the more damnable. Or even better, the sanctuary could be respected and the regicide Vellido Adolfo protected by the Zamoranos. The whole story would be one of vengeance and reprisal and would not be far from the pattern Pidal associates with the older Castilian epic.

Diego Ordóñez's challenge could have been answered in more straightforward fashion by Arias Gonzalo: there would be no need for him to comment on the picturesque form of the Castilian's speech. More important, perhaps, one of the puzzling details of the later *cantar,* the "jura de san Gadea," would for once make sense. As it stands in the *Primera crónica* it is completely anomalous.[10] Alfonso had no reason to resist taking the oath. Common law demanded that when a king dies a violent death, his successor must swear he had no part in that death.[11] The *Crónica* version gives no hint that Alfonso consented in any way to the murder of his brother, and so the oath should have been pure routine. But instead, the new king is angered and humiliated when the Cid obliges him to take the oath. In our hypothetical version

---

10. Horrent points out this anomaly (1961, 2:263).
11. Menéndez Pidal 1969, 195 and 197.

of the poem, however, Alfonso's hesitation and blanching would be explained purely and simply by his complicity in the murder. That he should have consented to Sancho's death in the poem is believable in that his brother had invaded his lands, and that throughout the whole episode he and Urraca figure as allies. It is remarkable that a contemporary document actually accuses him of having planned the murder himself.[12] This fact, interestingly, drives Menéndez Pidal to affirm that in one form or another the "jura de san Gadea" really took place, though this view is subject to serious doubts.[13] In any case, there are no reasons why the "jura" could not have been part of an old *Cantar de Sancho*. Professor Horrent argues to the contrary, saying, in effect, that in the only *Cantar* we know, the one in the *Primera crónica,* Alfonso knows nothing of the murder until he is informed of it during his stay in Toledo.[14] But this objection does not stand. The Toledo episode in the *Crónica* is based not on poetic sources but on chronistic,[15] and there is little evidence that any *Cantar de Sancho* ever had anything to say about Alfonso's exile. Thus, the "jura" narrative is compatible with an older Sancho poem on two premises: that such a poem made Urraca guilty, and that it did not totally deny Alfonso's complicity. Neither hypothesis is unacceptable.

But did a *Cantar de Sancho II* that displayed all the features we have spoken of actually exist? What do the two extensive texts we have mentioned, the Nájera chronicle and the work of Gil de Zamora, tell us in this regard? It is, after all, a plausible view that there lies a *cantar de gesta* behind the Nájera text, and even behind the Latin poem that is supposed to be its source. Entwistle and Menéndez Pidal both affirm this, though on different grounds.[16] Pidal also asserts, on weaker evidence, but not arbitrarily, that the Sancho episode in the *De preconiis* may have a vernacular poetic source.[17] How do these two narratives stand with respect to our hypothetical version? Each work presents a different problem. The Nájera narrative ends with Sancho's death and

---

12. Edited in Menéndez Pidal 1969, 711.

13. Menéndez Pidal 1969, 95–96. Horrent (1961, 241–61) argues that the "jura" did not take place.

14. Horrent 1961, 263.

15. Perusal of the texts in question makes this obvious, but Menéndez Pidal gives the sources in Lucas of Tuy and Rodrigo of Toledo in Alfonso 1955, 2:clxix–clxx.

16. R. Menéndez Pidal 1923, 349 and Entwistle 1928, 205–19.

17. R. Menéndez Pidal 1952, 85–87.

says nothing of the judicial combat. According to Entwistle, the *Carmen de morte Sanctii regis* probably ended the same way.[18] But as he points out, this hardly means that the vernacular original was lacking a combat scene. On the crucial matter of Urraca's complicity in the murder, the Nájera text is not absolutely explicit. But it does not give her the elaborate moral alibi we find in the *Primera crónica* version. It is not unreasonable to think her guilt clearly implied. What is more, there is no question about Nájera's hostility to her. It shows her as unchaste, proposing a love relationship with the savior of Zamora. To the narrator her lust is one of the most damning things about Zamora itself; the sinfulness of the princess accrues to the discredit of her city.

Fray Gil's text offers difficulties of another sort. It leaves no doubt at all about Urraca's responsibility for her brother's death. The phrase we have quoted above makes this quite clear. *De preconiis* also has a long episode about the judicial combat. But the account we find there of this event is different from both our hypothetical one and the version of the *Primera crónica*. Fray Gil's first pair of combatants, Fernando Arias and Diego Ordóñez, fight at length, and Arias, the Zamorano, in the long run has the best of it. But at this moment, when Ordóñez, beside himself, wishes to fight against impossible odds, the contest is interrupted by no less a person than the Cid. Sancho's greatest vassal is so persuaded of the innocence of the citizens of Zamora that he will not permit the combat to continue.[19] Now, the very divergence of this narrative from that of the *Primera crónica* is very significant. If the two texts were identical at this point, it would be the harder to suppose that the earlier poetic text told the story differently. As it is, not only does the character of the lost version become problematic, but we are actually permitted to guess that the old poet may have ended the combat so as to express his own moral judgment on the interested parties, the Zamoranos and the Castilians. In any case, this is exactly what Fray Gil does; his motives are transparent. Thus he insists particularly on the noncomplicity of the Zamoranos in the murder; it is stressed several times that aside from Urraca and Adolfo the people of Zamora were entirely ignorant of the fateful plot. Elsewhere in the Sancho episode a great deal is made of their heroism during the siege laid by the Castilians. The point of all this is that *De preconiis civitatis numantine* is a celebration of the greatness of

---

18. Entwistle 1928, 212.
19. Fita edition (1884), 164.

Fray Gil's native city of Zamora, identified by him with Numantia. Every episode in history that reflects on the heroism of Numantia-Zamora has its place in the work. It would be simply inconceivable that such a work would find the Zamoranos guilty. Fray Gil's solution of the problem is to dissociate them as much as possible from the manifestly guilty Urraca and Vellido, this by making them totally ignorant of the plot. The author's vested interest, so to speak, in his version of the story is beyond very much doubt.

If there is an epic song about Sancho older than the one preserved in the *Primera crónica,* it seems likely that it portrayed Urraca as guilty of her brother's death and contained a judicial combat whose issue was favorable to Castile. Much the same sort of evidence that supports these possibilities also points to another feature the older *cantar* may have displayed: it is likely that it made Sancho and not García the first of the sons of Fernando el Magno to make war on his brothers. Thus, all early versions of the story except the Alfonsine chronicle and works dependent on it make Sancho the first culprit: this is the account of the chronicle of Nájera, of the histories of Lucas of Tuy and Rodrigo of Toledo, and of the *De preconiis* of Fray Gil.[20] The most interesting texts in this connection are, once again, the *De preconiis* and the *Najerense.* The latter is a good witness for reasons we have already aired. It is based on a vernacular poem at one remove; if the chronicle makes Sancho the first warmaker, it is the less likely that the *cantar* went a different way. The work of Fray Gil brings forth testimony of a more complicated sort. The beginning of his Sancho narrative, where the Castilian's warlike initiative is recounted, comes from Rodrigo, and so far as I know, no one has ever suggested that Rodrigo drew on vernacular sources here. But Fray Gil does include material in his story that is most probably taken from epic. He draws on these poetic texts (if that is what they are) at the moments of his story when his Latin sources fail him; in every case the epic test supplies features missing in Rodrigo and Lucas.[21] Therefore, the fact that he makes the war start with Sancho may mean that his version of the poem told him nothing to the contrary. The evidence offered by the totally nonpoetic Sancho narratives of Rodrigo and Lucas

---

20. See *Crónica najerense* 1966, 110; Fita 1884; Lucas 1608, 57; Rodrigo Toledano 1987, 195.

21. The observation is mine. The start of Rodrigo's Sancho narrative, drawn on by Fray Gil, is, as stated in the preceding note, on pp. 194–95 of Rodrigo Toledano 1987.

is more diffuse. They simply round off the unanimity of all the pre-Alfonsine texts in this matter.

Now, Alfonso's work tells quite a different story. The *Primera crónica,* whose Sancho narrative is certainly based on a *cantar,* makes García, not Sancho, the man to break the peace. García invades the lands of his two sisters, anticipating his older brother's action in little, so to speak. The difference between the versions is crucial. The choice between García and Sancho determines the shape the whole narrative is to take. We will have more to say about this presently. For the moment let us note that if our hypothetical poem ever existed, García could hardly have been the first troublemaker. The whole economy of the story would have been destroyed. Our plot is logic itself: Sancho invades Urraca's lands; Urraca in revenge has him killed; the Castilians demand and get satisfaction in a judicial combat. There is tit for tat, not a character too many or an episode too many. The early appearance of García would have been very difficult to integrate into his scheme; indeed such a role for him would have dictated a totally different sort of poem, one whose logic had quite different premises.

We could sum up our argument to date as follows. The Nájera chronicle and the work of Fray Gil reflect in different ways a distinctive version of the *Cantar de Sancho* in which the hero is the first invader of his siblings' land, and in which Urraca is in league with Vellido Adolfo. If we try to correct the anomalies of the narrative in the *Primera crónica* and also bring to bear what we know about Castilian epic in general, we can guess that the *Cantar* continued with a judicial combat, which the Castilians win. The work may even have concluded with a "jura de san Gadea," in which Alfonso perjures himself, swearing that he had no part in his brother's death. So it is that without much straining of the evidence one may entertain the possibility of an early *Cantar de Sancho* that is much more conventional, much more like certain other Castilian epic songs, than is the version that survives in the *Primera crónica.*

In any case, our hypothesis allows us to perceive the very distinctive profile of the late *Cantar.* This poem is assuredly unconventional. In its sophistication of outlook, its complexity of theme, it resembles only the *Poema de mio Cid* among epics on Spanish themes. What information we possess about Spanish epic poetry makes the later *Sancho* and the canonical *Cid* stand dramatically apart from the rest of the literature. The difference between these two works and many of their fellows corresponds roughly to the distinction that one might make between a later

Romance epic about kings and political order and an early one about personal and family rivalries. We are, of course, speaking of the later *Sancho* as though we knew it well in all of its detail. Obviously we do not. As with the *Najerense* text the poem itself is lost, and the Alfonsine version has combined bits of the prosified *cantar* with passages from nonpoetic sources. All sorts of questions arise, as with the older poem. For example, do the portions of the text in the *Crónica* that come from Rodrigo Toledano ever replace portions of the *Cantar* that are therefore lost to us? Or again, have the editors of the *Crónica* tampered seriously with the design and sense of the poem? Their hands are hardly clean. We know the freedom they exercise in adapting other texts than this one to their purposes. All these difficulties notwithstanding, granting for argument's sake that much has been lost and much altered, the gross outlines of the *Cantar* are clear enough to see. They are, as we will try to show, easy to identify, and they have a consistency and logic about them that is hard to obscure.

The later poet has completely displaced the system of cause and effect of the older narrative. There are two details of plot in his *Cantar* that are decisive in giving the work its special profile. These are the very points that separate the poem from its predecessor: the fact that García, not Sancho, is the first to go to war, and that Urraca is presented as not guilty of the murder of her brother. These two features bear very much upon each other. Urraca's innocence represents a fundamental change; if she is innocent, then vengeance is no longer the motive power of the action. What takes its place? Ultimately and fundamentally, the new mainspring of the plot is the fact that Fernando has divided his realm among his children, this in violation of Visigothic law. At the deathbed division he binds all of them by oath not to invade each other's lands, thinking thus to assure the peace of the whole territory. The whole plan, in addition to being illegal—at least to the mind of the poet—is also impractical. The new situation is an invitation to mischief. The trap is set, so to speak. The temptation is great for one of the brothers to break the oath and try to recover some of what Fernando had destroyed. The inevitable happens. But as it turns out, it is not the powerful Sancho who initiates the bloodshed but the witless García, king of Galicia. García in this version embodies the principle of fortune: any of the three brothers *could* have gone to war, but he, perhaps the unlikeliest, actually did. García regards the land of his sisters Elvira and Urraca, territory ceded to them at the last minute by Fernando, as his own (García's), and so he seeks to recover it.

Now, García himself does not represent a serious threat to the peace. He is weak and not very talented, and in any case, his ambitions are limited. García's adventure, however small, is a spark that sets off a great explosion. He sets the example for the infinitely stronger and more resourceful Sancho, who also thinks himself wronged by his father's act. Sancho is not merely ambitious or willful. He is Fernando's firstborn and rightful heir and declares with some justice that the whole of his father's lands should have gone to him. Therefore, once the possibility of peace is gone, once García has made his move, he sees no reason why he should not recover by force what should have been his by right. It is then and only then that the bloody career of Sancho begins, hateful above all to poet and audience because Christians are slaughtering Christians. The fatal machine does its work: the chance circumstance that the weakest of the brothers is the one to break the impossible pact makes it inevitable that Sancho, with right on his side and actually bound by no oath,[22] should throw the land into disorder.

The difference between this version of the story and older ones—in historical sources still in existence, and in hypothetical epic texts—is palpable. Sancho's role comes to be a complex one. Rodrigo, after all, attributes the war between him and his brothers to the contrary temperament of the Goths, simply.[23] Other historical writings are not even so specific as that. If all of these texts taken together tell us anything about the lost *Cantar,* we would have to conclude that it too found little motive for Sancho's actions other than his intractable and rebellious nature. But in the later version everything is different. Sancho thinks his rights violated; such are his feelings on the subject that he refuses to swear the oath his father requires of him. But remarkably, he does not rush into war for all of that. Only when García marches on his sister's lands, in other words, only when the temptation is overwhelming, does Sancho act to recover his birthright. Fernando's deathbed disposition of territory, therefore, has the effect of ultimately deflecting the considerable goodwill of a Sancho whose moral character is far from contemptible. The new Sancho is by no means a total villain. The blame for the ills of Spain, once again, is laid at the feet of Fernando.

In time Sancho is brought up to the walls of Zamora. The action up to

---

22. The *Crónica* is contradictory; on his deathbed Sancho repents having broken the oath (Alfonso 1955, 512).

23. Rodrigo Toledano 1987, 189–94.

this point is logical, the motivation superb. What is more, this logic is something more than pure formalism. The plot is a sort of paradigm of political folly; it illustrates dramatically the risks involved in dividing the kingdom. But Sancho's death before Zamora seems to break this logic completely. What are we to make of it? Vellido appears from nowhere, as it were, and commits the murder virtually on his own. Urraca's innocence is obviously crucial here: she is no longer the one to spur him to action. The murder is thus decisively disconnected from the events that precede it. Now, this very curious disposition of the plot cannot but be deliberate; its function is to make it clear that Sancho's death is an act of Providence, a judgment of God. Divinity intervening takes the place of Urraca's revenge on Sancho as in the old poem. In the later *Cantar* the dying king is in fact made to admit that his fall was brought about by divine justice:

> bien entiendo que muerto so, et matome el traydor de Vellid Adolffo que se auie fecho mio uassallo; et bien tengo que esto fue por mios pecados et por las soberuias que fiz a mios hermanos, et passe el mandamiento que fiz a mio padre et la yura que fiz que non tolliesse a ninguno de mios hermanos ninguna cosa de lo suyo. (512)

> [I well know that I have been killed, and that the traitor Vellido Adolfo, who had become my vassal, has killed me, and I truly believe that this was in payment for my sins and for the arrogant things I did to my brothers, for I violated my father's command-ment and broke the oath that I made that I would not take any-thing from my brothers that was theirs.]

Sancho is not blameless. However much justice is on his side, he is the breaker of a solemn oath (the editors seem to forget that earlier they made Sancho abstain from this oath).[24] Perhaps even more important, he is a disturber of the peace of Christendom, a shedder of Christian blood; our text is at pains to tell us this many times. The above account of the episode may seem gratuitous or trivial. One might object that since medieval Christians thought Providence all pervading, it is unlikely that a narrator of those days would attribute one turn of his story to the hand of God, but not all. There are narratives in the Middle Ages about which such an observation might be true—in which every event is seen

---

24. In Alfonso 1955, 494a, Sancho is represented as refusing to swear.

as providential. The later *Sancho* is not one of them. There is a sharp contrast here between events that occur in the ordinary course of things and the one that comes about through the direct agency of God. The sequence of events up to the murder is presented as conforming to the law of natural cause and effect; to understand it one need not have recourse to the Unseen Hand. Breaking the statute that enjoins the king not to divide his domain is bad because of the enormous risks it entails, those of bloodshed and disorder. There is no need for God to deal out poetic justice; the interplay of human will and fortune is more than able to do the damage. But when we come to the murder narrative, so lovingly designed by the later poet, we are shown the notable coincidence of evident guilt on the part of Sancho and a quite fortuitous event that punishes him. We may note parenthetically that elsewhere the editors of the *Primera crónica* decidedly favor this clear distinction between the acts of nature and the acts of God, and that in this sense the later *Sancho* fits in very tidily with their schemes.

Crucial to the orientation of the later *Cantar de Sancho II* is the unfavorable view of Fernando. One of the grounds we have for considering the prosification in the *Primera crónica* reasonably faithful is that other portions of the larger work treat him very kindly. The portrait of Fernando inherited from the *Historia silensis* by Rodrigo of Toledo, Lucas of Tuy, and finally the editors of the *Crónica*[25] is of an ideal Christian king, just, pious, humble, a splendid warrior. The *Cantar* plainly represents a different strain, in that it associates Fernando exclusively with a single illegal, impolitic, and, indeed, immoral act, the division of the kingdom. Can it be that this discrepancy of texts is due in part to the milieu out of which the poem sprang, a milieu quite different from that which produced the *Primera crónica general*? There are reasons to believe as much, though of course the notion isolated that rule should be one and undivided is hardly in itself alien to the chronicle. A close look, therefore, may persuade us that some of the issues to which the poem speaks were not living ones for the Alfonsine compilers. Thus Sánchez Albornoz very reasonably offers us a *Sancho* that is a piece of propaganda in favor of the rights of primogeniture, an issue that arises when Alfonso VII divides his lands.[26] Concerns of this order are certainly not

---

25. The life of Fernando is found in *Historia silensis* 1959, 183–209; in Rodrigo Toledano 1987, 189–94; in Lucas 1608, 91–97; and in Alfonso 1955, 482–95.

26. Sánchez Albornoz 1945, 42 n, 50.

forcefully expressed in the *Crónica*. A second possible reading of the *Sancho* could be based on an observation of Menéndez Pidal; we could see in the work a protest against the notion of the kingdom as the prince's patrimony. In *La España del Cid* Pidal makes the point that in dividing the kingdom Fernando, a Navarrese prince, is conforming to a pattern of kingship normal in his own land but totally foreign to western Spain.[27] It is remotely possible that the *Cantar* was meant to express the displeasure of the westerner at the intrusion of an alien form of public life. This view taken whole is, however, implausible in the sense that our version of the *Sancho* in all likelihood comes so late. It is hard to believe that the whole question would have much urgency so many years after Fernando's death. But patrimonialism by itself raises an important point. A patrimonialist view of kingship, if we could speak of such a thing, is almost by definition one that makes no allowance for the public character of kingly office. If the king's lands are his property in the ordinary sense of the word, he can do what he likes with them, make grants of them to his nobles, divide them among his sons. His relations to the grantees of various sorts are private; indeed, strictly speaking, the distinctions public and private have little meaning applied to them. This issue was not entirely a dead letter at the time the poem was composed.

Fresh in the minds of the poet and his audience in the late twelfth and early thirteenth centuries was the case of another division of lands than that made by Fernando and of another time of troubles consequent to that division. The king in question was, of course, Alfonso VII, who formed a great empire in the feudal mode and then provided for its dismemberment. It is not necessary to specify fully what principles and precedents he stood on in breaking up his holdings. But is it not possible that the author of the later *Sancho* wished to express disapproval of Fernando's act— and, by implication, Alfonso's—on the grounds precisely that it violated the public nature of kingship? Our text gives certain indications in this sense. It condemns Fernando for putting asunder what God has joined:

> los godos antiguamientre fizieran su postura entresi que nunqua fuesse partido el imperio de Espanna, mas que siempre fuesse todo de un sennor, et que por esta razon non lo deuie partir nin podie, pues que Dios lo auie ayuntado en el lo mas dello. (494)

---

27. Menéndez Pidal 1969, 1:142–43.

[The Goths of old made an agreement that the Spanish domain should never be divided but that it should always be under one lord, and for this reason it should not and could not be divided, because God had joined together the land and everything that pertains to it.]

The words are Sancho's, spoken at Fernando's deathbed. Menéndez Pidal identifies these lines as part of the *Cantar de Fernando*,[28] but this work is so entirely of a piece with the *Sancho* that if the two do not actually form a single work, they must at the very least be thought of as forming a cycle. What needs stressing is the notion that for the Goths Spain was always to be under the rule of one man. Fernando's act is judged adversely on the basis of Spain's right to unity. Now, it is obvious that at this moment in history, when our *Cantar* was composed, the unified Spain of our text is purely and simply an ideal. Fernando's kingdom, which Sancho hopes to reunite, is assuredly not Spain *simpliciter*. Not even the empire of Alfonso VII, impressive as it is, corresponds entirely to the ancient Gothic domain. No post-Gothic Christian kingdom realizes fully and literally the meaning of the word *Spain*. The "España" of our text is plainly a myth, a sort of lofty fiction based on old memories. What, then, is the word supposed to mean in this context? Could the reference possibly be to a sort of ill-defined community or corporation, a public thing transcending private interests, a body politic of which Fernando is the head? If this is the case, the poem invites us to condemn Fernando on the grounds that a king conceived according to these principles cannot regard his kingdom as though it were his private property. The kingdom is from God and hence not the king's to divide.

It is well known that in the poet's time many jurists and writers on legal and political matters tended to base royal authority on something other than the king's title to land or his contractual relations with vassals and others. Thus, "lo Princep . . . es comuna persona a tots los habitadors de aquesta terra" [the king is the person common to all the inhabitants of this land], and again, "totes coses que són el regne són del rey *quant a jurisdicció*" (italics mine) [Everything that is of this kingdom is the king's *with respect to jurisdiction*]; that is, the king's "ownership"

---

28. Alfonso 1955, 494; Menéndez Pidal identifies the source in vol. 2, p. clxviii. Cf. R. Menéndez Pidal 1951, 240–56, for a more extensive relic of the *Fernando* than is found in the *Crónica*.

of his kingdom is restricted and has a very special sense. The quotations are from the writings of Pere Albert, the great Catalan jurist, who wrote not many decades after the formation of our poem. His sentiments are, of course, entirely typical of the legal thought of a whole epoch, but the testimony they offer is the more eloquent in that the legal norms he is speaking of bear almost entirely on feudal institutions.[29] Our *Cantar's* reference to Gothic law is, by the way, absolutely crucial. The Visigothic legal and canonical tradition understands fully the distinction between the public and private persons of the king and draws a clear line between the royal lands and the king's private property. Visigothic kingship is, of course, elective, not hereditary, and so the distinction has great practical consequences. For a king to distribute royal lands to personal heirs who have absolutely no claim on the throne would manifestly be an abuse, and in fact royal and conciliar decrees, preserved in the *Forum judicum,* specifically prohibit such a division.[30] Needless to say, the sense of these statutes applied to kingship that is not elective changes considerably. But the concept of king as public person implied in them survives.

In the *Cantar,* then, when Fernando divides his lands among his children, we are invited to see him as violating the high dignity of his office. In a particularly radical way the king fails as king. In a significant fashion Fernando's situation in the *Sancho* duplicates that of Alfonso in the *Poema de mio Cid.* Alfonso's delinquency is infinitely less serious: he has dealt unjustly with a faithful vassal. The acts of both monarchs are shown, however, as failures to realize the fullness of kingship. In the *Poema* the position of the king is very clearly defined. His authority over his nobles transcends by far the contract he makes with them as they become his vassals. This is, of course, the point in the Cid's fidelity. In a sense, once Alfonso has exiled him, his obligations as vassal are at an end. But Rodrigo to the last regards himself as Alfonso's subject. It can only be that he is so presented by the poet because he wishes to show the authority of the king as permanent,

---

29. Both quotations are from the edition of the *Commemoracions* of Pere Albert included in the edition of the *Usatges de Barcelona* prepared by J. Rovira i Ermengol (1933); the first quotation is on p. 158; the second is on p. 185. Maravall 1967, 141–56, is eloquent particularly on the emergence of a notion of the public character of the king, even in a feudal setting.

30. In *Fuero juzgo, en latín y castellano* 1815, the prologue, "De electione principis," ii, a decree of the eighth council of Toledo, and the decree of Receswinth, 5–6, both sustain this principle.

superior to, and different from any specific bond between an actual vassal and his lord, prior to and different from the character and acts of the man who exercises that authority.[31]

The two poems share a notion of king as public person preeminently. But the likeness of the *Sancho* to the *Poema de mio Cid* could perhaps be pushed further, and here again we are led to note a divergence between poem and chronicle. Could it be that the abstract view of kingship in the *Poema* is somehow of a piece with the premium the work places on law and legality? More specifically, is it reasonable to suppose that at the time of the poem's composition, the same men who presented Rodrigo as faithful to his sovereign first and last might ipso facto and automatically be inclined to present the trial at Toledo as a model of rational judicial process? Possibly. In any event, the *Sancho* poet has the same pair of prejudices. He at once deplores Fernando's failure to appreciate the absolute character of his office and treats as barbarous, irrational, and inimical to justice the traditional legal forms. The *Cantar de Sancho* is a rational jurist's poem and expresses his adverse judgment on archaic laws. In every case the Germanic customs important in the plot are treated as ridiculous or positively unjust. Arias Gonzalo's mocking speech in which he accepts the challenge of the Castilians is, in effect, the rational critique of the form of that challenge. The violation of the sanctuary claimed by Vellido Adolfo is manifestly an answer to the simple demands of justice. And most important of all, the judicial combat is made to turn out against expectations, with the pathetic deaths of the sons of the admired Arias Gonzalo, precisely in order to hold up that legal pattern to judgment. The traditional forms are hateful to the poet because they do not serve the right. The point of view, the critique, one might say, is that of a devotee, perhaps a practitioner of rational legal procedure. All of this might be drawn from a reading of the text of the *Sancho* preserved in the Alfonsine chronicle; the bias is simply there to be seen. But the same text also reveals that its author really knew the law; the reference to the *Fuero juzgo* is scarcely mistakable. But what is most remarkable about the allusion to the *Fuero* is that it bears precisely on the matter of the public character of kingship. The judgment on Fernando is in effect made on the basis of two or three texts in the Visigothic code. Everything fits, from the condemnation of Fernando to

---

31. The point is obvious, but see *Poema de mio Cid* 1972, lxi–lxii, and Hart 1962.

the dim view of judicial combat. The consistent pattern is one of criticism, the point of view, that of a jurist.

I conclude this section by observing that my view that the *Sancho* poet knew the law is not new. Professor C. C. Smith has spoken to this effect, on evidence more positive than mine.[32] The proposition that the *Cid* poet also was a lawyer has, of course, also been maintained, both by Professor Smith and by Professor P. E. Russell.[33] It now only remains to us to observe that law, legality, and legitimacy, which figure large in our *Cantar,* are not very important themes in the whole Alfonsine chronicle. María Rosa Lida de Malkiel has pointed to this lack as one of the important characteristics of Alfonsine historical narrative. She had in mind particularly not the *Primera crónica* but the parallel *General estoria,*[34] but the two works are not so dissimilar that her remarks might not be applicable in some way to both. In the *Crónica* the lack is, as I would think, especially conspicuous in those portions where the compilers have the greatest control of their material. We will allude vaguely to this problem in the section that follows. For the present, it could be useful to recall Américo Castro's remarkable characterization of the whole opus of the Learned King as a "suma pragmática."[35] The most authentic portions of the *Crónica* assuredly bear more on the practical problems of rule, the arts and skills of war and statecraft, than on questions of legitimacy. The *Cantar* plainly belongs to another world. The fact that its legalist bias is preserved by the Alfonsine compilers may well be a witness to their respect for the poem's text.

We now confront head-on the problem we have already dealt with only partially and indirectly: the place of the *Sancho II* in the *Primera crónica.* We can scarcely do less; the text we have been reading is the Alfonsine work. The question breaks itself in two: how the poem fits into the *Crónica* as a whole, and what its place is in the section on the reigns of Fernando, Sancho, and Alfonso. Before dealing with the first, however, we must make some general remarks about the broad design of the Alfonsine work, or of the lack of such design. Surely the first temptation of many readers is to see in the *Crónica* a vast, shapeless

---

32. Smith 1971, 593–94.
33. Smith 1971, 593–94, and Russell 1952.
34. Lida da Malkiel 1958.
35. Castro 1954, 309.

work, rather than a compilation, a catchall, in which criteria for inclusion or exclusion of sources are very vague, and in which the manner of articulating them, chapter by chapter, is totally unsystematic. It is one of the purposes of this study to dispel this impression. It needs to be stressed that parts of the work are put together with great care, that it is built around themes, that its design answered to certain plans. But there is no point in denying the obvious. The *Primera crónica* is a very miscellaneous work. For example, the preferred sources are not the same in the various sections. What is more, the actual techniques of compilation differ greatly from one part to another. What the editors do with the sources in the first 108 chapters, for example, is not at all like what happens in the chapters following. The quality of the narratives in the *Crónica* varies enormously. Some are articulated with great skill; others are loose and little organized. The themes of the work are distributed in curious ways. Some are scattered through the length of the work, others are restricted to one section. What follow immediately are a few modest examples of a solidarity between the *Sancho* and other parts of the *Crónica*. They speak for themselves and are not meant to give the impression that the large work is more systematic than it is. I would suggest that the search for intelligibility in the *Crónica* might begin with such essays as this.

There is one sense in which the coincidence of *Cantar* and chronicle is manifest. The main theme of the *Sancho* is sounded in a place no less important in the mammoth work than the prologue itself. That all-important introduction tells us that the history to follow is among other things a warning to rulers not to break up their kingdoms to distribute them to several heirs. The text is listing the subjects to be treated:

> del danno que uino en ella por partir los regnos, por que se non pudo cobrar tan ayna; et despues cuemo la ayunto Dio. (4)

> [concerning the ill that came to it [the land], how this ill could not be quickly righted, and afterwards how God reunited the land.]

The significance of these lines needs to be stressed. The bulk of the prologue is, of course, simply a translation of Rodrigo of Toledo's preface to his own history of Spain, but this particular passage is original. It is one of the handful of additions the editors make to Rodrigo's text, all of which add up to a scarce seven lines of one column in Menéndez Pidal's edition. The conclusion can only be that the editors thought the matter of the division of kingdoms important enough to add to a ready-made prologue already full of high purpose. This striking coincidence of *Cantar* and prologue raises serious problems. Menéndez Pidal has argued on the basis of the list of authorities cited in the prologue that it was composed with only the first 108 chapters in mind.[36] If he is right, how do we account for what seems a clear allusion to the *Sancho*? There are, after all, no narratives in the *Crónica* quite like it. The possibilities are several. The section on the Roman Civil War, which does fall within the 108 chapters, stresses heavily the risks in dividing rule between two powerful men and so could have been intended as a warning to princes not to break up their kingdoms. Then, too, the editors, without knowing the *Sancho* specifically, could have foreseen that the chronicle would eventually contain narratives dramatizing the dangers of division. The instances are several, of which Fernando is only one. It is, for example, pure accident that the Alfonsine work did not extend as far as the reign of Alfonso VII.[37] If the original plan had gotten that far, the narrative might have been shaped to bring into relief the theme of division.[38] But to my mind the simplest and most obvious possibility stands: that the editors of the prologue really did take into account the inclusion of the *Sancho*. The force of Menéndez Pidal's argument is limited, after all, in that the authorities named in the prologue are with one exception the same ones cited by Rodrigo. The list could be pure cliché and not meant to be exhaustive. Dating is apparently not a problem. Diego Catalán has presented strong evidence that the broad outline of the *Primera crónica* as we know it is genuinely Alfonsine up to a point well into the reign of Alfonso VI.[39] This covers the time of Sancho, obviously. The likelihood, therefore, that the *Cantar* was somehow alluded to in the prologue cannot be ruled out.

---

36. Menéndez Pidal, introduction to *PCG*, 1:xxii–xxiv.

37. Catalán cuts the Alfonsine project off in the middle of the reign of Alfonso VI (1963a, 205–10).

38. The *Crónica latina de los reyes de Castilla* (1964, 4) expresses great disapproval of Alfonso's act of dividing his empire; the chronicle's outlook on that event is in almost every way similar to that of the *Cantar de Sancho* with respect to Fernando. There is no evidence that I know that the editors of the *Primera crónica general* knew the *Crónica latina de los reyes de Castilla* or that they would have used it had their project reached the period in question. But the latter work is, in fact, an example of a literary text that does express a severe judgment on Alfonso. It is thus not at all inconceivable that another historical work, like the *Primera crónica general,* might have followed the same path.

39. See note 37.

A positive argument that the inclusion of the *Sancho* answered to some general program on the part of the editors is that there is one narrative in the *Crónica* that presents a striking parallelism to it. This is the episode we have mentioned, on the Roman Civil War, which has built into it a strong focus on the dangers of putting the commonwealth under the rule of more than one man. What makes this coincidence remarkable is that, unlike the Sancho passage, the structure, the design of the civil war narrative is entirely the creation of the Alfonsine editors; it is not ready-made. The thematic focus we have mentioned is literally forced on its sources. The bulk of the text is from the *Histories* of Paulus Orosius,[40] and yet, the editors manage by artful interpolations from other sources to alter completely the sense of the Orosian narrative. In Orosius the episode is one more item in his gallery of horrors, intended to show that public life and the careers of the great reflect the inherent inclination of man towards ill. But in the hands of the Alfonsine committee the story is one of Pompey's initial success; the jealousy of Caesar, which is at first hidden, but which little by little becomes manifest; the growing power of Caesar; and finally the inevitable conflict between the two. The moral of the story is explicitly stated more than once; when the fullness of power does not reside in one man, the commonwealth is thrown into disorder. The most complete and indeed dramatic statement of the theme is the brief chapter 79, worth quoting entire. It is a heavily amplified mixture of Lucan and Rodrigo;[41] note that the educational value of the whole episode is especially pointed out:

> Ponpeyo et Julio Cesar fueron suegro et yerno, ca era casado Ponpeyo con Julia, fija de Julio Cesar; et que auie ya en ellos sos fijos, dond se fazie el debdo entrellos tamanno, que seyendo catado, non deuiera por ninguna manera contecer lo que oyredes adelant que y contecio. Mas por que eran amos estos principes de muy alto linage, otrossi eran de grandes coraçones et muy esforçados en armas, et de grandes fechos et bien andantes en guerras et en lides,

---

40. The civil war proper is covered in Orosius 1882, bk. 6, chaps. 14–15, but the material used by the Alfonsine editors for the whole episode I am speaking of is in Orosius 1882, bk. 6, chaps. 1–15, passim.

41. Menéndez Pidal (Alfonso 1955, 1:lxxxi) gives as the sources of this chapter verses 109–14 of the first book of the *Pharsalia* and a couple of lines from chap. 10 of the *Historia romanorum* of Rodrigo (1793, 220). A scrutiny of these passages shows that the Alfonsine text is very free with both; the dependence on Rodrigo is especially loose.

et uenturados de uencer las mas uezes; e tan poderosos fueron en el
sennorio de Roma sobre los otros principes romanos del so tiempo
et sobre los de las otras tierras, por que cada uno quiso seer sennor.
Ca del comienço de los consules fastal so tiempo dellos siempre regnaron dos o mas cadanno en uno; cuemo lo departiremos adelant en
so logar. Mas agora contaremos de los fechos que amos estos principes fizieron daqui adelant, sobre que ouieron guerra et lidiaron muchas uezes ellos e los otros cibdadanos de Roma por las razones
dellos; et de los fechos que ellos fizieron por las otras tierras diremos
ende algunos: lo uno por que fueron amos sennores de las Espannas, pero que en sennos tiempos, lo al por que uienen y razones en
que puede aprender quien quisiere exiemplos de castigos. (57–58)

[Pompey and Julius Caesar were son-in-law and father-in-law, for
Pompey was married to Julia, daughter of Julius Caesar and had
his children by her. On this basis the familial bond was so great that
what did come to pass, as you will hear presently, should never
have come to pass. But since both were princes of very high lineage, and moreover were of great spirit and very bold in arms,
doers of great deeds and very successful in wars and conflicts, and
fortunate in that they prevailed most of the time, and since they
were so powerful in the lordship of Rome, more powerful yet than
other Roman princes of their time and than those of other lands
[for all these reasons], each one wished to be [exclusive] lord. For
from the beginning of the time of the consuls, as we will explain in
due time, two or more people ruled, but one at a time, one year
each. But now we will tell of the deeds of both these princes from
this moment on, how they made war on each other, and how for
their own interests they very often made war on the citizens of
Rome; we will tell also of some of their deeds in other lands; we
will do this for two reasons, because both were lords of Spain but
at different times, and because there is matter here for whoever
wishes to profit from the example.]

The parallelism between the civil war episode and the *Sancho* is manifest
above all in one particular turn of the plot. The senate, seeing the
danger in the rivalry of the two great men, divides the Roman lands
between them, giving each authority over certain territories. They see
this as a sure road to peace, and they believe they have averted the

conflict (chapter 86). Events, of course, very quickly show them their error. The boundaries laid down by the senators came to mean nothing, and before long Caesar is at the Rubicon, about to invade Italy and start the war. The role of the senate is here obviously like that of Fernando, who also believes falsely that dividing his lands is a way of avoiding war. We should stress here particularly that this whole development in the narrative is entirely the work of the Alfonsine compilers. Thus, the only thing Orosius contributes to the passage is the information that certain provinces were conceded to each of the two men.[42] From Rodrigo of Toledo's Roman history comes the detail that the rivalry was a threat to Rome's stability.[43] The notion that the granting of provinces was a measure for peace is simply a deduction made by the editors. We thus cannot in the least doubt that the element that this chapter adds to the political and moral lessons taught by the civil war episode is fully intended and is by no means an accident.

In general the control the editors exercise over their material in this whole section is very close. A few more instances suffice to show this. The text of Orosius, which supplies most of the thread of the narrative, is abandoned several times in ways that tighten the structure visibly. Two very brief interpolations come from Lucan. One tells of the death of Julia, Caesar's daughter and Pompey's wife. The other relates the death of Crassus, who is presented as a peacekeeper between Caesar and Pompey (chapter 91). The latter substitution is striking in that it replaces lines in Orosius that actually make Crassus entirely hateful.[44] The *Crónica,* following Lucan, presents him as admirable, exercising a laudable civic function. These interpolations bring the story a completely distinctive pattern of motivation. The point is that, alive, Julia and Crassus are the two bonds between the rivals, the two forces that keep hostilities from breaking out. Dead, they can no longer play this important role, and indeed, once they are gone, the dreaded civil war does begin. Thus, what in Orosius is pure happening is here turned into a consequence; the start of the war is the effect of certain immediate causes. But more than a love of logic is involved. The passage is weighty with doctrine and illustrates two themes. First, it shows the play of

---

42. Chaps. 7 and 15 of book 6; we may note that this information is not even in one place in Orosius's work.

43. Rodrigo Toledano 1793, 221.

44. Orosius 1882, bk. 6, chap. 13.

fortune, the "ventura" so beloved of the Alfonsine editors: the unfore-
seeable deaths seriously alter the course of events. Second, it illustrates
the great importance for statecraft of the personal relationships between
leaders. The vagueness of the boundary between public and private is a
significant fact of medieval life, both in literature and in practice. The
matter is highlighted here. As in the *Sancho,* the chain of cause and
effect brought into the narrative is made to express practical wisdom.
The logic of the events narrated becomes in itself an exemplary pattern,
full of high doctrine.

The roles of Julia and Crassus are obviously secondary in the
Alfonsine narrative. The principal, all-important strain of motivation in
the civil war narrative is the envy of Caesar. This passion is, in point of
fact, the one and only cause the *Crónica* speaks of for the war itself;
quite simply, this is how the war is explained. The declared theme of the
whole episode is, of course, that rivalry between the great brings disaster
to the commonwealth. But the emulation here is all in one direction.
The personal blame is all Caesar's. Curiously, Pompey does not recipro-
cate: he is presented throughout as modest and generous, and it is never
suggested that he bears his father-in-law any ill will at all. The rivalry is
entirely a one-way affair. It is the envy of Caesar that is the complete
and sufficient cause of the war. Now, to implant into the narrative this
crucial and central piece of explanation, the editors are, once again,
obliged to use considerable surgery. The actual text on Caesar's envy
comes to them from Rodrigo of Toledo; more than a quotation, however, what we have here is a sort of interpretation by the editors of a
passage in the brief chapter in the *Historia Romanorum* given over to
the civil war.[45] Remarkably, the *Primera crónica* uses the fragment several times, at various points in the narrative. As Pompey's star rises, as
his power and prestige come to be ever greater, the compilers press the
Rodrigo bit into service to tell of Caesar's envy at his rival's triumphant
return from Spain, at his military successes in Asia Minor, and at his
victory over Mithridates. This repeated use of a single passage tells a
great deal about the intentions of the compilers. The doctrine of María
Rosa Lida de Malkiel, in large part true, that in the Alfonsine histories
completeness of information is the one basis for including a given
source[46] clearly does not hold here. Rodrigo may be an obligatory

---

45. Rodrigo Toledano 1793, 220–21.
46. Lida de Malkiel 1958, 112.

source, so to speak, but it is hard to see how a desire to present all information available would force the editors to use the same fragment over and over again, in contexts unlike that of the original. Their choice of this source was a free one. The resulting logic for their narrative is in fact impressive. One case in point involves still more surgery. As we have noted, Caesar in the *Crónica* is jealous of Pompey after his military victories in Spain. A long section is devoted to the triumph accorded him on his return. The passage is not from Orosius; it is a mosaic, made up of bits and pieces from several other sources (chapter 78, pp. 56–57). It is, in other words, virtually an original passage. But immediately after this the interpolation from Rodrigo appears for the first time. As the *Crónica* tells the story, then, it is the glory surrounding Pompey on his return from Spain that first arouses the envy of Caesar. The sources of the civil strife are traced back to the most specific circumstances, and the sequence of events is logical, plausible, and exemplary.

In this respect the *Crónica* passage is much like the *Sancho* narrative, one might say. But as we have pointed out, the difference between them is that the *Cantar de Sancho* came to the Alfonsine editors whole, or nearly so, whereas they were obliged to make up the other well-formed narrative on their own. The likeness and unlikeness seem to me significant. In a word, it is believable that the *Sancho* could have found its way into the *Primera crónica* complete with its stress on the evils of division without this last feature being part of the overall scheme of the compilers. We have already pointed out a few thematic strands in the poem that enjoy no great fortunes elsewhere in the *Crónica*. But the fact is that the editors went to great pains to construct elsewhere in their work a tight and articulated narrative on a theme similar to that of the *Cantar*. The conclusion can only be that they saw the drift of the *Sancho* and thought it valuable for their purposes, perhaps valuable enough to copy.

One last link can perhaps be found between the *Sancho* and the civil war episode. It is a cliché, a commonplace, taken from the *Pharsalia,* used over many centuries to express the evils of divided rule. It is the poet's remark about Caesar and Pompey on the eve of their conflict:

Nulla fides regni sociis, omnisque potestas
Impatiens consortis erat.

[There will be no loyalty between those who share governance, nor will power tolerate a partner.] (trans. Fraker)

J. A. Maravall has shown that these lines from Lucan appear in a wide variety of Spanish texts touching on the matter.[47] This is possibly significant in itself. The theme of the division of rule calls to the medieval author's mind the *Pharsalia* or a fragment of it. Since the *Pharsalia* is about the civil war, and since it is, in fact, the second most extensive source for that episode in the *Primera crónica,* the compilers may well have been forced to view it and the Sancho section as parallel narratives. But seen in detail the problem is much more complicated. The phrase does occur in Rodrigo of Toledo's account of the struggle between the children of Fernando.[48] That passage in Rodrigo is in fact translated in the *Crónica,* but in neither text is the sentiment identified as Lucan's. In the *Crónica* it is specifically attributed to Rodrigo:

> assi como dize ell arçobispo don Rodrigo, el sennor non quiere otro par en el sennorio. (495)

> [as Archbishop Rodrigo says, no lord wants a peer in his lordship.]

On the other hand, in the civil war passage in the *Crónica* the notion, the idea that the great cannot bear rivals, is everywhere, but the actual phrase is simply not translated. This is the more remarkable in that the passage on the bonds between Caesar and Pompey, Julia and Crassus, is heavily dependent on Lucan, and it is here in the *Pharsalia* that the critical phrase occurs. Thus, the link between Lucan and the Sancho episode is obscured, if it is there at all. It may be there, nevertheless.

We turn now to the second large question on the place of the *Sancho* in the *Crónica:* how does the *Cantar* fit into the section of the chronicle dealing with the reigns of Fernando, Sancho, and Alfonso? This question is perhaps more straightforward in that we are dealing with a smaller body of evidence. In a sense it is also a prior question. The unit we have been in effect discussing is the complete narrative in the *Crónica,* the fragments of the poem along with the passages from other sources. This is, indeed, a remarkable and original unit. The poem is assuredly its backbone but is far from being the whole narrative. What is it like, and what do the interpolated passages add? To answer we must observe that in the short run, at least, the added matter is of two sorts:

---

47. "Un tópico medieval sobre la división de reinos" (Maravall 1972, 91–101).
48. Rodrigo Toledano 1987, 194.

that which obviously harmonizes with the poem, and that which does not. The latter at first has the look of the compiler's nightmare, passages on Sancho that they can hardly neglect—Rodrigo, for example, is their most respected authority—but that do not seem to tell the same story as the main source. Yet, contrary to appearances, both sorts of additions, tractable and otherwise, enrich the narrative visibly.

The tractable additions are easy to dispose of. The passages inherited from Rodrigo that tell of the difficult and contrary temperament of the Gothic kings are harmless enough:

> los reys de Espanna uinieron de la fuerte sangre de los godos, por que acaescio muchas uezes que los reys godos se mataron hermano a hermano por esta razon. (495)

> [the kings of Spain are from the strong blood of the Goths, for it has happened many times that the Gothic kings killed one another, brother killing brother, for this very reason (the Gothic inheritance).]

The events narrated surely bear witness to the contentious nature of Sancho, and this passage therefore is a good generalizing signpost. More interesting, perhaps, is the information Rodrigo brings the story about García. The García of the poem, we recall, is at bottom its most hateful character. Sancho's career is a perverse and destructive one, to be sure, but certain things weigh for him: the folly of Fernando, the fact that Sancho is his firstborn son, and the fact that García was first to break the oath. But no good whatever can be said about García's adventures. They are quite without dignity. The editors of the *Primera crónica* hardly miss their cue. The sections from Rodrigo that they add tell of his cowardice, his inability to work in concert with his great nobles, the contempt in which they hold him. One passage tells of a shameful overture he makes to the Muslims, which they refuse. The relief of the Sancho narrative is manifestly heightened by these additions.[49] They do not destroy its logic; in many ways they enhance it.

A third nonepic detail included by the editors, perhaps the most

---

49. The passage from Rodrigo is chap. 17 of bk. 7 of the *De rebus hispaniae* (Rodrigo Toledano 1987, 194); this matter appears in Alfonso 1955, in chaps. 819, p. 499, and 821, p. 500.

striking one of all, comes from Lucas of Tuy and is part of the section
about Alfonso's stay in Toledo. It is the pair of lines that tells how the
exiled king hoped eventually to take the Muslim city. We should explain
that this fragment is itself part of a larger interpolation, mostly from
Rodrigo, which covers the whole period of the exile. We can easily guess
why this section was added. It is possible that the *Cantar* had little to say
about the Toledo period, and that the editors were obliged to turn to
Rodrigo to fill the gap in information. There is, after all, analogous gap-
filling through the whole length of the *Crónica*. The handiest parallel is,
perhaps, the Cid narrative, where the periods not covered by the *Poema
de mio Cid* are supplied by Ben Alcama and the *Historia Roderici*. But if
this explains and justifies the larger interpolation, it hardly does the
smaller. It does not really supply information at all; it only expresses a
state of mind. Here is the passage:

> El rey don Alffonso ueyendo el bien et la onrra daquel rey Al-
> memon et de como era sennor de grand caualleria de moros et de
> la mas noble çibdad que en tiempo de los godos fue, començo a
> auer grand pesar en su coraçon et de cuedar como la podrie sacar
> de poder de los moros si Dios le diesse tiempo en que lo pudiesse
> fazer. (503)[50]

> [King Alfonso—when he saw the splendor and honor of that king
> Almemon, and how he was lord of a great body of Moorish knights
> and of the noblest city of the time of the Goths—began to feel
> great sorrow in his heart, and he began to think about how he
> could take the city out of the power of the Moors, if God granted
> him the time to do it].

What is likeliest is that these lines are brought in for what they add
thematically to the passage. Effectively, this is what they do. Alfonso
plans for the first time what is to be his great contribution to the Reconquest, this with God at his side. He regrets the subjection of the ancient
Christian capital to Muslims and with God's help proposes to win it
back. It is only here in the episode that the text speaks of strictly Christian motives for the recovery of Toledo: the graft brings the theme of

---

50. The lines in Lucas are on p. 98 of Lucas 1608: the large passage in Rodrigo consists
of chaps. 15–19 of bk. 7 of the *De rebus hispaniae* (Rodrigo Toledano 1987, 195–201).

Reconquest as Christian enterprise to the narrative. It is not entirely an accident that this interpolation is from Lucas, whose chronicle has a more sacral and providentialist bias than Rodrigo's. I believe that it could be shown that whether by design or simply de facto many of the short interpolations from Lucas in the *Crónica* serve to sound a specifically religious note in passages that otherwise lack it.

The lines about Alfonso's thoughts in Toledo function very neatly within the narrative. In the first place, it makes the Toledo episode itself more coherent. Later in the story, as we recall, the men at the court of Almemon are fearful that Alfonso will eventually return to capture the city. Almemon, unwilling to do away with him, actually makes him swear that he will not make war on him or on his immediate heir. The passage from Lucas belongs to the same series. It makes it stronger and more logical, indeed, by showing explicitly that Alfonso, from the beginning, almost in principle, hoped to recover Toledo for Christendom. A second sense in which the bit from Lucas adds to the Sancho narrative is that, as we have pointed out, Alfonso's thoughts embody the spirit of holy war, of crusade. The passage should be seen in contrast to those that tell of the conflict between the children of Fernando. The *Crónica* sets forth on one hand the unedifying spectacle of warfare between Christian princes, but on the other the prospect of a holy war waged against the very enemies of Christendom. It is a question of legitimate warfare against illegitimate. Parallel texts abound. At least one epic song touches on the theme. In the *Girart de Vienne* (1977), the war between Charlemagne and his vassals is brought to an end only to have the now united Franks march off to do battle with the Moors. Fulcher of Chartres in his chronicle makes Urban harangue the Christian princes, telling them to cease disturbing the peace of Christendom and march instead to the Holy Land to recover her from the control of Islam.[51] Other instances are too numerous to mention. The fragment from Lucas thus brings a new dimension to the Sancho story and makes it give utterance to one of the most widely sounded themes in medieval literature.

This disposes of the easy interpolations in our narrative. What about the difficult ones? These all bear on one theme, the excellence of Sancho. In the short run the passages that favor him are manifestly out of accord with both the detail and the general drift of the later poem, as we

---

51. *Historia hierosolymitana* 1876, 322–23.

can see. The *Cantar,* exceptionally among Spanish epic poems, is pro-
León and anti-Castile. The Castilian king's position is treated with fairness, but on balance the poem is strongly unfavorable to Sancho. By
contrast, the compilers have managed to put into the Sancho narrative a
few passages very friendly to him. Pelayo de Oviedo supplies one: Sancho is characterized as "muy fermoso et cauallero muy esforçado" [he
was handsome and a very bold knight] (Alfonso 1955, 505).[52] It is easy
for the modern reader to underestimate a cliché of this sort. In any
event, this one was put in by conscious choice of the editors and so can
hardly be overlooked. A more significant graft, perhaps, consists of two
chapters in the *Crónica,* based on a source not yet identified,[53] that treat
Sancho very splendidly. The pair, 815 and 816 (495–97), are the ones
that tell of his campaign against the Moorish king of Zaragoza and of the
consequent struggle with Ramiro of Aragón, respectively. The chronology disposed of, the first of these begins:

> el rey don Sancho en este segundo anno del su regnado, pues que
> ouo uisto su regno et sus pueblos et fechas sus cortes, con la grand
> fortaleza et el grand esfuerço del su coraçon trabaiosse de cometer
> contra moros grandes fechos a onrra de Dios et a pro de la
> cristiandad, et saco su hueste muy grand.

> [in the second year of his reign, King Sancho, when he had seen his
> kingdom and his people and had convoked his court, out of the
> great fortitude and strength of his heart, was at pains to honor God
> and benefit Christendom by launching campaigns against the
> Moors, and his host was very large.]

These lines may seem to be little more than the conventional praise a
chronicler might grant an admired king. It is rather fulsome, however,
and what is more important, expressions like these applied to Sancho
are almost totally lacking in either the parts of the narrative that come
from the *Cantar* or those from Rodrigo or other sources. In the case of
Rodrigo, a perusal of his text will show that there is nothing of this sort

---

52. "Fuit homo formosus nimis et miles strenuus" [He was handsome and a bold
knight] (*Crónica del obispo don Pelayo* 1924, 78).

53. Menéndez Pidal has "fuente desconocida" [unknown source] as his entries for both
chapters in the index of sources (Alfonso 1955, 2:clxviii).

there that the editors of the *Crónica* have left out.[54] The praise is
evidently meant seriously. Moreover, in the second of these chapters
Sancho is shown unwilling to press his advantage in battle with the
Aragonese, because, since fighters on both sides were Christians, Christendom would lose from any further slaughter:

> Et por que eran cristianos todos della et della part, touo el rey don
> Sancho por bien, maguer que era muy fuerte rey, que la cristiandat
> non se perdiesse por tal razon et tan torticera, et mando a los suyos
> que non firiessen et que estudiessen quedos.

> [And since they [the warriors] were Christians on one side and on
> the other, Sancho, even though he was a king of great prowess,
> decided that Christendom not be diminished [in effect, that Chris-
> tian blood not be shed] for a motive that was so at odds with
> justice, and he ordered his men not to attack and to stand still]

This is obviously meant to be an act that would honor any Christian
prince. What, then, are we to make of the discrepancy between passages
like these and the rest of the narrative? One answer is simple and obvious. The *Primera crónica* is a compilation, and the editors do not always
attempt to harmonize their sources. We recall that elsewhere the
chronistic matter and some of the text derived from epic poems favor
Fernando, while another epic fragment does not. In a situation analogous to this one, the section on Alfonso III, we have even wider discord.
The chronistic sources make Alfonso one of the great kings of Spain,
while the passages from the Bernardo del Carpio epic depict him as an
archvillain. All the scholarly rhetoric in the world cannot plaster over
that crack.

But still, the breach in the Sancho narrative is not so great as that. A
king who is full of "esfuerço," "fortaleza," and the rest may, for a fact,
also be willful, imprudent, and destructive. Indeed, it is hard to imagine
a man without great warlike and kingly virtue doing the things the
chronicle attributes to Sancho. I would further say that, if the juxtaposi-
tion of texts favorable and unfavorable is an accident, it is a happy
accident. As it stands, it has point. Moreover, there is evidence that it is
not an accident. The whole story of Sancho conforms to a pattern that

---

54. See Rodrigo Toledano 1987, 194–99.

can be found more than once within the *Primera crónica* and even more
frequently outside it. It is the pattern of the overreacher. The overreacher is the man of heroic qualities whose very heroism leads in some
way to his fall. The overreacher is, in a word, the hero of medieval
tragedy, the subject of the fall of princes. The pattern of Sancho's career
as told in the *Crónica* is thus one of the most widespread clichés of
medieval literature, the story of the great man come to ruin. But we
must proceed with caution. The notion of medieval tragedy brings to
mind a certain very specific literary genre, the exemplary biography,
heavily moralized, in the manner of Boccaccio, Lydgate, and the rest. A
mammoth history written several decades before the *De casibus* is hard
to throw into the same category as certain later works. Then, too, Boccaccio admits quite a variety of types into his collection of tragic falls,
whereas the requirements for an overreacher are rather narrow. The text
that presents him must be worldly: his virtues must be purely warlike or
civic. If they are strictly moral and Christian, the hero is no longer an
overreacher but simply a man who falls from grace. The overreacher's
strength is also his weakness. The very qualities that make him great also
bring about his fall. He remains the same throughout and does not
abandon them. Most typically his human greatness is at odds with his
moral state: he is an exemplary warrior and ruler, but he is proud, or he
overestimates his powers or fails to take into account the designs of
Providence. But if, indeed, providentialism is part of the outlook expressed by the text, the scope of this theme is limited. God appears, if at
all, playing a small role, occasionally striking down some of the great
and proud. Thus, the moral world of the churchly, monastic chronicle, in
which the Unseen Hand is everywhere exerting its power, is not very
propitious for the creation of overreacher narratives.

This is not so in vernacular texts of the thirteenth and fourteenth
centuries, where overreachers abound. A work as familiar as the *Libro
de Alexandre* is a perfect case in point. In learning, prudence, modera-
tion, prowess in war, and capacity for rule, Alexander is without peer,
but as his career goes on, things go wrong. His unreasonable ambition
and pride lead him to extravagant deeds that only he can perform, but
that eventually cause him to be cut down. Similar things could be said of
the hero of another thirteenth-century work, very well known in its
time, the *Fet des romains*.[55] The *Fet* is a life of Julius Caesar, compiled

55. *Li fet des romains* 1938, 2 vols.

out of unexceptionable sources: Sallust, Lucan, Suetonius, and Caesar's own *De bello gallico*. In many ways—in style, scope, technique of translation—it reminds one a great deal of the *Primera crónica*. In particular, the way the sources are subtly modified so as to produce a consistent text is very reminiscent of Alfonsine procedures. A great portion of the *Fet* treats Caesar as entirely admirable. Such are the sections on the Catiline episode and the Gallic campaign, based on Sallust[56] and Caesar, respectively. With the civil war, taken from the unfriendly Lucan, things begin to darken, though it is remarkable that some of the most violently anti-Caesar passages in the *Pharsalia* are either suppressed or attenuated in the *Fet*.[57] The effect is to salvage something of the picture of Caesar as exemplary warrior and leader of men, while admitting fully his unreasonable ambition and the injustice of his cause. The end of Caesar's life completes the story. The source in this case, Suetonius, is followed scrupulously; the last few unfriendly chapters of his life of Caesar are translated with scarcely any modifications. The pattern of the fall of the great is manifest; the disastrous end of the hero is prepared by his progress from total excellence, so to speak, to a mixed state, and finally to a condition of largely unrelieved vice. The very medieval character of the whole book is particularly evident in two of its details. First of all, one of the last chapter headings announces that the narrative is to tell of Caesar's fall through pride: "Dou grant orgoill ou Cesar chut" [on the great pride by reason of which Caesar fell] (1: 735). The actual text does not tell quite so simple a story: Suetonius is too unsystematic and inclusive. In the second place, under pressure of the lexicon of Old French, the translator at one point makes his text again favor the notion of Caesar's fall through pride. Suetonius is leading up to one of Caesar's outrageous acts: "Adiecit ad tam insignem despecti senatus contumeliam multo arrogantius factum" [to this most remarkable insult to the despised senate he added a much more arrogant deed].[58] But Suetonius's arrogance, a note of one particular act, becomes the more absolute and fundamental pride. The *Fet* thus says: "A cest grant depit que il ot eü dou senat ajouta il un mout plus

---

56. The mention of Sallust here is not meant to imply anything about that author's intentions in the *War with Catiline*. The passages from Sallust in the *Fet* do show Caesar in a favorable light.

57. For example, the *Fet* picks up Lucan only at verse 185 of the first book (cf. *Li fet* 1938, introduction and commentary, 2:147).

58. Suetonius 1886, chap. 79.

orgueuillex fet" [to this great contempt he had towards the senate he added a very *prideful act*] (1:735–36); (italics mine). A specific accusation in Suetonius is changed to a general one of pride. The full parallelism of the French work to the *Primera crónica* will become evident presently. For the moment let us note that the presentation the *Fet* makes of Caesar as an overreacher did not escape medieval eyes. One of the Italian offshoots of the work has an original prologue that speaks eloquently of the ambiguity of human accomplishment:

> Nostro Signore Dio stabilio lo mondo, e sottomiselo a la subiezione d'Adam nostro primo padre. Adam fu tutto solo, et ebbe lo mondo e le cose del mondo tutte sotto la sua signoria. Et cosi per natura li suoi descendenti filliuoli ciascuno la signoria del mondo pienamente desidera, e non guardano l'altro mirabile numero de'filliuoli d'Adamo che ciascuno ne die avere parte. E cosi la ragione è vinta da la volontà e sottostata lunghissimi tempi; e le sfrenate voglie sono per lo mondo trascorse, uccidendo e robbando l'uno l'altro, ordenando le battallie e'pericoli per mare e per terra. Unde sono fatte molte rimembranze, ma sempre li vincitori sono rimasi vinti, e li pazienti infine sono rimase vincitori.[59]

> [Our lord God established the world and made it subject to Adam, our first father. Adam was all alone and held the lordship of the world and of all the things of the world. And so it is by nature that each and every one of his children and descendants strongly desires the lordship of the world, and not one takes into account the enormous number of other sons of Adam, or that each of these has a right to a part (of the world). Thus reason is overcome by will and is subject to will over long periods of time. These unfettered wills (of power-hungry persons) go about the world killing and robbing, planning battles and dangers on land and sea. The memory of these deeds is preserved, but in time the victors become the defeated, and in the end, the long-suffering are the (genuine) victors.]

The message of these lines is distinctive: it is not entirely cliché. Especially as applied to the life of Julius Caesar, it conveys perfectly the notion that the great fall precisely because of their greatness, not in spite

---

59. *I fatti di Cesare* 1863, i.

of it. In this sense one could not imagine a better definition of the overreaching attitude. Our point in going into such detail in our examination of the *Fet des romains* is to show that at least one work that displays generally great kinship with the *Primera crónica* reflects an acute understanding of human greatness gone wrong. The point is not trivial. The severe judgment on the overreacher in the two books is the sacral dimension of works of history whose focus is predominantly this-wordly and pragmatic.

The overreacher is already to be found in Alfonso's most important source author in the *Crónica,* Rodrigo of Toledo. At least twice in the histories of the latter do we find examples of admirable and heroic figures who meet disastrous ends: Theodoric, the Ostrogothic king of Italy, in the *Historia ostrogothorum;* and 'Abd al-Rahman ben 'Abd Allah al-Gafiqií, the emir of Cordoba, in the *Historia arabum.* Both figures pass virtually without modification into the *Primera crónica.*[60] Rodrigo, learned cleric, archbishop of Toledo, is indeed just the sort of churchly writer one would expect to lack the secular perspective we thought essential to a good sense of the strictly human qualities of his great men. But paradoxically, there is a sense in which his very estate would lead him to treat Theodoric and 'Abd al-Rahman the way he does. Neither are Catholics—one is a heretic, the other a Muslim—and so if he is to take account of their excellence at all, it must be in purely natural human terms. But since their lives are ultimately hateful to God, he must express this by having them be cut down. Then, too, churchman though he be, Rodrigo also is a great man in public life, indeed a great warrior.[61] His writings, which in so many ways fall well within the range of what we expect from learned clerical historians, also express high regard for worldly estates, for chivalry and nobility. One must not think of him as a scholarly recluse, totally insensitive to secular values. Rodrigo's Theodoric and 'Abd al-Rahman are in the *Crónica.* Overreachers other than Sancho are thus no strangers to the Alfonsine histories. But the Alfonsine compilers themselves are entirely capable of constructing biographies of this sort on their own. The central exemplary figure in this sense is none other than Julius Caesar. The

---

60. Rodrigo's Theodoric is on pp. 224–27 of Roderigo Toledano 1793; his 'Abd al-Rahman is on pp. 255–56. The *Crónica*'s Theodoric is on pp. 242–51 of Alfonso 1955; its 'Abd al-Rahman is on pp. 331–33.

61. See Ballesteros Gaibrois 1936, and Linehan 1971, passim. The latter account is more up-to-date by far and is by no means so favorable to the prelate.

Caesar in the *Primera crónica* is not at all inherited from any single one of its sources. It is built up mosaic-style out of a variety of Latin texts: Rodrigo, Orosius, Lucan, Suetonius. Curiously, Alfonso's hero is almost the mirror opposite of the one that appears in the *Fet des romains*. The latter work presents a basically good man who is brought down by the sin of pride. The *Crónica*, however, shows us a contentious, envious, willful man who is nevertheless a great general and man of state. In this latter case it is as if the hero were not able to achieve his vices without an element of greatness.

The *Primera crónica* is assuredly severe with Julius Caesar. It preserves texts that attribute to him all sorts of faults—restlessness, hatred of peace, contentiousness—as we have noted. Our chronicle stresses three vices in particular, however: envy, greed, and pride. All of these are made to figure large in the narrative, entirely by the will of the editors. We have seen how this works out in the case of envy. The situation of the other two is identical. They show up prominently both in the civil war passage and in the account of Caesar's own reign, and in almost every case the words about his pride and greed are the editor's own: they do not belong to the texts translated. In some cases they are simply added, while in others they are a part of the generous amplification typical of Alfonsine translations. Thus, the *Crónica* says that the senate denied him Pompey's consulate because they knew he wanted it out of pride and greed: "E sobresto entendieron la soberuia que traye e la cobdicia con que andaua" [In rejecting his requests they understood the pride that was in him and the greed which moved him] (65). The "soberuia" and the "cobdicia" are nowhere to be found in any of the obvious sources—Orosius, Lucan, Rodrigo.[62] The editors, also on their own, make much of a special modality of pride that they find in Caesar, his attributing to his own powers what he really owes to God and to good fortune. This is what the reader is asked to impute to him after his initial triumph in Spain, for example (chapter 96), after his African campaign (chapter 116), and after his second foray into Spain (chapter 117). Again, in none of these instances can the mention of the vice be traced to any of the editors' normal sources. Even the location in the text of these passages is significant. They straddle one of the *Crónica*'s important boundaries, discovered by Menéndez Pidal, the end of chapter

---

62. Menéndez Pidal (Alfonso 1955, 1:lxxxiii) cites as sources Lucan 1.291–93; Orosius 6.15.1–4; and Rodrigo's *Historia romanorum,* chap. 10 (1793, 221).

108.[63] Thus, even though the first 108 chapters form a unit structurally as well as linguistically, the compilers saw enough importance in the over-reacher's vice to attribute it to Caesar both before and after the fissure.

But vice is not all there is to Julius Caesar. The *Crónica* makes no effort to disguise his greatness as a military leader. For example, it preserves and amplifies the passages in Lucan that show him as fore-sighted, shrewd, and resourceful in the Spanish campaign. But even if we discount one entirely laudatory portrait based on Suetonius (via Vincent of Beauvais), we can see that the chronicle is setting forth more than his purely technical competence. The text associates with him acts that the editors and their contemporaries ordinarily connect with the greatest and most noble princes. One such act slips out almost by acci-dent. The Latin text of Orosius tells how Orgetorix, about to face Cae-sar in battle, orders his men to set fire to their villages and lands. Caesar prevails and simply sends the survivors back home: "cetera in terras proprias missa sunt" [the rest he sent back to their own lands]; "cetera" agrees with "milia") (7.7). The *Crónica,* however, amplifies:

> los otros que ficaron biuos ouieron su pleytesia con el, e enuiolos a
> sus tierras, que auien ellos mismos destroidas, que las poblassen e
> que fuessen del sennorio de Roma. (62)
>
> [the ones who survived parleyed with him, and he sent them back
> to their lands to (re)populate them and to submit to the power of
> Rome.]

The repopulation is the telling detail. Any reader of medieval chronicles knows full well that one of the acts that honor the most admired kings is the population or repopulation of desert areas. One may almost speak of the editors betraying themselves in one of their most routine acts, the amplification of a text. They interpret as admirable an act Orosius pres-ents without comment as a simple fact.

But we can do better at finding a virtuous Caesar in the *Crónica.* In one passage of some length, a fair-sized chapter, the editors show Caesar performing an act they obviously find admirable, conquering through love and goodwill, rather than through force of arms. This is at the beginning of his first Spanish campaign. Now, we should note that the

---

63. Alfonso 1955, 1:xxii–xxiv.

conquest by love is a significant theme in the early portions of the
Crónica. Once again, it is so by the design of the compilers. In a long
and important episode we learn that Spain under Scipio was at peace
and submissive to Rome thanks to his gentle and loving treatment of the
Spaniards, but she rebelled when his successors followed more violent
ways. We cannot doubt that the *Crónica* presents the capacity to conquer through love as an ornament in the prince. In the case of Caesar
peaceful conquest was not usually his choice, for the prince who is not
feared cannot rule effectively, but Spain was an exception:

> E dizen del las estorias que en las otras tierras numqua se el pagara
> tanto de conquista que fiziesse en paz, como daquella en que fallaua
> contienda et lid, e que se mostraua brauo et cruel en sos fechos por
> fazerse temer; e que esto era lo que querie siempre, quel temiessen
> todos: por que ningun princep non puede tener bien a derecho sus
> yentes ni castigarlas como deue, sil no temen. Mas demudos desto
> aqui en el fecho de Espanna, e puso en so coraçon que de quanto y
> pudiesse ganar por amor o por abenencia, que lo no leuasse por
> guerras nin lides nin muertes ni por esparzer sangre &c. (69)

> [And the histories tell of him that, in other lands, he never took as
> much pleasure in the conquests that he made peacefully as in those
> in which he encountered opposition and warfare, and he made a
> show of ferocity and cruelty in his deeds so that he might be feared;
> and this is what he always desired, that everyone fear him; for no
> prince can govern his people well or justly, or command and counsel
> them as he should, if they do not fear him. But he changed plans
> here in the Spanish campaign, and he set his heart on gaining as
> much (territory) as he could by love and the union of minds rather
> than by war or conflicts or deaths or bloodshed.]

These lines are clearly favorable to Caesar throughout. Even his prefer-
ence for warfare is seen in a good light. Once again, the passage is
virtually original. A glance at the bits of Lucan it is based on will show
how little it owes to its source.[64]

---

64. Menéndez Pidal gives as sources Lucan 4.1–3 and 1.143–47, "combinados ambos
passajes, y muy amplificado el primero" [both passages combined and the first greatly
amplified] (Alfonso 1955, 1:lxxxiv).

Caesar, a perfect warrior, a ruler through fear, also a ruler through love, is very nearly an exemplary prince. His vices are, in effect, the very ones a great prince might possess—pride and an overestimation of his own powers. It should come as no surprise, for example, that the lauda- tory Suetonius chapter we have spoken of, which calls him "uno de los meiores caballeros del mundo" (chapter 117, 94) [one of the best knights in the world], follows immediately the one that at greatest length calls him an overreacher. It is this amalgam, by no means a wholly hateful man, who is made to fall. His death is told in such fashion that its meaning cannot escape us. The chapter that tells of his murder (chapter 119) is preceded by one given over almost entirely to the omens announc- ing it. A violent death may itself invite the reader to judge that the victim is being dealt some kind of justice, but a murder preceded by omens can hardly be read otherwise. We must add that these tragic events are not as elaborately staged by the compilers as are their empha- ses on Caesar's pride and envy. The sequence of omens and murder comes largely from Vincent of Beauvais's version of Suetonius. It is remarkable, however, that the most important modification of this text is in the passage on the omens. Vincent's list is augmented by items from Paul the Deacon and Lucas of Tuy. The charge of meaning is made a little heavier.

The biography of Caesar, then, is a classic medieval tragedy, the exemplary story of the fall of a great, though flawed, man. The drama is strictly the creation of the men who formed the *Primera crónica general.* If, therefore, the *Crónica's* version of the history of Sancho II also presents him as in many ways excellent, though in the long run damna- ble, we need not attribute this duality to incompatibility between the *Crónica's* sources or to any lack of control on the part of the editors. It is at least possible that the two elements are part of the plan, the pattern of the overreacher, the genuinely great man who oversteps the bounds Providence sets for him. There are, after all, in the *Cantar* itself certain factors that would encourage the editors to see more than one side to Sancho. The hero of the poem is not devoid of positive elements. There is the very palpable fact of his military prowess, which allows him to prevail over his brothers. Then too, although the poem does not other- wise show admirable qualities in him, it makes much of the fact that justice is in some sense on his side. His father, in an illegal act, has cheated him of his birthright as firstborn son. He is righting a wrong done to him. Also, the Sancho of the *Cantar* has certain traits of character that might assimilate him to figures of the sort of Julius Caesar. Caesar is envious and proud; Sancho is impetuous, headstrong, imperious. But Caesar's vices belong, in fact, to a great man. Likewise Sancho's qualities are not incompatible with the view of him conveyed by the two chapters that speak kindly of him. A king who is zealous to fight Islam could well be impulsive. The Sancho who shed Christian blood when his presumed rights were at stake might also be reluctant to shed it when they were not. Like Caesar's, his flaws of character do bring about his fall, but there is nothing in the narrative to keep us from regarding him, as we do Caesar, great in that fall.

The Beginning of the *Cantar de Sancho*

In 1974 I launched a set of hypotheses about the lost *Cantar de Sancho* prosified in the *Primera crónica general;* this epic song, as I would remark, must have been, along with the *Poema de mio Cid,* the flower of the Castilian *cantar de gesta.*[1]

I set forth the view that the poem known to the editors of the chronicle was a late version of an older text, and that certain features of the Sancho poem in the *Crónica,* joined to information about Castilian epic in general, might give a fair idea of what an earlier song of Sancho might have been like. In broad terms, my argument was that the *Sancho* known to the prosifiers was built around learned themes, such as the royal dignity and Christian Spain's claim to unity, whereas the primitive version looked to notions based on custom and oral tradition, such as personal honor and the law of vengeance and reprisal. Ordinarily, as I suppose, there might be little reason to recall this old article. But occasions conspire. For one thing, traditionalism in epic studies, long in crisis, is now in convalescence: it might strike some that the old questions about lost epic songs and multiple versions might well be worth asking again. My own special motive in doing a new study on the *Cantar de Sancho* is that there are to my mind serious flaws in the old: it is time I set the record straight about which motifs belong to the primitive poem and which to the revised version. I remark finally that Dr. Brian Powell's searching study of the lines in the *Crónica de veinte reyes* covering the last days of Fernando I[2] obliges me to pose my own questions in more exact terms: in my essay of 1974 I assumed that the passage in the

---

1. I refer to the preceding essay in this book.
2. Powell 1984, 459–71.

chronicle on the division of the kingdom and the death of the monarch was a coherent text, and Powell's plain evidence to the contrary, his discovery of its many inconsistencies and contradictions, forces me to recast certain parts of my argument.

My analysis of 1974 ran along two lines. First, I tried to show that the Sancho song in the two *Crónicas* displayed a series of plain anomalies, all of which could be resolved if we assumed that there existed an older song on the Sancho theme, one that was more like its Castilian fellows, the *Siete infantes de Salas,* for example, or the *Infante García.* Second, I tried to state as well as I could the premises on which the later singers of the song based their production, and the motives they had for parting company with the older text. I must explain these matters more fully, beginning with the anomalies.

Menéndez Pidal always maintained that one of the distinctive marks of the Castilian *cantares de gesta* was the fact that their narrative world generally reflected Castilian legal customs—social norms that were traditional, were transmitted orally, and were in some broad sense Germanic.[3] Now, on this basis the *Cantar de Sancho* both is and is not a traditional or typical epic text. The Germanic matter is there, surely enough, but the treatment it receives in the *Crónica* text is in many ways strange. I will cite three examples. First, there is the matter of Urraca's mantle. Vellido Adolfo murders the Castilian king, rushes to the walls of Zamora, enters through a postern gate, and finally claims sanctuary under the mantle of his lady (that is, the lady of the city). The sanctuary is violated as he is led away. Now ordinarily in the world of the *cantar de gesta* the violation of a traditional rule tends to bring very serious consequences. One such breach actually involves the matter of sanctuary. We recall that in the *Siete infantes de Salas* Doña Lambra's servant seeks out her mantle for protection. When the seven heroes of the song drag him away and kill him, their destruction by treachery is not far off. But in the *Cantar de Sancho,* as we know, the analogous bad outcomes do not materialize: no one attempts to punish the violators, openly or otherwise. One can only conclude that the definitive poet does not expect his audience to take the sanctuary business very seriously.

Second, there is the matter of Diego Ordóñez's challenge to the people of Zamora and Arias Gonzalo's response. The former plainly

---

3. Menéndez Pidal 1955, 12–27.

follows some sort of deeply traditional usage: don Diego blames the death of Sancho on the inhabitants of Zamora, dead, living, and yet unborn; the stones in her walls; her waters; and so on. The issue is obviously collective guilt, the notion that the offense committed by one can be attributed to the whole tribe or community. "How silly!" says Arias Gonzalo in answer to don Diego's speech. Don Arias of course accepts the challenge, but he asks sensibly how the dead or the unborn or the stones or water could have anything to do with the murder. His critique, if we could call it that, is a serious one: the assumption that the collectivity is responsible for the fault of any one of its members is assuredly an important provision of the traditional code we have been speaking of and is also a basic premise in the plot of a great many Romance epic songs, Castilian or otherwise. Don Arias's words are therefore not idle. It is precisely the idea of collective guilt that is the butt of his sarcasm. The poet could hardly have introduced this element accidentally, but in the short run, at least, it is hard to see what the issue is he wishes to raise.

Finally, there is the whole set of uneasy questions posed by the judicial combat between the champions of Zamora and of the Castilians. We must understand that the judicial combat is in principle a device to establish guilt or innocence: a just God is supposed to intervene and choose winners and losers. In this case the issue of guilt is clear: Sancho was killed by Vellido Adolfo and by him alone. If we consider the generally bad press that attends the princess Urraca, the least that we can say about that in our version of the story is that her complicity is seriously attenuated:[4] as we know, earlier texts (and later) accuse her explicitly of being party to the crime. I in fact believe now, as I did in 1974, that the *Crónica* text indeed tells us that in a moment of rage she thinks and speaks of having her brother destroyed, but in her crucial interview with Vellido Adolfo she says that, while she would welcome an end to the siege, she does not assent to the murder: her language is indirect, but her drift is clear. If, then, Urraca is innocent, what are we to make of the combat scene? It would have been very easy for the definitive poet to have the contest run its course and to let victory, in justice, go to the champions of Zamora. He does neither. He has the first three combatants on the side of the city fall in succession, and to

---

4. Cf. Deyermond 1976.

complicate things, he has the combat cut short, never to be decided. The whole sequence appears to be an embarassment to him.

In all three of these cases we have an ancient custom that we could call Germanic, the significance of which seems to be lost or gutted. Nothing appears to work out in the right way. If we look at other Castilian epic legends, or, indeed, at the Romance chanson de geste generally, we find that this failure to make the plot run according to rule is virtually unique: other poems simply do not take the liberties with these social norms that our Sancho song does. The intentions of the definitive poet aside, can we imagine a Sancho text in which the Germanic motifs work out in a more normal way? To answer this question I hypothesized in 1974 a simpler, briefer *Cantar de Sancho* with more or less the following characteristics. In my version, the first character to break the peace and march on his siblings' lands would be not García but Sancho himself. The text that Menéndez Pidal calls *Cantar de Fernando par de emperador,*[5] which I thought was certainly a section of the later poem, was to my mind not a part of the older text. One of my reasons for saying so was simple: the later version attenuated Sancho's guilt. Fernando foolishly divides the kingdom and tries to oblige his children to respect each other's inheritance. Sancho hates Fernando's disposition of the lands, because he believes that as firstborn the whole of his father's kingdom should have been his. But in spite of the injustice his behavior is noble: he stays at home and poses no threat to any of his siblings. But when García makes the first move and marches on the lands of his sisters, Sancho sees no reason for not claiming what he regards as his own, and so the generation of warfare begins, on García's own turf. On this score we simply cannot find fault with Sancho. Peace is to his mind holier than justice, and so at first he puts his just interest aside for the sake of peace. But when all hope of peace is shattered, he can see little reason not to pursue what to his mind is both right and to his advantage. An initially faultless Sancho, as I thought, did not fit into the more traditional epic song I envisioned. My primitive version would have focused mainly on the conflict between Sancho and Urraca. Sancho, wrathful and strong-willed, breaks all the laws of God, takes by force the lands, in turn, of García and Alfonso, and then attempts the conquest of Zamora. Urraca's reaction to Sancho looks in two directions. On one

---

5. Menéndez Pidal 1951, 240–56.

hand, in planning to have her brother destroyed she is taking legitimate vengeance. But on the other, she fully consents to have him put to death by treachery: in my version Urraca is a genuine accomplice. Her action is therefore plainly heinous, and the Castilians can do no less than demand satisfaction. The judicial combat takes place, and the outcome decisively favors the offended Castilians. I remark now that the conception of Urraca in this version would be completely of a piece with that of certain characters in other Romance epic songs. When deeply vicious figures in these poems make their decisive moves, they often do so to right what they perceive as wrongs done them, but they overstep the bounds of the law by taking vengeance treacherously. This is the case with Ganelon, humiliated at Charlemagne's court; with Ruy Velázquez, intent on avenging the deep affront to his wife—the matter of the mantle, once again, and the protection it was supposed to afford—and eminently with the Infantes de Carrión, mindful of "lo del león" [the matter of the lion].

As I thought, this version of the *Cantar de Sancho,* if it ever existed, would have respected fully the provisions of the customary law. The judicial combat would have been effective both in giving satisfaction to the Castilians and in confirming the guilt of Urraca and her city. Arias Gonzalo would have had little reason to make light of the challenge. The sanctuary offered by Urraca's mantle might well have been respected in this version, giving the Castilians one more complaint against the people of Zamora, that they were protecting the murderer. As I will explain presently, my whole outline for this hypothetical *Cantar de Sancho* fails badly on several grounds: as I think now, some of my old judgments can stand, but others are surely faulty. I cannot open this question, however, without first reviewing the other wing of my argument, what I considered to be the rationale and general scheme of the song prosified in the *Crónica.*

In examining this later text, much of the focus must pass from Sancho to his father, Fernando. Fernando's act of dividing his kingdom among his children is, of course, impolitic to a remarkable degree; the unwisdom of the act is compounded when Sancho and García are forced to give Urraca portions of their land. But in the *Crónica* version this is only part of the story. Fernando's move also raises the very gravest issues of statecraft and public law. As the character Sancho points out, the division of the lands violates a provision of the Visigothic Code—he in fact speaks of the ancient customs of the Goths, but texts in the *Fuero juzgo* he is referring to are easy to identify.[6] The article in question says exactly what the *Cantar* implies; it is illegal for the king to distribute the lands of the kingdom itself among this personal heirs. The immediate practical issue for the (historical) Visigoths was of course the fact that kingship among them was elective and that there was no assurance that any of the heirs would actually come to the throne. But more fundamental here is the Roman principle that the king's authority (or the emperor's) entirely transcends any of the circumstances of his personal life, and that what he does as a public person has no legal connection with his private interests or those of his family. Fernando in this sequence is represented as violating his own royal character and dignity. A second serious issue raised by the division of the lands (a matter I did not discuss in my old essay) is that of the unity of Spain. Sancho in the same utterance echoes Christ's dictum on marriage, that what God hath joined man should not put asunder, and applies it to Christian Spain herself. Fernando's act is offensive to God, because Spain under Christian rule has a right to be and remain one; the old king's act destroys what unity is left. Maravall, in a now classic text, has told us eloquently that the notion of a Christian Hispania, heir to the kingdom of the Visigoths, was very much alive during the years of the Reconquest.[7] The profile of the new *Cantar de Sancho* emerges. The question posed by this extraordinary poem is the following: once legitimacy or some portion of it is lost, what is left? The implied answer offered by the song itself is very clear: peace and stability. The role of Sancho in the new *Cantar* takes on Shakespearian dimensions. At first he favors peace over legitimacy: he does not lay claim to what is rightly his. But from the moment García takes over Urraca's land, Sancho changes course and conducts a relentless pursuit of legitimacy, this in violation of the one sacred bond of Christendom, which is peace. God, therefore, through the agency of Vellido Adolfo, strikes him down before Zamora.

Let me remark out of hand that I now see little to criticize in this account. The two motifs in Sancho's crucial speech, the appeal to Visigothic law and the theme of the unity of Spain, are there to be seen, staring us in the face: there is no use in pretending they are not there.

---

6. *Fuero juzgo, en latín y castellano* 1815, prologue, "De electione principiis," ii (eighth council of Toledo) and the decree of Recceswinth, 5–6.

7. Maravall 1954; the whole second half of the book is interesting for our theme, especially chaps. 5–8, pp. 201–501.

The rest of my reading of the poem is, as I believe, simple logic: it follows as a conclusion from fairly certain premises. But one of my greatest mistakes was, as I think, to bind these large issues of public law so very closely to the rest of the texts preserved in the *Primera crónica* and eminently in the *Crónica de veinte reyes*—the passage Menéndez Pidal calls *Cantar de Fernando*—which tell of the division of the kingdom. The argument in my first essay was to say that the later poet incorporated the lofty themes I speak of into the new *Cantar* by composing precisely these verses, the ones that tell of Fernando's deathbed decisions. Obviously, there is nothing compelling about this conclusion: most of the motifs in the supposed *Cantar de Fernando* are perfectly compatible with my scheme for the earlier poem. If we were to delete from Sancho's speech the bits about Visigothic law and the unity of Spain, allowing him to protest simply that as firstborn he should have inherited the whole of his father's kingdom, we would be left with a text that would in no way jar with my hypothetical *Cantar.* It is worth mentioning in this connection that Sánchez Albornoz has actually asserted that the *Sancho* was a piece of propaganda in favor of the rule of primogeniture.[8] This view is striking because in the *Primera crónica* the arguments that are put into Sancho's mouth on the matter of succession run along very different lines. If Sánchez is right, if the issue is less the unity of Spain than the right of the eldest son to succeed to the throne, then it is all the more plausible that an earlier version of this *Cantar* would have had Sancho's speech stress the latter theme. This simpler disposition of the plot would of course change considerably the moral status of Fernando's act. He would indeed be guilty of violating custom (albeit not of very long standing, since the rule of primogeniture is relatively modern), but his breach of the law would not have been presented as a violation of his very nature as king, and since the sacred unity of Spain was not at issue, he could not be accused directly of offending God. But the division of the kingdom would in any case stand as a very imprudent act, a genuine invitation to disaster. If, then, we still have two *cantares,* as I believe we do, why could not this whole sequence, or some variant of it, belong to the old version?

To try to carry this argument still further and show that the old song might have begun with the deathbed scene—to suggest, in other words,

8. Sánchez Albornoz 1945, 42 n, 50.

that the old version and the new may have been less unlike than I had thought—I would like to call to mind certain other Romance epic poems whose design and layout is something like those of the *Sancho*. One song in particular is notable for its plot, which is in some ways very similar to that of our *Cantar*. I mean the *Raoul de Cambrai*.[9] The disposition of lands is an issue here, as it is in the Sancho poem. The heavy, so to speak, the culprit analogous to Fernando, is no less a person than Louis the Pious. French epic singers, by the way, seem to have been of one mind about this poor man: virtually all portray him as a remarkably bad king, cowardly, imprudent, and malicious. The *Raoul* poet is no exception. The end of the song is entirely symptomatic of its whole tendency. When the surviving heroes of both factions that, thanks to Louis, have been at war for years finally make peace, the first thing they think of doing is to turn on the king that caused all the trouble: the poem ends with the firing of Paris at the hands of the former rivals. Louis's fault is hardly negligible: he takes one man's land away from him and in compensation gives him another fiefdom, but on condition that he take it and keep it from another family by force. Bloodshed over two generations is the sorry consequence. The first part of the plot of the *Raoul* runs as follows. Louis decides to marry his widowed sister, Aulais, to Gibouin, a favorite of his; Gibouin is also to receive Cambrai, her late husband's inheritance. Aulais flatly refuses the match with her suitor, but Louis, determined to do great things for him, gives him Cambrai regardless. The dispossessed heir, Aulais's young son Raoul, is in time brought to court and is eventually dubbed knight. Some time later this spirited young man approaches Louis and demands to have Cambrai restored to him. The king refuses, saying that he cannot dispossess Gibouin, but promises to compensate Raoul: when the next of his great vassals dies, the young man will come into possession of the dead man's lands. One year later, surely enough, Herbert of Vermandois dies. But nothing at Louis's court happens automatically: Raoul must once again approach his sovereign and demand that he keep his promise. Louis does so, but on one condition: Raoul must make war on Herbert's heirs and take the lands by force. The details of the rest of the story do not concern us at this point. As I have said, the conflict between the two families, Raoul's and Herbert's, lasts two generations. Bernier, even though he is Her-

---

9. *Raoul de Cambrai, chanson de geste du XIIIe siècle* 1924.

bert's nephew, is at first Raoul's squire and vassal, and he fulfills his duties to his lord in an exemplary way. But at one point in the very bloody struggle, Raoul orders the firing of the abbey of Origny, where Bernier's mother is abbess. The poor woman dies with all her nuns, and Bernier has no choice but to change sides. He emerges as the leader of the Vermandois faction. Several episodes later, the great Raoul himself dies begging for mercy, put to death by none other than Bernier, his former squire. At last there is peace. But in time, Raoul's nephew Gautier comes to maturity, swearing to avenge his uncle's death. Inevitably the war begins again under the two leaders, Gautier and Bernier, and it is only after years of bloodshed that both parties decide to settle things by single combat, Bernier against Gautier. The contest takes place, but neither man prevails, and both are grievously wounded. Their time of convalescence is decisive: during that long period the pair are finally reconciled thanks to a generous concession by Bernier. The end of the story is remarkable, showing Louis at his worst. With peace and a reasonable settlement in sight, the king announces that on the death of Ybert, father of Bernier and brother of Herbert, he, Louis, means to take over Vermandois for himself. Ybert protests, saying that he has settled on Bernier as his heir. Impossible, says the king: Bernier is a bastard and cannot inherit the lands. Thereupon, all heap reproaches on Louis, reminding him that the long war is entirely his fault. The former enemies then join hands to attack the king in his own city. This remarkable poem has a history, just as to the mind of some the Castilian songs do. The details of this matter do not really concern us, but we cannot fail to observe that whatever its past may have been, the brilliant Chanson in its final form has an architecture, an intention, and a logic that are impressive, and that the signs that the text shows of this complicated history do not in any way diminish its power.

There are several points to be made here. The first is that the *Raoul* and a *Sancho* that would include elements of the so-called *Cantar de Fernando* have a great many features in common. I am not suggesting that there was direct influence either way, although such is conceivable. I am in fact more inclined to think that the number of narrative motifs in Romance epic generally is limited, and that on this basis, wholly independent poems are at some point bound to go down the same path. In the short run, however, it is the similarity we must concentrate on, origins regardless. What we should note in particular is that both heroes are in some sense men of mixed character, or if I may say so, of mixed careers.

On one hand, both Sancho and Raoul are violent and impulsive. This nature is highlighted in both poems by the presence of a contrasting character, the Cid in one case and Bernier in the other; the prowess-wisdom topic is realized by both contrasting pairs. In the parts of the *Raoul* in which the hero and Bernier are enemies, it is always the latter who attempts to bring peace, who makes concessions, but it is the contentious Raoul who always frustrates these initiatives. Both heroes are deaf to advice. When Louis finally offers his nephew the new lands on condition that he fight for them, there is no lack of voices telling him to refuse. Aulais ends by cursing her son for his ill-fated decision once it is taken. Sancho too, as we recall, is warned not to pursue his warlike course: the Cid is at his side, urging him to abandon his plans. In a word, both heroes are blameworthy, at their worst caring little for peace and shedding blood recklessly. But both are wronged, and both have a degree of justice on their side. Is it, indeed, so easy to tell a victim of injustice to abandon his cause? My point is simple. There is nothing whatever unique in the fact that the *Cantar de Sancho* places its hero in a genuine moral dilemma, or that the issues of right or wrong are for him less than clear. Such characters and circumstances are in fact legion in Romance epic; the *Raoul* is but one witness among many. To be sure, Sancho's response to his difficulties is subtler than Raoul's: he chooses peace when we do not expect him to and war when circumstances drive him to it. But that is simply an interesting wrinkle on the surface of the poem, nothing great enough to put it at odds with its genre and tradition.

The difficult moral choice is a basic element in the plots of both the *Sancho* and the *Raoul*. There is an important conclusion to be drawn from this coincidence. It is this: the dilemma facing Sancho in his *Cantar* has no necessary connection to the questions of public law that are raised in the *Crónica* version of the piece. One might conclude as much from the simple observation: the song as I have described it, one that includes elements of the *Cantar de Fernando,* can stand as a coherent whole even if the crucial bits about the *Fuero juzgo* are left out. But the testimony of the *Chanson de Raoul* carries us still farther. The *Raoul* and the Castilian song are in so many ways similar, and yet the French piece is, unlike its companion, an entirely normal chanson de geste, and it is wholly innocent of themes of the kind that appear in some versions of the *Sancho*. The work is entirely traditional, so to speak—entirely Germanic. The description that Menéndez Pidal makes of the Castilian epic and its constraints applies equally well to the *Raoul,* just as it does to nearly every other chanson de geste. (The one French song that shows any of the distinctive thematic stuff of the *Crónica* version of the *Sancho* or of the *Poema de mio Cid*—that is, that displays some concern for what we could call public law—is the *Coronemenz Loois*. In this work the loyalty of William to the crowns of king and emperor is absolute, even when the man that wears them is unworthy; the parallels to the *Cid* are obvious. But one swallow does not make a spring; French epic is pretty much of a piece, and we should not, therefore, claim some special privilege for the *Sancho* based on the unusual thematic substance of just one of its versions.)

"The king's to blame"—so says Gertrude in her latest breath. She speaks more truly and more generally than she could have guessed. The king's guilt, obviously, is the crucial matter. The most important motive common to the *Sancho* and the *Raoul* is the king's faulty initiative, which triggers a period of useless bloodshed. This narrative element is very widespread: it is not at all peculiar to the *Sancho*. In the Romance epic corpus, kings are forever landing their faithful vassals into perfectly odious dilemmas. Often the latter find themselves obliged to rebel against their lords in order to protect what is rightfully theirs, a step they are deeply reluctant to take.

In *Girart de Roussillon*,[10] the emperor of the East, well served by Charles Martel and his vassal Girart in his struggle with the Saracens, rewards them by giving one of his daughters in marriage to each. Charles, betrothed to Berthe, is nevertheless wholly charmed by Elissant, the younger daughter intended for Girart; the Frankish king obliges him to take to wife the older sister. Serious contention ensues, and the plan goes through only after Charles releases Girart from all his obligations as a vassal. Girart is told to hold Rousillon freely, and the only right the king is to retain is to hunt on his former vassal's lands. Time passes. Charles goes on a hunting expedition and actually sees Girart's splendid castle in Rousillon, and disregarding his old promise, he lays claim to it. War is the result, and Girart, after losing the fortress, recovers it heroically. Once victorious, he seeks peace by a means common in the world of epic: he makes a concession to his enemy. Charles, in turn, deeply humiliated, demands a trial of arms between the two forces; this struggle turns out to be bloody and very costly to both sides. The rest of the story does not concern us.

---

10. *Girart de Rousillon, chanson de geste* 1953–55.

As I have suggested, this is by no means an unusual plotline. Reynaud de Montauban, in the chanson named after him,[11] is attacked by Charlemagne's nephew Bertolai in a quarrel over chess. Reynaud demands satisfaction from the king. When the latter refuses, the young man has no recourse but to kill Bertolai himself. Charlemagne then lays violent hands on him and in effect declares permanent enmity toward him and his brothers. After many more bloody episodes, Reynaud receives the castle of Montauban, not from Charlemagne, obviously, but from Yon, a king of Gascony, who is repaying him for aid in the struggles against the Saracens. Charles gets to see the imposing structure and ends by attempting to take it, even though he has no claim to it whatever. Once again, the king is at odds with his own vassals through his own evil initiatives. Charles's hostility to Reynaud and his brothers is in the first place unjustified and in the second relentless, indeed, prodigious.

Girart de Vienne, hero of another song,[12] also fares ill with his sovereign. Charlemagne seems incapable of dealing fairly with Girart or his brother Renier except under pressure from the great barons of the king's court. The pair are repeatedly humiliated by the king, and only when the nobles insist does he finally concede Gennes to the faithful Renier. Girart remains at court, an exemplary vassal, but, once again, is rewarded by Charles only at the strong urging of the barons. The young man is to marry the duchess of Burgundy and to take over her great fiefdom. But alas, Charles, in a change of heart, wishes to take duchess and duchy for himself. The good lady, not caring in the least for the match, herself proposes marriage to Girart, who nobly refuses. This woman scorned promises no good for the young knight. Again, under pressure from the great nobles, Girart is given Vienne, but the queen, under very complicated circumstances, manages to have him kiss her foot at the very moment when in respect he thinks he is kissing the foot of the king. This act, utterly humiliating to Girart and his family, remains a secret, even to him, but one day all is revealed when the queen boasts of her ruse to Aymeri, a nephew of Girart. Charles is given the opportunity of satisfying the offended family by punishing the queen, but he refuses, and war breaks out: Girart and his family cannot remain at peace if they are to retain their honor. The moment comes when

---

11. *La chanson des quatre fils Aymon* [also called *Reynaud de Montauban*] 1909.
12. *Girart de Vienne* 1977.

Girart is obliged to defend Vienne, the very fiefdom he has received from Charles himself.

In these songs Charles Martel, Charlemagne, and Louis the Pious are to some degree malicious in their dealings with their vassals: there is more than bad judgment involved. But even benevolent monarchs in epic are capable of making trouble for others. The superhuman Charlemagne of the *Chanson de Roland* is seriously flawed as a decision maker. He sends Ganelon on his mission to Marsile even when this vassal shows plain signs of ill will. One could add that at the initial stormy board meeting, Charles's consultation with his vassals about Marsile's offer, everything goes wrong. He receives excellent advice from Roland and rejects it, instead following very bad advice from his other barons. And in the end he does send Ganelon to Saragossa, even though there are very clear signs that he should not. What is much worse, he sets Roland and Oliver at the head of the rear guard against the warnings of Heaven itself. There is no missing the point: he tells us plainly in a speech that he knows the danger he is exposing them to. Charles is clearly a link in the chain of causes that produces the disaster at Roncevaux. A still more familiar example of a well-wishing king who makes bad judgments is no one less than Alfonso in the *Cid*. It is he who, wishing to reward Rodrigo, marries his daughters to the vicious Infantes de Carrión.

The flawed king is simply a topic of Romance epic poetry: he may take many forms, but what his avatars all have in common is that certain of his initiatives produce bad results, destructive of individuals, of groups, or of the public peace. The motifs of the *Cantar de Fernando* that have to do with the division of the kingdom are obviously well within the range of this commonplace. In the light of all this review of epic literature, I feel it necessary to revise my views on the *Cantar de Sancho* in the following sense. The oddities of the *Crónica* version indeed cut two ways. The fact that the later poet does not expect his audience to take the laws of sanctuary seriously or to respect the legal validity of the judicial combat fits with his concern for legal patterns of another kind. In other words, the allusions to the Visigothic code, or to the idea of the unity of Spain, and the anomalous bits belong to the same text and reflect the same views about life and law. For their part, the references to customary law are indeed relics of an older poem, one of more traditional character. In it Urraca beyond any doubt shares the blame for the murder of Sancho. This means that the issue of collective guilt is taken seriously: since Urraca is the lady of Zamora, Diego

Ordóñez's challenge could properly accuse the city as a whole, and Arias Gonzalo's response would have been different from the one preserved. As I suggested before, the poet may have seen no need to have the sanctuary sought by Vellido Adolfo violated; Urraca would have had no reason not to protect him. However, the song surely would have begun with the division of the kingdom as told in the so-called *Cantar de Fernando,* but without the allusions to the *Fuero juzgo* or to the sacred unity of Spain. What makes this inclusion verisimilar is that the man of mixed qualities, the difficult or costly choice, and the flawed king are all topics in epic texts that in Pidal's terms are entirely traditional and Germanic. All of these motifs are sustained if the old *Sancho* began with the division of the kingdom, and there is no reason whatever to exclude them from an epic song that in principle and by definition is supposed to be traditional and Germanic.

I conclude with some observations about some of the Fernando material preserved in the *Crónica de veinte reyes.* As I have implied all along, it is obvious to me that certain motifs in this passage are certainly parts of our poem. As Powell has demonstrated,[13] stretches of this chaotic text belong to the version of the song preserved in the *Primera crónica:* one should point out, incidentally, that once the crucial Fernando story has been disposed of, the two chronicles do not give significantly different versions of the history of Sancho. The *Primera crónica* at one point refers to Arias Gonzalo's prophecy that the division of the kingdom would set brother against brother (Alfonso 1955, 499). The prophecy is missing from this chronicle, but it stares us in the face in the Fernando passage in *Veinte reyes* (Menéndez Pidal 1951, 256): it is part of don Arias's lament for the dead king and includes the very words "parientes con parientes" [relatives against relatives], which figure in the *Primera.* It is hard to believe that the two texts do not come from a single source. The *Primera crónica* passage is actually headed by the formula "cuenta la estoria" [as the history tells], which suggests that the compiler could be quoting from the same *Cantar* that is prosified in the *Veinte reyes.* I would add on my own one further piece of evidence that the editors of *Veinte reyes* and the *Primera* have the same song before them. As I have pointed out often, the *Primera* version makes García the one son of Fernando to break the peace after his father's death. But the chronicle

---

13. Powell 1984, 459–60.

leaves that tragic move wholly unexplained: the audience must assume, simply, that García is willful and lawless. But *Veinte reyes* does supply a motive. Fernando originally gives him Portugal and Galicia free and clear but later takes back some of this land and transfers it to Urraca. On this basis García is not simply making trouble: he is trying to make up for what he lost in the second disposition of territory. Once again, Fernando is at the heart of things. Had he had the foresight to provide for Urraca from the first, the likelihood of general warfare would have been less.

PART 2

The three essays that follow have a common theme, Rome as conceived by Alfonso and his associates. In point of fact, two of the three essays begin by addressing certain narrow issues in literary history and theory. One tries to vindicate the idea that formal patterns can have a history, just as themes or commonplaces can, and that the appearance of such a formula in more than one text can be as sure a sign of literary borrowing as a verbal or thematic coincidence. The other essay airs the possibility that Alfonso and his collaborators were open to diffuse literary influences, just as a modern author might be, as, for example, Wordsworth was influenced in a general way by Milton. My aim, in other words, was to show that the inclusion in the Alfonsine text of bits of Ovid or Paul the Deacon was not the only way in which the compilers showed their debt to their literary past. But once these studies get down to Alfonso's own subject matter, the focus is Rome.

The word *Rome* signifies two rather different things for the Alfonsines. On the one hand Rome is what one might call the exemplary civilization, and on the other it is an institution, the empire, which had its beginnings in the remote past, but which was in existence in the Learned King's own day; we must of course understand that, for medievals, the German emperor was the successor of Augustus in the most literal sense. In mapping out the first area, Rome as example, one must begin by saying that the *Estoria de Espanna* is not easy to read. To comprehend fully the place of this theme in the work, one must take into account its structure and, in particular, one of its important boundaries. This dividing line comes immediately before chapter 108 of the *Estoria*, that is, well into the Roman section of the work—recall that the whole of the *Estoria* is divided into long sections, one each for every people or nation that ruled Spain. As we shall see, there is good reason to believe that this pre-108 portion of the history was given some sort of special treatment and was perhaps composed by a different group of editors than was the rest. Chapters 1 through 107 carry us in time up to the end of the Roman Republic. But at chapter 108 the narrative flow stops completely. Starting at that point there is a stretch of text that informs the reader generally about Rome and its past: we are given a chronological list of kings, another of consuls, a historical description of the principal Roman offices, the etymologies of *Caesar* and *imperator*, and similar matters. When the narrative gets under way again in chapter 115, we launch into a major division of the *Estoria* and of its Roman section, the one about the empire, properly speaking, from Julius Caesar on; Julius is for the Alfonsines the first emperor. This long set of chapters, as we should note, scarcely mentions Spain; it is primarily and fundamentally about the imperial monarchy that ruled the Roman world over several centuries. By contrast, the *Estoria*'s chapters on Rome before the fall of the republic are primarily about Rome and Romans as they affect the fortunes of Spain; the passage includes generous portions of Roman history as we would understand it, but despite all of that, the principal focus of the section is Spain.

The boundary I speak of occurs very close to another one, this time not before but after chapter 108. Years ago Menéndez Pidal pointed out that the language of the Alfonsine history before the end of 108 was more archaic than that of the rest of the text; he observed further that the list of authorities in the prologue to the *Estoria* seemed to have been framed with only this early portion of the work in mind. The language of the first chapters, as he thought, represented the linguistic preferences of the Learned King himself, and it was don Ramón's judgment that Alfonso may have intervened more directly in the composition of the early chapters than in that of the following ones (see Menéndez Pidal's introduction in Alfonso 1955, 1:xxiii–xxiv). What is certain is that the editors on either side of the boundary could not be entirely the same. A superficial reading of the text itself and, above all, a study of Menéndez Pidal's index of sources (Alfonso 1955, 1:lxxxvi) suggests that indeed a change of the guard has taken place; a new set of *auctores* seems to hold the stage, and the style of presentation is rather different.

It is also very clear that the all-important theme of Rome as example belongs almost entirely to the earlier portion of the *Estoria de Espanna:* the chapters between the beginning of the Roman section of the chronicle and the boundary or boundaries I have spoken of seem to have a near monopoly on this matter and are plainly designed to make Rome and Romans memorable and exemplary. We should understand that these pages are, for one thing, put together with great care, perhaps more so than any other part of Alfonso's historical production. The best and most elaborately designed narratives belong to this set of chapters. In my general introduction I tried to show how the art of the Alfonsines shaped, out of unpromising sources, the well-formed, well-articulated story of the beginnings of Scipio Africanus's greatness. The essay following this introduction to part 2 of this book continues the analysis of the Scipio passage, arguing, once again, that the compilers' craft gives their product a shape and design that its immediate sources lacked completely. In the first essay in this book, the one primarily on the epic *Cantar de Sancho*, I attempted to show how the *Estoria*'s fine account of the Roman Civil War has an architecture that is the compilers' own doing and that owes little to any of the *auctores* that are its basis. In the latter case, the set of chapters on the struggle between the forces of Pompey and Caesar, there is a significant counterexample. In book 5 of the *General estoria* the *Pharsalia* is translated whole; that is, the story of the civil war is told not in some version of Alfonso and his assistants but in more or less that of Lucan himself. The fact that the compilers of the first part of the *Estoria de Espanna* followed a different course from that of the editors of the *General estoria*, and that the former set out to compose an integral and independent narrative about the civil war, one with its own design and focus, tells us clearly that their whole project was generally quite different from what the compilers might have intended in the longer history. On these grounds and generally, one must conclude that the compilers of the pre-108 portion of the *Estoria de Espanna* were far more active and aggressive before their sources than the composers of the *General estoria*, or indeed than those of the rest of the Spanish history.

The Alfonsine editors did not make up their fine stories simply to entertain us. The narratives in the early Roman section of the *Estoria de Espanna* have a design and an intention; they are organized to make a point. Scipio is prudent, has great practical sense, and is resolute against great odds. Great leaders maintain their authority by inspiring either fear or love; Scipio is wise to the ways of the doughty Spaniards and chooses love rather than fear. Dissension breeds disorder; it is a rule forever that rivalry among the great leads to disaster. Events in Rome bear out this principle: Pompey's great power awakened the envy of Caesar, and the slaughter of thousands of Romans was the result. Both men are exemplars—the older man of the mean and of statesmanship, the younger of immoderation and ambition. It should be emphasized above all that these are Roman stories. Their heroes are Roman; this observation is in no way trivial. The art of the Alfonsines is aimed at nothing less than making its Roman characters memorable; this is its function. There is more. Rome is the theater; the texts make frequent mention of Rome itself and tell us plainly that the virtues and vices of Rome's heroes accrue to the general good or ill of the Roman commonwealth. All of the *Estoria de Espanna* is edifying, needless to say, but its Roman narratives are so in an exceptional and striking way.

The possibility that Alfonso's history of early Rome is meant especially to dramatize the city and make it an example is confirmed by a remarkable paragraph at the very head of the Roman section of the chronicle. These lines answer the question: why did Rome achieve universal power? Chapter 23 begins as follows:

Las estorias antiguas cuentan que por tres cosas fueron los romanos sennores de toda la tierra: la primera por saber, la segunda por seer bien acabdellados, la tercera por suffrencia; ca ellos fueron omnes que sopieron los grandes saberes et ayudaron se bien dellos, et ouieron sabiduria por allegar grand auer pora acabar con ello lo que querien, e sopieron tomar conseio a las cosas ante que uiniessen, e fazien sus fechos cuerdamientre et con grand seso; otrossi ellos fueron los meiores cabdiellos del mundo et los que meior sopieron traer sus yentes acabdelladas et auenidas; e quando auien guerra sabien soffrir lazeria mas que otros omnes, et por esso conquirien las tierras et sapoderauan dellas. (Alfonso 1955, 1:18)

[Ancient histories tell (us) that there were three reasons why the Romans became the lords of all the earth; the first was knowledge, the second the fact that they were well led, the third that they were long-suffering; for they were men who knew the great sciences and made good use of them, and they had the wisdom to accumulate great wealth so that they could carry out whatever plans they wished, and they had the wit to take counsel concerning things (i.e., emergencies) before they occurred, and they carried out these projects wisely and with good sense; and besides this, they were the best leaders in all the world, and the ones who best brought out their hosts united and under the best leadership, and when they went to war, they could undergo trials and sufferings better than other men; and this is why they conquered (many) lands and took control of them.]

One should note first of all that these lines are entirely original; "estorias antiguas" does not seem to refer to any particular *auctor*, and the passage has nothing whatever to do with Rodrigo Toledano, with Paul the Deacon, or with any of the prevailing sources of this portion of the *Estoria de Espanna*. What is more, the first of the three themes given here, the importance of learning and wisdom, is the Alfonsine theme par excellence. It is a leading motive in the life and practical affairs of the Learned King himself, obviously, but it is also a persistent strain in the two histories. In the *General estoria* major figures like Adam, Seth, Abraham, Hermes, and Jupiter are men of science and knowledge, and although in the Spanish history the gallery of wise men is not as large, these are not missing; Julius Caesar is remembered as a man of letters (Alfonso 1955, 1:94), and astonishingly, Mithridates, the enemy of Rome, is singled out as a model learned king, a wise and lettered man himself, and a patron of philosophers (Alfonso 1955, 1:60).

In a word, the opening fanfare of the Roman section of the *Estoria de Espanna*, the list of reasons for Rome's greatness, is as Alfonsine as one could imagine. It is unique in Alfonso's historical corpus. It is also distinctive. Rome is admirable, but the Goths are violent and contentious. The latter theme is a topic throughout the Gothic section of the history; Sancho II of Castile, for example (a Goth by Alfonsine standards), is restless and disposed to conflict, thanks to his Gothic inheritance (Alfonso 1955, 2:495). The dozen or so lines about Rome are significant in themselves, but they also point to the Roman character of the very Alfonsine narratives that follow them. The theme of Rome as example is articulated first in general terms, but the text then turns to particulars, presenting the deeds of memorable Romans in original and distinctive narratives, products of the compilers' high art.

As I have suggested, the themes of Rome as example and Rome as a continuing institution are not at all the same. They are related, obviously; the editors who wish to tell us that Frederick Barbarossa and Frederick of Sicily are Romans might also want to insist that ancient Rome was a fine and splendid place. The imperial theme in Alfonso is troublesome, mainly because, over the acres of the Alfonsine historical text—compilation, or miscellany, that it is—the empire is presented in more than one way. Let us begin on safe ground, with some clear terms of contrast, some well-articulated texts that tell us more or less what Alfonso's thought is not. Dante, as we have seen, turns Roman history into theology. Rational civic life is a natural good. Nature is, of course, established by God, and so the norms for wholesome public life are of divine origin, but they do not belong to the order of grace, and knowledge of them does not depend on revelation. However, the great agency that in point of fact brought good civic life to the world, Rome itself, was under the direct protection of God and was guided by him in a special and unique way throughout its history. Such is Dante's vindication of empire as a living institution; Rome, by God's special design, is the unique civilizer of the world. Centuries before Dante, Eusebius of Caesarea framed another theology of empire. For him Christianity came full flower when the emperor accepted the religion of Christ, and the empire became the protector of that religion. The Christian order for Eusebius was a mixture of sacral and civic elements. The first came from the teaching, practice, and experience of the Church, until then an underground organization, while the latter came from the laws and institutions of the empire itself in its non-Christian years. God prepared this union of elements from the first, and the empire grew, from Augustus on, under divine tutelege, so that in time it could become part of the great amalgam.[1]

As we shall see, neither of these views is very much like those expressed in the two Alfonsine histories, but Dante and Eusebius are of a piece with Alfonso in one respect: all three authors represent the empire as something positive. In other words, none is Augustinian; none regards political order as evil, though necessary, and none regards the empire in particular as a witness to the fallen state of humanity or to the human propensity to sin. Alfonso and his collaborators could not possibly have known Dante, and most of Eusebius was in fact a closed book to them, Greekless as they were. They did, however, know the *Historia ecclesiastica*, turned into Latin and expanded by Rufinus of Aquileia; they knew this text partly through Vincent of Beauvais's *Speculum historiale*, but there is also plain evidence that they were acquainted with

---

1. I am simplifying. The views I attribute to Eusebius here are, more than anything else, those set forth in the *Tricennial Orations*, book 16 (Drake 1976, 119–23). For a general account of Eusebius's view of history see D. S. Wallace-Hadrill 1960, chapter 9, "The Purpose of God and Human History," pp. 168–89.

Eusebius-Rufinus directly.[2] Now, the greater part of Eusebius's theology of history belongs not to the *Historia* but to his other works; the outline of his thought I have made is, for example, a paraphrase of part of the *Tricennial Orations* (Drake 1976, 119–23). But one important piece of his theory is in the former work. In a passage in the first book of the history, we find two remarkable propositions. The first is that human beings after the Fall were uncivil: "City and state, arts and sciences meant nothing to them; laws and statutes, morality and philosophy were not even names." The second notion is that God sent Moses to the Jews as a remedy for barbarism, and that "from the Jews the movement spread, and soon the characters of most heathen races began to grow gentler, thanks to the lawgivers and thinkers in every land."[3] Moses, called by God, emerges here as the civilizing hero of humankind at large. The gentler ways Eusebius speaks of—the high culture, the laws and civil institutions of the heathen nations before Christ—all, therefore, had a divine origin. It is remarkable in a way that the Alfonsines, who must have known these lines, took so little note of them.[4] The passage of humanity from savagery to civilization does have an important place in the argument of the *General estoria* (as several essays in this book try to point out). So also does the notion that the empire was the eminent civilizing force. The Alfonsines are of course thinking of the

2. Menéndez Pidal correctly attributes to Rufinus the *Estoria*'s chap. 319, on the Council of Nicea, and chap. 320, on the Invention of Holy Cross; he assigns the first to Rufinus 10.1–6 and the other to 10.7–8. The book should be 11, but the chapter numbers are correct (Alfonso 1955, 1:cxi). These passages are in fact from Rufinus proper, not from the parts of the *Historia* that are translated from Eusebius. The *Estoria*, however, plainly attributes the material in the Nicea chapter to "sant Eusebio, obispo de Cesarea la de Palestina, en un su libro que a nombre la Estoria eclesiastica" (190) [Saint Eusebius, bishop of Caesarea, in Palestine, in a book which is called Ecclesiastical History.]. Vincent of Beauvais' accounts of Nicea and the Invention of Holy Cross do not match (Vincent 13.lxii and 13.xciv, respectively). Elsewhere in his index of sources Pidal correctly identifies the passages from Eusebius-Rufinus that come to the compilers from Vincent. All these facts suggest to me that the editors of the *Estoria* know Eusebius-Rufinus firsthand.

3. The first of my two quotations is from Eusebius 1989, 7; the second is from p. 8. Williamson's translation is of course from the Greek, but his rendering is in fact an adequate version of Rufinus's Latin (Eusebius [1479?], bk. 1, chap. 2; the folios in the Mantua edition are not numbered).

4. As I point out in an essay in this book, "The *General estoria*, Material Culture, and Hermeticism," the *Pantheon* of Godfrey of Viterbo, which was known to the editors of the *General*, does quote the bit of Eusebius on the barbarism of early humanity but does not include the part about the mission of Moses or about the spread of civilization among the Gentiles.

empire as beginning not with Julius Caesar or Augustus but centuries earlier: Jupiter replaces the tyrannous Nimrod and his successors as world ruler and is the founder of the line that runs down not only to the Caesars but to Frederick of Sicily, who is, of course, Alfonso's predecessor on the imperial throne. Jupiter is the civilizing monarch par excellence who first brings law and learning to a barbarous humanity. Had the editors of the *General estoria* chosen to heed Eusebius, the Eusebius they had at hand, it would have been supremely easy for them to theologize empire and to present that institution as God's direct handiwork. The result would have been a view with affinities to the views of Dante or perhaps even more to those of Eusebius. But the compilers of the *General estoria* show little consistent interest in theories of this sort; assuming their acquaintance with the *Historia ecclesiastica,* the absence of a fully sustained theological motive may have been deliberate.

What, then, is the concept of empire that the two *Estorias* do set forth? This question is vain. The Alfonsines do not write "apologetic history"; their two historical texts are not concentrated, programmatic, centered on a few large themes. The empire, very real to them, indeed central for them, is presented under several aspects. It is in the first place, more than a concept, a continuity. It is, from their point of view, contemporary: there is in their day a living emperor, but he belongs to a line that stretches far back into the past. This continuity is laid out differently in different passages. In one, taken whole out of Orosius, there are four world empires, the Babylonian, the Macedonian, the Carthaginian, and the Roman. The last is still in existence in Alfonso's day (in its German form, obviously). The middle pair, Macedonian and Carthaginian, last a much shorter time than the others, and therefore, Rome should be regarded as the genuine heir of Babylon; Macedonia and Carthage are to be seen as the tutors and guardians of the youngest offspring. The editors of this chapter add as a sort of afterthought the alternate sequence of the Eusebius of the chronologies and of Petrus Comestor: Assyria, Sidonia, Scythia, Egypt; then they try to reconcile this list with Orosius's (Alfonso 1930, 79–81, and Orosius 2. prologue). One should add that the compilers retain Orosius's statement that all four of his universal kingdoms enjoy divine sanction. We will return to this matter presently.

A quite different version of world rule and its continuities is presented in the *General estoria* a few chapters further on, in a passage I have just alluded to. In this account the equitable and humane Jupiter

replaces the wicked Nimrod and his succession; Jupiter's descendants—
we must take Alfonso very literally here—are the kings of Greece and
Troy generally: Troas and Dardanus, Alexander the Great, Aeneas,
Romulus, the Caesars, and, finally, Frederick Barbarossa and Frederick
of Sicily. In the short run this olla podrida of names sounds arbitrary and
fanciful, more like poetry than history. In point of fact, the design and
intention of this passage are very clear. The purely human, historical,
euhemerized Jupiter is the ancestor of kings. The real point of this
proposition is that Jupiter is the founder of the line that ends in the
reigning German emperor. As we know, the kings of Christendom in the
Middle Ages claimed ancient lineages, derived from personages of
hoary antiquity; these long lines of succession gave them legitimacy. The
kings of Spain, for example, are successors of Hercules, as the *Estoria de
Espanna* tells us (Alfonso 1955, 1:7 and the chapters following). The
link between Frederick and Jupiter is obviously of this type. Then, too,
we should note that not all the persons on Alfonso's list are universal
rulers; Aeneas is not, Romulus is not, and neither are all the kings of
Greece and Troy. There are actually not one but two lines of succession
here. We have on one hand the world monarchs—in order, Jupiter,
Alexander, the Caesars, and the two Fredericks; the German emperors,
as we must understand, are universal rulers by right, if not in fact. On
the other hand, there are the lesser monarchs, the ones that make up the
Trojan-Roman line. Aeneas is, of course, the founder of Rome, and so
the successions of Dardanus, Romulus, the Caesars, and the two Fredericks make up a compact group. The continuities of empire for Alfonso
are therefore threefold. There is first the actual succession of world
monarchies—Jupiter's, Alexander's, the Caesars', and the two Fredericks'. Second, there is Frederick of Sicily's lineage, traceable to Jupiter.
And finally, there is Rome itself, with its origins in Troy, linking Jupiter
and Frederick via Dardanus and Aeneas.

The first thing we should notice about this system is that it is completely secular. We should understand that the lines of succession outlined here are not anecdotal or in any way frivolous. They signify legitimacy. Their relevance is strictly legal. Rightful inheritance is equivalent
to title, and therefore the reigning German emperor is universal monarch by right, being the heir of the person who, at the dawn of history,
brought learning and law, justice and civilized ways, to the human race,
and who imposed his benign regime on the whole world. It is almost
humorous to observe that in this pattern the source of legitimacy is not

God but Jupiter. One must point out that the Alfonsines do not in turn claim legitimacy for Jupiter from some other source—one perhaps linking him in some way to sacred history—or by pointing to some kind of divine sanction. He is plainly presented in the *General estoria* as the source of his own legitimacy, a nonsacred personage in a nonsacred narrative.

Is this nontheology of empire the Alfonsines' last word on the subject? The true answer is, of course, that in the two histories there are no last words, that each passage and section speaks for itself. There is, however, one passage in Alfonso in which the editors surely do wish us to see the hand of Providence guiding the destinies of empire. This is the section of the *Estoria de Espanna* on the reign of Augustus. In chapter 151 the all-important point is made that the conception and birth of Christ occur at a time when the whole world is at peace, the gates of the temple of Janus are closed, and the empire is at the height of its power under the rule of an admirable *princeps* (Alfonso 1955, 1:108–9). The highlighting in the *Estoria de Espanna* of this match is supported by two other motifs. In chapter 122 (p. 96), which is partly on the accession of Octavian and the prodigies that attend this event, we are told that there appeared in the East three suns that blended into one. This marvelous occurrence had two meanings. On one hand it symbolized the transition of power from the First Triumvirate to Octavian alone, and on the other it signified the trinity and unity of God; in the latter sense the prodigy signaled the fact that Christ was to be born in the reign of Augustus. The other moment in the narrative when the special status of the emperor's reign is underlined is in chapter 140 (p. 106), where it is suggested that Augustus is a virtual Christian, *anima naturaliter christiana*. The text says that he threatens to punish anyone who calls him "lord of all the world" and demands that he be addressed instead as "lord after the Lord of all the world."

One should emphasize that this sequence in the *Estoria de Espanna* is unique; nothing in the preceding chapters prepares us for it, and nothing that comes afterward echoes it until, perhaps, we come to the Christianization of empire under Constantine, where we could hardly expect even the cold-blooded Alfonsines to abstain from a bit of providentialism. This special case and that of Augustus aside, Alfonso and his collaborators show little interest in tying the fortunes of empire to the designs of Providence. The closest we come is in the passage I spoke of in the *General estoria* on the four world monarchies—Babylonian, Macedonian, Carthaginian and Roman. Its argument is not very strong. The *General estoria* translates faithfully some lines from the prologue to the second book of Orosius to the effect, first, that the life of fallen humanity is miserable, thanks to a perpetual food shortage; second, that all power is from God, and that political order is a merciful concession of His to His unhappy creatures; and finally, that if any political power whatever is by His will, so especially must the great powers be, particularly those of the four great monarchies. If what we are looking for is some statement that the whole profile of imperial history is the direct handwriting of God, this passage falls short in two respects. First, it fails to differentiate enough between great powers and small. If any rule whatever enjoys divine sanction, the text says, then so must Babylon or Rome to a high degree. This is, perhaps, excellent Christian doctrine, but it is hardly commensurate with the unique place the *General estoria* assigns to Rome and the empire. Second, Orosius focuses simply on the origin and plain existence of political power and says nothing about the sequence of events within or surrounding a particular institution or about God's role in regulating that flow.

Where do we finally stand? Is the special status of empire in the two Alfonsine histories always presented in a nontheological or nonphilosophical manner? Is their account simply narrative and anecdotal, or is there somewhere in the two works a hint at a grand theory? One notable passage in the *General estoria* seems to answer this question: it speaks plainly of the unique destiny of Rome and the empire. Its message is clear: from the very first it is determined that, of the four world monarchies, the Western one is to prevail over the other three, and that it is to last forever. This is as positive and hopeful a view of Rome, the Caesars, and their predecessors and successors as one could imagine. Dante, with his extraordinary reading of Roman history, could hardly have done better. But alas, in the Alfonsine account it is not God who is the architect of this splendid past and future; it is his ministers, the stars. As we saw in the introduction to this book, the great prophecy is put into the mouth of the singular wise man and astrologer Yonitho (in Alfonso, Yonito). Nimrod, craving power for himself and his heirs, covets Europe, known to be the fairest part of the world; he therefore consults his uncle Yonitho, son of Noah, and wise in the way of the stars, who, drawing on his star-lore, tells "the mighty hunter" of the special destiny of the Western monarchy. On the force of the older man's words, Nimrod goes to settle in what is later to be called Rome, which is ruled by his

other uncle, Janus, also a son of Noah (Alfonso 1930, 72). The fact that
to the mind of the Alfonsine editors the lofty future of the Western
kingdom is written in the stars, not directly in the mind of God, is
significant in two senses. First of all, the sentiment is very Alfonsine.
Astrology at the court of Castile in the late thirteenth century is not a
frivolous subject: I do not have to remind my readers of the Learned
King's serious and dedicated patronage of astrological studies and of the
production under his guidance of more than one treatise on the stars
and their influence on things here below. Star-lore is, also, everywhere
in the *General estoria*. Adam, Abraham, Atlas, and Hermes are, for the
editors, all astrologers. What is more, astrology is presented in the
General estoria as a sacred science and is literally a gift of God. As the
last three essays in this book point out, that work traces the prodigious
knowledge of Seth and his descendants to his father and teacher Adam,
who in turn receives it directly from God. At the center of this knowledge is, of course, astrology. Given the astrological ingredient in the
Nimrod story, we cannot doubt that the lines on the mighty Nimrod's
journey to Rome and on Yonitho's words that moved him to look west-
ward and found the empire were written in earnest and were meant to
be taken very seriously.

This passage and its message are significant in another sense. They
tell us as clearly as we could hope that Alfonso in his histories is more
concerned to speak of secondary causes than of primary, more about this
world than about the other. Even in what we could call Alfonso's theology, the focus is more on creatures than on their divine source. The
patriarchs think of God because they study the stars; this very special
science raises their minds to higher things. Seth and his progeny are
presented this way in the *General estoria:* they were liberal artists and
astrologers and were thus men of God (Alfonso 1930, 21). Abraham, for
his part, is able to preach monotheism, because he can show that the
collective labor of the stars in benefiting humankind would not be possible were they not guided by the divine hand (Alfonso 1930, 68). And in
civil history proper, the Alfonsines tell us more about how the world
works by itself than about how it is guided by Providence. In the long
run, of course, all power comes from God, but what gives legitimacy to
Frederick of Sicily is his descent from the very human Jupiter, King of
Thebes, whose wise governance brings peace, laws, and justice to the
human race. In a word, Alfonso's *General estoria* and its companion are
secular books. They are about this world and its inhabitants; the wisdom

they convey is worldly. This does not mean that the editors of these works despise the divine or that they forget completely the supposed role of God in history. But, left to themselves, the editors focus on humans and their activities and leave the otherworld out of account.

In conclusion, I wish to make a very concrete reference to one of my essays. In "Alfonso X, the Empire, and the *Primera crónica*" I suggest that the Learned King and his collaborators abandoned work on the *Estoria de Espanna* shortly after 1274, because that was the year he was forced to drop his claim to the imperial throne. My argument runs as follows. Fundamentally, the *Estoria* has a twofold personality: it is not only a Spanish history but, at least secondarily, a Roman one. Its narrative would have ended in the reign of Alfonso himself, who would have been the latest monarch in the two lines, Gothic—that is, Spanish—and imperial. My point was, of course, that once the empire eluded him, he might have seen little point in finishing a history with this design. But certain difficulties have been posed for this view. It has been observed that there are many more references to empire in the *General estoria* than in its companion, and that these allusions cannot be dated so tidily, before the fateful date 1274. The time at which the Spanish history was abandoned thus becomes less significant (Fernández Ordóñez 1992, 38). I do not believe, however, that my hypothesis is seriously damaged by these facts. What is at issue is not any allusion whatever that the histories make to the empire, but in particular allusion to what would have been Alfonso's double role as Gothic king and emperor. When one element of the pair failed him definitively, so also, I think, did an essential part of his projected history, and that may explain why work on it came to an end.

Scipio, and the Origins of Culture:
The Question of Alfonso's Sources

Love rules the world, so it seems. In the passages about Scipio Africanus's Spanish campaign in the Alfonsine *Estoria de Espanna,* the word *amor* and its cognates appear several times, and their use, as we will see, is an index to an important stratum in the makeup of that work. Having taken Cartagena, so Alfonso tells us, Scipio resolves to make further conquests on the peninsula, and in order to win the Spaniards' goodwill he shows them love by freeing some prisoners: "E por mostrar mayor *amor* a los espannoles tomo todos los presos que dellos tenie, e diolos a sos parientes en don" [To show the Spaniards greater *love,* he took all the prisoners that he held from among them, and he gave them to their relatives as a gift] (Alfonso 1955, 22). After his gracious treatment of the woman prisoner, things begin to go in his favor. Many Spaniards pass over to the Roman side and win for him fortified places, some of which yield to force, others freely, out of love: "fezieron ques le tornaron muchas uillas e castiellos e todo lo demas de la tierra, e algunas dellas por lit, pero la mayor partida por *amor*" [they made them turn over many towns and castles and all the rest of the land, some of these by force, but the greater part through *love*] (22). Scipio's fortunes rise and Hasdrubal's fall, for the Spaniards transfer their love from the Carthaginian to the Roman: "Mas Cipion, que era muy sabidor de guerra e dauer las gentes de so part, sopolo fazer de guisa que *amauan* a el y *desamauan* a Asdrubal" [Scipio, who was very wise in the ways of war and in getting people to be on his side, managed to get them to *love* him and *hate* (*des-amar,* as it were, to dis-love or un-love) Hasdrubal] (22). The *amauan-desamauan* pair occurs again a few lines further on in exactly the same sense (23). Though Carthaginians threaten further, Scipio prevails, sometimes by force, but other times through love: "Cipion uencie siempre e ganaua la tierra lo uno por *amor,* e lo al por fuerça" [Scipio always prevailed and won territory on one hand through *love* and on the other by force] (23). As we will see presently, *amor* and *fuerça* parallel the pair *amor-force* in an interesting passage in the *Fet des romains.* The Spanish campaign goes on, and Scipio wisely makes alliances, "friendships": "puso otrossi *amiztades* con aquellos que touo por que podrie meior acabar so fecho" [he established *friendships* with those he had (in the territories he had conquered), so that he could better carry out his campaign] (24; "friendships" = *amiztades,* which has the same root as *amor,* "love"). However, one Spanish king is intransigent, but once he is conquered, Scipio shows his love by demanding no hostages: "E maguer era costumbre de los romanos que quando uencien a algunos, e depues uinien a adobo, que tomauan grandes arrahenes dellos por que les non mintiessen de lo que con ellos ouiessen puesto, tanto fue grand ell *amor* que mostro Cipion a aquel rey, que non gelas quiso tomar, maguer gelas el querie dar" [And even though it was the custom of the Romans when they conquered someone and then came to peaceful terms with them that they take important hostages from them so that they not lie about what they had agreed to, so great was the *love* that Scipio showed to that king that he refused to take hostages from him, even though he was willing to give them] (24). Scipio's benevolence is decisive in Spain. Once he and his love are gone, the peace he established falls apart: "Ya oyestes de suso cuemo Scipion se partio dEspanna quando la ouo toda metuda so poder de los romanos, e se fue pora Roma; mas desque los espannoles sopieron que era passado a Affrica, touieron que numqua tornarie a ellos; e por que los otros romanos que y ficaran no les sabien fazer onra ni *amor,* assi com el, despagaron se dellos e alçaron se luego; e començaron los a guerrear" [You have already heard how Scipio left Spain after he had placed it under the power of the Romans, and how he went to Rome; but from the moment the Spaniards found out that he had gone on to Africa, they judged that he would never come back to them; and because the other Romans that remained there (in Spain) did not know how to render honor or *love,* the way he did, they took a dislike to them, and after a while they rose up and began to make war on them" (26: italics mine throughout).

The above group of passages is interesting on several counts. In the first place, in only one instance does *amor* or the related word have any sanction in the source texts underlying the lines quoted. Of the king from whom Scipio demanded no hostages, Eutropius-Paulus Diaconus says, "regem Hispanorum magno proelio victum in *amicitiam* accepit et primus omnium a victo obsides non poposcit" [he (Scipio) received the king of the Spaniards in *friendship*—the one he had beaten in a great battle—and he (Scipio) was the first not to demand hostages of the defeated] (Paul the Deacon 1914, 50; italics mine).[1] In every other case *amor* and cognates are the invention of the *Estoria*'s compilers. In some cases the words and what they express do fit into the translated text very gracefully, as when the "lover's" goodwill can be deduced from the context: Scipio's freeing of the hostages would be an example. But in other cases word and context alike are quite new: thus, only the freest sort of interpretation of Eutropius or Orosius would justify the notion that Scipio formed "amiztades." I must insist that these changes are in no way capricious. As we can see, all bear on the benevolence of Scipio and its consequences—the conquest through goodwill, in a word—and this indeed is meant to be an important theme in this episode and in the *Estoria* generally. The compilers of the work put this element there precisely where their sources did not have it and did not demand it. That the ingrafting of *amor* and cognates is really meant to sustain this large new theme is entirely evident from our last quotation, which is wholly original: so important to Spain was Scipio's goodwill, we are told, that its withdrawal led directly to rebellion.

Let us consider the words first. *Amor, amar, amiztad,* as brought to the text of the *Estoria* by the compilers, and as used by them, offer us an eminent case of what has so often been called medievalization. The cluster of terms referring to the relationship of the great to each other, or of the great and the less great, expressing, in short, a public, military, or even political reality, is everywhere in medieval literature. The characterization of Rodrigo Manrique as "amigo de sus amigos" is a pertinent locus. In epic, French and Spanish alike, *amor* and its cognates are ubiquitous. In this corpus *amor* is sometimes given certain specific and technical meanings—the favor of a lord to his vassal or a voluntary legal alliance between equals.[2] But it can also express a more general and

---

1. Paul the Deacon incorporates into the *Historia romana* much of Eutropius's *Breviarium,* as is well known. Although Menéndez Pidal cites the two works as separate sources of the *Estoria,* it seems to me likeliest that for the Alfonsines and for most medievals this was one text, the copies that circulated containing elements of both where they differed. For simplicity, therefore, I refer to Eutropius-Paul as one work and cite texts exclusively from Paul. Anyone who consults copies of Eutropius will in all but a few cases find that his wording of my quotations is identical to Paul's.

2. Jones 1963, chaps. 1 and 2 and the references there; Menéndez Pidal 1976, 2:464–65, 463. My comments are largely based on my own reading of chansons de geste.

informal goodwill. Twice in *Girart de Roussillon* (1953), for example, *amor* characterizes those who simply favor peace. We have a wise counsellor, for instance, about to speak "a gize de baron qui amor quer" [in the manner of the baron who seeks love] (line 2965). Charles and Girart are contrasted: "Vos cai vengiz por gerre e por folor, / el conte por paz e por amor" [You vindicate yourself by war and madness, the count by peace and by love] (lines 9413–14). Still more general is this: "Franceis a Borgignons non unt amor" [The French and the Burgundians do not have love (between them)] (line 8242). Other examples from epic could be urged of *amor* within much the same range of meaning of the word in the *Estoria*. The *Fet des romains* comes still closer to our target. This work, itself heavily influenced by epic, uses *amor* once in a context identical to that of the word in one of our Scipio passages: a city or fortified place yields to a conqueror willingly, "par amor." As I will try to show presently, this very passage may have influenced the compilers decisively in their determination to use *amor* and to accept everything the word implies.

One could argue against the notion that all of these uses of *amor* and cognates were strictly medieval by advancing the case of Eutropius's *amicitia,* dating from the fourth century. Indeed, the *Oxford Latin Dictionary* (Oxford: Clarendon, 1968) cites instances of *amicitia* meaning "friendship between states or rulers" starting in time with Cicero; it also quotes three cases of *amor* meaning "affection of peoples, between nations," from Hirtus, Virgil, and Tacitus. The issue this matter raises is the classic one of genesis, and one could ask how pertinent the genetic question was at this point. The authors of the chansons de geste or medieval chronicles and histories had certain quite contemporary and unclassical things in mind when they wrote *amor* and *amiztad/amitié,* and the practice of a handful of ancient authors hardly explains why the later ones wrote precisely as they did. What is more relevant in any event is the fact that in every case but one, *amor* and cognates are brought to the *Estoria* by the compilers: the Alfonsines use the words where their sources do not. They plainly mean to bring to these old texts a pattern of meaning, a message, indeed, that is quite their own, and that is thus inevitably medieval.

Why did the Alfonsine editors wish to stress the benevolence of Scipio? One among several possible answers is the following. A later very significant passage in the *Estoria* presents us a notion of a Spain singular among nations: she and her people are out of the ordinary in that only the gentlest methods of rule work with them. In the section on

the war between Caesar and Pompey the point is made that order in
Spain is normally to be kept not by violent means but by peaceful. The
prime text is in a passage about Julius Caesar: it tells us that the great
general, violent by nature, as a rule took no pleasure in peaceful conquests, but that in Spain he was wise enough to realize that more benevolent measures were necessary. The paragraph is, incidentally, quite original: it is made up in part of scraps of Lucan, but they are joined together
in such a way as to produce a virtually new text. Of Caesar's change of
heart we read: "Mas demudos desto aqui en el fecho de Espanna, e puso
en so coraçon que de quanto y pudiesse ganar por amor a por abenencia,
que lo no leuasse por guerras nin lides nin muertes ni por esparzer
sangre. E assi cuemo fue entrando por la tierra, trabaiosse de auer las
uillas e los castiellos e la otra yent lo mas en paz que el pudo, dando a los
unos sos dones granados et prometiendo a los otros. E dizen que lo fazie
por las yentes de las Espannas que sabie el que eran muy fuertes en
armas" [But he followed a different plan in the Spanish campaign, and he
set his heart on the notion that insofar as he gained as much (territory) as
he could by love and by agreement, to that extent he would not have to
do so by wars nor battles nor deaths nor bloodshed. And as he went
deeper into the territory he made every effort to take towns and castles
and other peoples as peacefully as he could, giving great gifts to some
and making promises to others. And it is said that he did this because of
the (special character of the) Spaniards, because he knew that they were
powerful men at arms] (69). In a piece of a speech in the *Estoria* spoken
by Caesar himself we get a similar sentiment: "ca en toda Espanna non
quiero yo desta uegada fazer batalla ninguna que con sangre sea, en
quanto lo yo pudier escusar" [for if I can help it, this time in no part of
Spain do I wish to fight in a battle that is bloody] (75). This is also new: it
is not to be found in Lucan. Supporting these passages are others that tell
us that the fortunes of Spain are an important strand in the civil war
narrative. Thus, at the beginning of the section the deeds of Caesar and
Pompey are made to bear upon Spain: "Mas agora contaremos de los
fechos que amos estos principes fizieron daqui adelant, sobre que
ouieron guerra et lidiaron muchas uezes ellos e los otros cibdadanos de
Roma por las razones dellos; et de los fechos que ellos fizieron por las
otras tierras diremos ende algunos: lo uno por que fueron amos sennores
de las Espannas, pero que en sennos tiempos, &c." [But now we will tell
of the deed these two princes performed from this point on, as a result of
which they made war (on each other), and they waged war and fought

many battles, and so did other citizens of Rome on their account; and we will tell about some of the deeds they performed in other lands; we will do so for one thing because they were both masters of Spain, though at different times] (58). The whole string of chapters is further decorated with lines telling us what is happening (or not happening) in Spain in the meantime. One example will do: "Pero en estas contiendas de los principes de Roma e de sos cibdadanos que en aquella sazon se fazien, las Espannas estauan quedas e assessegadas con los fijos de Ponpeyo e con sos cabdiellos que las tenien" [But during the struggles that were taking place in those days between the princes of Rome and her citizens, the Spains were quiet and peaceful under the sons of Pompey and the leaders under them] (66). Thus, although the civil war episode is not primarily Spanish, the theme of Spain is nevertheless in one way or another present in it, and at the heart of this significant presence is the proposition that Spanish dignity will not tolerate a violent ruler. The *Estoria,* a compilation, is not therefore a rag-heap. The Scipio passage plainly is meant to be a prefiguration of the section about Pompey and Caesar. The reason why the compilers took such pains to make benevolence the mainspring of Scipio's actions in Spain was to announce for the first time a theme that would be articulated later more explicitly, the special disposition and dignity of Spain and of Spaniards.

We observe, finally, that *amor,* significantly, figures in our passage about Caesar.

As I have suggested, there is a detail in the *Fet des romains* that may lie behind the use of *amor* in the *Estoria* and ultimately behind the conquest-by-love idea found there. I tried to show in another article that the *Fet* was probably known to the Alfonsine compilers.[3] The older history, like the *Estoria,* is a compilation: it is a mammoth biography of Julius Caesar, formed in great part out of large pieces of Sallust, Caesar himself, Lucan, and Suetonius. It is in many ways like its Spanish successor, particularly so in style and in translation-technique. Nearly all of the *Pharsalia* is preserved in its French text. Now, one of the passages in Lucan that unquestionably underlies the *Estoria*'s crucial paragraph about Caesar's changed ways in Spain is a phrase from book 2 on the Roman's warlike disposition: "Non tam portas intrare patentes / Quam fregisse iuvat, nec tam patiente colono / Arva premi quam si ferro

---

3. I refer to the essay immediately following this one in this book.

populetur et igni" [He would rather burst a city gate than find it open to
admit him; he would rather ravage the land with fire and sword than
overrun it without protest from the husbandmen] (Duff's translation)
(Lucan 1959, bk. 2, verses 443–45). (Menéndez Pidal does not list this
bit among the sources for chapter 96 of the *Estoria* [Alfonso 1955,
lxxxiv], though he plainly should have.) The version in the *Fet* has the
word *amor:* "Plus li plesoit entrer ez citez par force et brisier portes et
barres que se l'en li rendit par amor" [It pleased him more to take cities
by force, by breaking down gates and bars, then when they surrendered
to him out of love] (*Li Fet des romains* 1935, 1:372). The *amor* obviously
is alien to the Latin. Now the *Estoria* phrase that is closest to this bit of
Lucan assuredly does not have the key word: "E dizen del las estorias
que en las otras tierras numqua se el pagara tanto de conquista que
fiziesse en paz, como daquella en que fallaua contienda et lid" [And the
histories tell of him that, in other lands, he never took as much pleasure
in the conquests that he made peacefully as in those in which he encountered opposition and warfare] (69). But the very following sentence, the
one we have quoted, uses *amor* in a way that recalls the Scipio episode:
"Mas demudos desto aqui en el fecho de Espanna, e puso en so coraçon
que de quanto y pudiesse ganar por amor o por abenencia, &c." [But he
changed plans here in the Spanish campaign, and he set his heart on
gaining as much (territory) as he could by love and the union of minds.]
The fact that the *amor* in the *Fet* and that in the *Estoria* are on opposite
sides, referring in one case to the goodwill of the conquered toward
Caesar, and in the other, the other way around, seems to me hardly
significant: the former situation certainly presupposes the latter. The
Estoria uses the word *amor* in our sense perhaps less than a dozen times
in its whole extent, and it is surely remarkable that one of the occur-
rences comes precisely after a paraphrase of a bit of Lucan that the *Fet*
translates also using *amor.* We must remember two things in this connection, that we have independent grounds for thinking that the French
work was known to the Spanish compilers, and that the appearance of
amor in the *Fet* is itself significant, since the original Latin does not have
it and in no way compels its use. What seems likeliest, therefore, is that
the use of *amor* in the Caesar passage was suggested to the compilers by
their reading of the *Fet.* What is further possible is that this occurrence
of *amor* in the French work, along with the correlative *force,* may have
suggested the benevolent conquest theme to the Spanish compilers as a
straight reading of Lucan's Latin might not have.

The *Fet* thus may well have an important role in the formation of the *Estoria*. But a broad reading of the Scipio episode suggests another possible source, one of much greater scope and importance. The possibility, incidentally, is not one we should entertain lightly: we are in for serious difficulties. The source is Livy. The matter is not a simple one. A sober study of the Scipio narrative and its known sources—Orosius, Eutropius-Paul, and Rodrigo Toledano—would lead us to think that the central theme of conquest by benevolence is simply a new strain brought by the compilers to their old texts, one Alfonsine initiative among many. But what is wholly disconcerting is the fact that the end result, sources plus new material, gives us a conception of the Roman hero that is very close to the portrait of him that we find in Livy, who also presents him as a conqueror through benevolence. I must explain: the accessibility of Livy is not a problem. Portions of *Ab urbe condita* were well known in the Middle Ages, and many of the surviving manuscripts dating from before Petrarch's ambitious study of the text contain the passage about Scipio.[4] We know in particular that there may have been copies of the work in Spain.[5] There is nothing wholly ridiculous in the thought that the compilers of the *Estoria* knew Livy. But what is completely anomalous is the fact that they do not at any point cite him textually. As we know, the *Estoria* is largely a catena of translations and adaptations of texts, ancient and modern, put together with a certain amount of order and system, and accommodated to their new setting. The translations run from strict to quite free, but ordinarily one has little difficulty matching them with their originals—Orosius, Paul the Deacon, Rodrigo Toledano, and so on. But as far as I know, one cannot find so much as a single line of Livy, not a scrap of continuous prose that can be identified as a translation of *Ab urbe condita* (*AUC*). More than that, the Scipio narrative in the *Estoria* seems to owe little, broadly speaking, to the Roman work. Even with respect to the texts that are explicit about Scipio's goodwill, there is not much coincidence. Indeed, the first *amor* passage cited at the beginning of this article does have its analogue in Livy: in *AUC*, Scipio, at the point of freeing the hostages, says that the Romans prefer to prevail over their enemies by awakening their gratitude rather than by inspiring their fear (26.49). To this detail we should add the whole episode of the Roman's generous

---

4. Manitius 1935, 72–76. For the state of the text of Livy, see Billanovich 1951, 131–208, esp. 143, 144, 148.

5. See preceding note. The allusions to copies in Spain in Manitius are all late.

treatment of the beautiful young woman hostage, which indeed comes to the *Estoria* from Livy (ibid.) by way of Eutropius-Paul the Deacon. Aside from these cases none of the *amor, amauan, amiztades* passages owes anything to *AUC*. By the same token the rest of Livy's texts on Scipio's generosity find no echo in the Spanish work. Two refer globally to the general's goodwill (27.17 and 27.20), and three others tell of acts of kindness that are omitted from the *Estoria* and its sources (27.19, all three). The proposition in the Spanish work that the un-Scipionic violent ways of Scipio's successors in Spain inspired rebellion does have a sort of parallel in Livy: we are told that Indibilis rose up against Rome because to his mind every Roman officer seemed base by comparison to Scipio (29.1.19). But this is flimsy enough and not a very convincing likeness. What we have, then, is a possible global influence of one text on another, with little if any borrowing of details. This is in the face of the fact that practically the whole of the *Estoria* is one endless verbal borrowing: the ipsissima verba for the Scipio bit come not from Livy but from Rodrigo, Orosius, and Eutropius-Paul the Deacon.

If, indeed, Scipio's benevolence in Alfonso comes from Livy, we must ask why the compilers treated that valuable text as they did. Their interest in Scipio was very great; Livy's account of him was quite what they needed. Why, then, did they not treat *AUC* as an immediate source to be quoted extensively? Why, indeed, did it not occur to them to draft Livy to do heavy labor for them, as they did Orosius, for example? Above all, it seems so generally and wholly alien to their practice to draw a broad conception from one author but the actual words from another. The normal case would be one in which a large idea or theme—and the details and, broadly speaking, the words also—does come from an older text. Thus the compilers' conception of the times of Sancho II is almost entirely that of the *Cantar,* which, as we know, is quoted at length. To a lesser extent one could say that their view of the Roman Civil War owes much to Lucan, who also supplies much of their text on the subject. The borrowed text of course need not enforce its views on the compilers, but it sometimes does. Literary influence in a conventional sense takes this form in the *Estoria*—it rarely takes any other—and it is this uniformity in the work that makes the Scipio-Livy connection there seem so strange. It appears, then, given our evidence, that we cannot do without Livy, but at the same time we cannot do with him. Can this paradox be resolved? Could, for example, the *amor* passages be traced to a source other than the ones Pidal proposed for the whole passage? This question, promising as it may seem, is in essence not a fruitful one, since in most cases the new material expresses notions that the compilers obviously deduced from the known sources. Besides the instances I have already given, one could point out that the *amauan-desamauan* pair is most probably derived from Eutropius-Paul's "omnes fere ad eum [Scipionem] transierunt" [almost all went over to him] (Paul the Deacon 1914, 49), and that the *amor-fuerça* pair derived from the remark in Orosius (also in Rodrigo) that Scipio took eighty cities, some of which surrendered freely, others after a struggle, "lxxx ciuitates aut deditione aut bello in potestatem redegit" [he reduced to his power eighty cities, either thanks to their [free] surrender or by war]. (Orosius 1882, bk. 4, chap. 18) That leaves the genuinely new *amiztades* passage, which is hardly crucial anyway, and the much more interesting section about Scipio's absence from Spain, and in fact I am unable to find a post-Livy source for it. But if we ask globally what texts the Alfonsines might have read aside from *AUC* that could have contributed to the idea of benevolent conquest, the answer is, practically none. Florus, whom Pidal cites a few times in his index of sources, is of no help. Vincent of Beauvais's *Speculum historiale,* a work that contributes heavily to the Alfonsine work for later Roman history, does have a solid chapter on Scipio, but not a word about conquest by goodwill. Other medieval compilations in Latin and in the vernacular leave us high and dry. Otto of Freising, for example, or Ekkehard of Aura, or the very widely read *Orose en français* (*Histoire ancienne jusqu'à César*), which on Scipio follows Orosius and Eutropius slavishly.

One of our known sources does offer a glimmer of hope; it is a text that in fact preserves elements of Livy that bear heavily on our problem. Eutropius-Paul, omnipresent in the *Estoria*'s Scipio passage, may well be the medium we are looking for. That text, as we know, contributes the episode in which Scipio, against all precedent, demands no hostages from his conquered enemy. It also preserves the episode of the woman hostage: Scipio, having taken New Carthage, is faced with a test of character in the form of an attractive young prisoner. Young himself and all-powerful, he nevertheless hands her over to her betrothed, a local noble, a generous act that wins him the goodwill of many: as we know, most Spaniards go over to his side in the war: "omnes fere ad eum transierunt." The compilers, incidentally, strengthen this motif only slightly: they specify that Scipio's few allies win for him a number of fortified places of strategic value. These elements, straight out of Livy, by themselves give the Alfonsine committee a very gallant and generous

Scipio and an effective conqueror through goodwill. But the mere accessibility of this material from Eutropius-Paul does not explain why the compilers chose to make benevolent conquest the dominant theme of the episode. They go far beyond Eutropius. After all, the very uses of *amor* and its cognates connect the theme explicitly with certain other turns of the narrative in the sources. As we have seen, Orosius's "aut deditione aut bello" (as in our quotation) surfaces in the *Estoria* in two separate *amor* passages, in the bit about the consequences of Scipio's treatment of the hostage and once afterward: this is a plain sign the compilers were carrying the ball. A similar initiative is involved in the three expressions traceable to the "omnes fere ad eum transierunt," in its proper place after New Carthage, and in the two *amauan-desamauan* lines. Most important of all, the account of the disastrous state of Spain without Scipio and his benevolence, a pure invention, tells us in the clearest terms that the compilers mean to foreground that benevolence. Why all these extra steps? The likeliest answer is to be found in the lines about the benevolence of Caesar. If this passage had already been planned, we can understand why the editors would choose to amplify the strain in Eutropius-Paul: the chapters on Scipio would thus prepare the way for the ones on Caesar. Perhaps, then, we can do without Livy. What Eutropius preserves of Livy, joined with certain initiatives of the compilers, might, in a sense, have restored some strains in the great historian they had lost.

If, however, we choose to keep Livy, we are left with the diffuse influence. If we prefer not to account for the coincidence between the *Estoria* and *AUC* by appealing to an intermediate text, we may find it likeliest that the compilers read Livy, borrowed themes from him, but did not incorporate bits of his history into their work. Setting aside other difficulties, how plausible is the notion of a diffuse influence? Menéndez Pidal virtually answers this question in many entries in his index of sources. The authors and texts he mentions sometimes contribute little to the actual words of the *Estoria* but do supply general ideas. Thus, in the civil war episode, once again, we read several times that the envy of Caesar was the basis for his hostility to Pompey: for each of these passages Pidal sends us to the last chapter of the *Historia romanorum* of Rodrigo of Toledo. But if we look at Rodrigo, we find this envy set forth only once, rather broadly, and we find no text of his that is actually translated, freely or otherwise, in the *Estoria*. There are many instances like this in Pidal's index. Mainly these judgments of his are in no way rash or unreasonable. To my mind there is in the Alfonsine corpus one spectacular instance of a global influence, a diffuse echo in the Spanish text of an author the compilers knew well, Cicero. The passage in question is not in the *Estoria de Espanna* but in the *General estoria (GE)*. It is in the remarkable account of the early life of humankind, of man's progress in culture and religion, in the third book of the first part—the chapter "De las primeras costumbres delos omnes" [Concerning the first customs of men] and those following. Humans at first had no religion, no legitimate marriage, and men did not recognize their children. All lived like animals, ate what nature provided, did not prune trees or cultivate crops; their clothing was of the simplest. Then began the slow climb upward: on one hand material culture emerged and became more and more satisfactory and refined, and on the other religion advanced from the cult of stones, plants, and animals to that of the four elements in upward order, on to that of the stars, and ultimately to that of God Himself, creator of the rest. In a sense, our source hunt is easy here. Bits of the *De inventione* of Cicero are strewn all over this passage, and at one point that work is named— "Tullio enla su primera Rectorica [Tully in his First Rhetoric] (i.e., the *De inventione*). The abject state of early man—his savagery and lack of religion, marriage, and legitimate offspring—is out of Cicero. So also, probably, is the account of house building, at an early stage of progress, when the art had barely been invented: "començaron a fazer casas de maderos mal dolados e tuertos, quales seles acahescien, e atados con uelortos de mimbres e de piertegas, ca non sabien aun ellos mas de mahestria nin de carpenteria pora aquello, e morauan en ellas" [they began to build houses of pieces of wood that were rough-hewn and twisted, just as they found them, which they bound together with shoots of reed, for they did not know about craftsmanship or carpentry, and they lived in those houses] (Alfonso 1930, 63). This passage may well have been suggested to the compilers by the "tectis silvestris" [rustic shelters] that, according to Cicero, humans began to build once the great culture hero taught his fellows gentler ways (1.3). Much indeed in the whole passage could be read as a typical Alfonsine expansion of the source text. The list of deficiencies of uncultivated man is a little longer than Cicero's, but not at all in a way that would surprise readers of the two great chronicles. Of course Cicero and the *GE* give very different accounts of the progress of the race. *De inventione* gives us a single leap out of savagery, led by a civilizing hero, whereas the

Spanish work conceives of a number of steps toward a better life, which in every case but one—the coming to a belief in God—are not connected with the teaching or activity of any single person. One would therefore hardly expect Cicero's description of early civilization to contribute very much to the Alfonsine picture of the better life, and in fact, the "tectis silvestris" is, at the outside, one of the few traces here of *De inventione*. Progress in religion is, however, the showpiece of the *GE* passage: the slow approach through one stage, to the next, to the notion of a single supreme God, the lord of nature, is presented as the greatest cultural achievement of all. This very original development, a series of imaginative deductions from a text of Lucas de Tuy, could also be read as a mirror image of Cicero's proposition that the first humans had no religion. To put things simply, *De inventione* gave the Alfonsine compilers two elements, the account of the original uncivilized state and the account of what came afterward. The editors indeed rejected the latter, but in their own story of civilization, they were free to invert, to give a reverse account of, what Cicero has about the first stage: what humans did not have at first, they learned or acquired later. Since *De inventione* gives us humanity without religion, the *GE* will give us religion with a vengeance. Thus the discussion of the subject in the *GE* could be read as a sort of deduction from the Roman work.

Alfonsine editorial procedures are admittedly extraordinary, but as I have been observing, many elements in the passage on the progress of the race may be considered traces of Cicero, identifiable and typical, if we remember more or less what those procedures are. This outlook on a very original series of chapters gives us a wholly inaccurate idea of their character and distracts us from our real purpose, which is to give an example of a diffuse influence. The passage presents us with a bold vision of the human situation, absolutely unique, I believe, in medieval literature. What, if anything, inspired this large and ambitious conception? What factors, if any, might explain its emergence? We could pose our problem in a special way. The Alfonsine scenario is remarkable for its general likeness to similar scenarios for the presumed growth of the world of man that we read in certain ancient authors: these plots are one of the manifestations of the phenomenon Lovejoy and Boas call "antiprimitivism."[6] As we know, there was a strain in Greek thought

---

6. Lovejoy and Boas 1935 [1965], chaps. 7, 8, 9, 12. See also Cole 1967.

that exalted arts and civlization over nature and that asserted that the lot of humans improved as human-made things and institutions were perfected. Not all the texts that set forth this point of view were narrative in design, but many were, telling in detail the several stages the race passed through to reach the high state of things in the writer's own time. Now, it is a plain fact that none of these latter texts could have been read by the Alfonsines: one would have to recast completely all one's notions of medieval literary culture before we could affirm that Polybius or Diodorus Siculus influenced the editors of the *General estoria*. What, then, could explain the general likeness, the approximate copy that appears suddenly after so many centuries? If we cannot have Diodorus as a source, who is to take his place?

The answer, as I would suggest, is Cicero himself. The long narrative, the unfolding saga of progress, is assuredly not his, but the proposition that the decent life is not natural but civilized and artificial can be found frequently in his writings, including some of those best-known to medievals. The passage from *De inventione* is in its way a prime example. Similar in design and scope is a passage in the *Tusculanae Disputationes*, in which a variety of arts, artifacts, and sciences are attributed, at least in principle, to individual heroes. Most pertinent of all from our point of view is a discussion in book 2 of *De officiis,* in which human ingenuity generally has attributed to it all sorts of blessings. I quote at length:

> As for mutual helpfulness, those very things which we have called inanimate are for the most part themselves produced by man's labours; we should not have them without the application of manual labour and skill nor could we enjoy them without the intervention of man. And so with many other things: for without man's industry there could have been no provisions for health, no navigation, no agriculture, no ingathering or storing of the fruits of the field or other kinds of produce. Then, too, there would surely be no exportation of our superfluous commodities or importation of those we lack, did not men perform these services. By the same process of reasoning, without the labour of man's hands, the stone needful for our use would not be quarried from the earth, nor would "iron, copper, gold, and silver, hidden far within," be mined.
>
> And how could houses ever have been provided in the first place for the human race, to keep out the rigours of the cold and

alleviate the discomforts of the heat; or how could the ravages of furious tempest or of earthquake or of time upon them afterward have been repaired, had not the bonds of social life taught men in such events to look to their fellow-men for help? Think of the aqueducts, canals, irrigation works, breakwaters, artificial harbours; how should we have these without the work of man? From these and many other illustrations it is obvious that we could not in any way, without the work of man's hands, have received the profits and the benefits accruing from inanimate things.

Finally, of what profit or service could animals be, without the co-operation of man? For it was men who were the foremost in discovering what use could be made of each beast; and to-day, if it were not for man's labour, we could neither feed them nor break them in nor take care of them nor yet secure the profits from them in due season. By man, too, noxious beasts are destroyed, and those that can be of use are captured.

Why should I recount the multitude of arts without which life would not be worth living at all? For how would the sick be healed? What pleasure would the hale enjoy? What comforts should we have, if there were not so many arts to minister to our wants? In all these respects the civilized life of man is far removed from the standard of the comforts and wants of the lower animals. And, without the association of men, cities could not have been built or peopled. In consequence of city life, laws and customs were established, and then came the equitable distribution of private rights and a definite social system. Upon these institutions followed a more humane spirit and consideration for others, with the result that life was better supplied with all it requires, and by giving and receiving, by mutual exchange of commodities and conveniences, we succeed in meeting all our wants. (Cicero 1913, 179–83)

The coincidences of this account with the one in the passage in the *GE* are twofold. First, Cicero does allude here, at least in principle, to the state of humankind without one or another civilized advantage: where would we be, we are repeatedly asked, without medicine, without decent housing? The deprived state is, of course, very conspicuous in the later work: under pressure of *De inventione* it places man without arts and artifacts in an original early and unhappy time. Second, *De officiis* and *GE* are alike in that they both mention a great number and variety of civilized blessings. The differences between the two passages are obvious. First, there is no chronology, no temporal sequence in Cicero. We will return to this matter presently. Second, the two lists of human-made goods are not very much alike. Any attempt, for example, to see in the Spanish account an influence in detail of Cicero's text would be wholly frustrating. But this very discrepancy raises what to my mind is the basic issue. If we ask ourselves where the Alfonsine story of the growth of civilization came from, we could answer more or less as follows. The compilers' school training would have put before them a group of texts of Cicero that set forth in some detail the excellence of civilized life and the poverty and misery of any other. One of these texts, *De inventione,* is actually in narrative form and describes an early savage state in fairly specific terms. The lot of these passages would become, as it were, the mental furniture of our editors, which would put a large theme or thesis about the human species in their awareness in global terms. Mutatis mutandis, I have in mind the sort of general literary influence we were brought up on, that of Milton on Wordsworth, of Verlaine on the Modernists. If we reflect further that the Alfonsine world is full of civilizing heroes—hardly any of the editors' own invention—such as Ceres who invented agriculture and Cadmus who invented letters, we can see that the Ciceronian themes might also have easy access to it. Ultrapositivist zeal should not hide from us the merits of vagueness. We are all influenced in vague ways, we learn many important lessons vaguely, we change our minds for vague reasons. We need not imagine that our predecessors were different.

There remains the matter of the chronological sequence in Alfonso. I believe that it got into our passage in the *GE* for reasons having little to do with Cicero or antiprimitivism. A tiny scrap of Lucas of Tuy's *Chronicon mundi* was the initial fillip. Different groups of men in olden times worshiped the different elements, one each: "nam alii colebat igne, alii aquā, alii sole, & sic de aliis elementis" (Lucas of Tuy 1608, 7). I would remark that Lucas's passage makes more sense, if we change *solem* to *solum,* "earth": this gives us all the elements. The English would run "for some men worshiped fire, some water, some earth, and some the other elements." We can be certain that the compilers of the *GE* have this passage in Lucas before them. In their discussion of the cult of fire they tell us that the Chaldeans worshiped that element (65): the detail comes to them from Lucas (8). They could scarcely have taken note of this bit of the *Chronicon* and been ignorant of the other: the two are a scant dozen lines apart. The fact that Lucas's simultaneous worship of the elements is certainly the source and basis of the *GE*'s successive cults further suggests that the Alfonsines also read "solum." Why indeed did the compilers choose to make these religions go stepwise in time instead of leaving them simultaneous, as in their source? The answer is complicated. Josephus gives the compilers two connected notions, that men worshiped the stars for their evident power (evident in Alfonso's day, as in Josephus's, and, as presumed, in biblical times), and that Abraham taught that the cult of one God was superior to that of the stars, as He was more powerful than they (1.7). The natural philosophy known to the Alfonsines would have told them that the idea of stellar influences explains more about the universe than the notion of the elements. So it is that the movement from a cult of elements to a cult of stars might seem natural to them, just as the movement from a cult of stars to a cult of God was for them both logical and authorized. The other two steps then were simple. They prefaced the cult of the elements with the less rational worship of stones, plants, and animals, and then they put the cult of the elements in an order of their excellence and of their closeness to heaven, earth, water, air, and fire. The result is a magnificent, quite original *itinerarium mentis in Deum* in the history of humankind, in which humans looked for more and more general and universal causes as the object of their religion until they finally came to the one and only God. The rest of the conception was equally brilliant and new. They turned the growth of religion into the heart and soul of a larger growth, that of culture and civilization. Hence we have the historical, narrative account of arts and artifacts.

We thus conclude our account of the complex and disquieting passage in the *GE*. The temporal sequence probably grows out of a thematic exigency, and the antiprimitivism is a general, undetailed reflection of ideas expressed in certain ancient texts. If these two propositions are true, I have succeeded in explaining why our string of chapters revives, after such a long stretch of time, a very old theme. More important for us, it opens the possibility of a diffuse, global influence on the Alfonsine works. In trying to list the preexisting elements that helped form it, we need not limit ourselves to sources that supply verbal parallels: general ideas will work too. If we return, then, to the question of whether Livy influenced the compilers of the *Estoria de Espanna* in their conception of Scipio Africanus, we are permitted to say that in principle it is not impossible. The large difficulty remains, however. If the compilers indeed had as splendid an account of Scipio's career as Livy's, why were they content to copy textually nothing more exciting than Rodrigo of Toledo, Orosius, and Eutropius-Paul the Deacon?

The *Fet des romains* and the *Primera crónica general*

It is odd that so little has been written about the relationship between the Alfonsine histories and certain older French compilations of similar scope. If impressions count for anything, it is worth assuring readers of the *Fet des romains* or of the work P. Meyer calls *Histoire ancienne jusqu'à César* that they might well feel at home in the *Primera crónica* or the *General estoria;* the reverse is also true. The two French compilations each have features of content, structure, and texture that recall in various ways the Alfonsine works. Style is not the first object of this essay, but we note that remarks by the modern editors of the *Fet* about that work's style and technique of translation are similar, often in detail, to parallel comments about the Alfonsine histories by María Rosa Lida de Malkiel and others.[1] Are these various similarities reflections of a common heritage? Did the older works influence the newer directly either in general or in detail? Are the likenesses significant at all?

One could answer these questions in various ways, depending on the scale of the inquiry, the sort of data one was looking at. An examination of the *Fet* and the *Crónica,* however, suggests a set of very specific answers. There are, for a fact, a few significant features of the Spanish work that may have come to it from the French. The dissimilarities are also considerable, needless to say. We must make this clear: precisely in

---

1. On the style of Alfonso, see Lida de Malkiel's comments on the techniques of translation in the *General estoria* (1958, 122–31) and Lázaro Carreter 1961. For the style and translation techniques in the *Fet des romains,* see *Li fet des romains* 1938, 2.29–31 and passim in the commentary, 61ff. Volume 1 is the text of the *Fet* and page references to either volume will be to this edition. See also Sneyders de Vogel 1933.

the area in which we would expect our texts to run parallel, they do not. Both compilations depend heavily on Lucan. The *Fet* translates nearly all of the *Pharsalia,* and the *Crónica* has among other things Lucan's version of Caesar's Spanish campaign. But the hastiest glance at parallel passages shows that the Spanish version is quite independent of its predecessor. Nothing fits: the amplifications do not in the main coincide, Latin place names are translated differently, and, with insignificant exceptions, mistranslations are quite unlike.[2] Actually a Spanish Lucan taken from a French is an impossibility in any case. The two come from Latin texts, which must have been unlike.[3] We know besides that the *Crónica* version was translated directly from a Latin copy, one not wholly unknown to us.[4] The almost total independence of the two versions must stand.

There are curious oases, to be sure. The two compilations, as is well known, translate their Latin texts with great freedom. By turns they amplify, they alter, they condense, they add explanations, they omit. Sometimes these new departures coincide. Both the *Fet* and the *Crónica* change *Pharsalia* 1.165 ff. in the same way: Lucan's account of the crossing of the Rubicon comes before the description of the river itself, but for the sake of a more logical order, perhaps, our two medieval texts

---

2. One such coincidence is noted in Sneyder's commentary to the *Fet,* 2.2:167.

3. The matter from the glosses on Lucan is distributed very differently in the *Fet* and the *Crónica;* on this basis alone we might conclude that the respective Lucan texts are different. The glosses coincide only in the following instances: the "acequias" used to lower the level of the Segre, according to the *Crónica* (Alfonso 1955—we will henceforth give page references in this edition), p. 71b, line 23, comes from a gloss on Lucan 4.141–43, also used by the *Fet,* 1:425, line 10 (see commentary, 2:168); *Crónica* "los de Salamina," p. 78a, line 38 follows a gloss on Lucan 3.183, like that used in the *Fet,* 1:396, line 21 (see 2:161); the *Crónica*'s "Menelao" could be from the gloss on Lucan 3.286, used by the *Fet,* 1:402, line 17; "Menphis de Egipto," in *Crónica,* p. 78, line 18, is from a gloss on Lucan 3.222, used by the *Fet,* 1:397, line 12 (see 2:161). According to Menéndez Pidal (Alfonso 1955, 1:lxxxiii–lxxxiv), chaps. 93–100 and 102 all have matter from Lucan's "comentaristas" unspecified; this must include more material than from the above. In the passages of Lucan used by the *Crónica,* the *Fet* draws on glosses on 3.188, 198, 210, 227 (noted in the *Fet,* 2:161), 253, 266, 269–70 (*Fet* 2:162), 284 (*Fet,* 2:167); 4.28–29 (*Fet* 2:167), 333–34 (*Fet* 2:169). These discrepancies probably show that the *Crónica* and the *Fet* used dissimilar texts of Lucan and almost certainly show that the *Crónica*'s editors did not use the *Fet* for their translation.

4. The Lucan copy used by the Alfonsine editors came from the cathedral of Albelda (see Alfonso 1955, introduction by Menéndez Pidal, 2:xx–xxi); there cannot be the slightest doubt that the Alfonsine versions of Lucan came directly from a Latin text.

put the description first.[5] French and Spanish compilers also react alike to another passage in Lucan's fourth book that tells of how the two forces before Lerida, Caesarian and Pompeian, were in sight of each other, and how the members of both armies felt shame at the damage they were working on Rome. Both the *Fet* and the *Crónica* heighten the drama by concluding that members of the opposing groups recognized each other. The two sets of editors may have drawn an analogy with a later passage in the *Pharsalia* in which soldiers in the same two forces do recognize friends and relatives among their opponents.[6] There are other less interesting coincidences between our two versions of Lucan, some of which are pointed out by the modern editors of the *Fet.* How significant all these very occasional parallelisms are is hard to say. So infrequent are they that it is safest not to draw any conclusion at all. But in any case the good evidence of a possible influence on the Alfonsine editors by the *Fet* is of quite a different order.

There are two formal features that the *Crónica* shares with the French history that are hard to attribute to simple chance. The first of these is the fact that the vernacular works are in part translations *with commentary* of ancient texts; they are not simply amplified versions of Lucan or Sallust but have the look of a text plus gloss or scholia. The appearance of this pattern in the *Fet* and in its successor forces on us the large problem of continuing influence of the old arts curriculum, especially of grammar and the study of the *auctores,* this at a rather late date. We must remark that the lore of arts and *auctores* is part of the background of both works. The matter is not a simple one, as we will see, but a plain list of the sources of the *Fet* and of the early portions of the *Crónica* is the best sort of witness in this sense; most of these old works either are themselves curriculum authors or are texts generally well known to "artists" of those days. But the mixture of text and gloss is also a striking testimony. It has been pointed out that many passages in the *General estoria* are simulations of a *lectio* of a grammarian or *auctorista.*[7] As has been shown, such sections

---

5. In the *Pharsalia,* 1:185 ff. have the apparition of Rome, her exchange with Caesar, and finally the crossing of the Rubicon; only at 213 ff. do we have the description of the river. In the *Primera crónica,* chap. 92 (Alfonso 1955, 67a) we are given the description in lines 35–38, followed by the rest of the passage, apparition, dialogue, crossing. The *Fet* has the description in vol. 1, from p. 347, line 22, to p. 348, line 6, and the rest from that point on.

6. The mutual recognition in the *Crónica* is in chap. 96, (Alfonso 1955, 70b, lines 22–23); the *Fet* has it, 1:422; this is based on Lucan 4.24–26. The later passage begins at 4.168.

7. Rico 1972, 167–88.

put into a continuous text portions of the author in question and their respective glosses, just as a grammarian before a class would by turns read his *auctor* and make his own comments. The structure of these passages in the *General estoria,* Ovid plus his known glosses, could in fact be viewed as a special case. We could also speak rather more loosely of an *explained* version of an ancient text, one in which, for example, persons and places named are identified, mythical allusions accounted for, certain figures of speech paraphrased, and obscure words defined. It matters little for our purposes whether these explanations actually come from a gloss or from another source or are entirely original. In this broad sense we could say that much of the *Crónica* is disposed this way, just like the *Estoria,* and in Rico's narrower sense one may see it extensively in the *Crónica*'s Lucan passages. In some parts of the *Fet* it is simply universal, in both senses. It is in fact no great surprise to discover that the lore that comes to both texts from the glosses is in some cases the same.[8]

Our purpose at this point is not to show some broad parallelism between the two works. As we will see, what we have is almost certainly a case of direct influence. One critical matter here, however, is the stretch of time in which grammar and the *auctores* generally enjoyed prestige; if this period ends sometime in the first half of the thirteenth century, we would be led to consider the *Fet des romains* a moderately conservative work. It is, for example, not incredible that the editor might have been a cleric trained in the old way. But the later date of the *Primera crónica* makes of it an anomaly, a monster: arts and authors in late thirteenth-century Castile constitute a striking archaism. One is obliged to give the Rico thesis a close look. But Rico's answer is there: arts *are* flourishing in Alfonso's time. A scrutiny of the *General estoria* tells us that his classification of the sciences is indeed out of step with its time, as we might suspect. Whereas the University of Paris and others of those days treated the arts as merely a stepping-stone to other disciplines, the Learned King regarded them as autonomous, as containing very nearly the whole of knowledge: only metaphysics and ethics of the sciences he valued lie outside their range. Lest we think this Alfonsine disposition of sciences a bookish matter entirely, Rico reminds us that Alfonso in 1254 extended special favor and protection to the chairs of dialectic, music, *and* grammar at the University of

---

8. See n. 3.

Salamanca.[9] In a word, we in no way need to regard the sandwiching of text and gloss in the *Crónica* as in any way incongruous. Grammarians and *auctoristae* must have been there in Castile in Alfonso's day to set the example to the compilers, just as they were in France at the time the *Fet* was being composed.

But does not this very parallelism make it unnecessary to suppose an influence of the *Fet* on the *Crónica*? Could not the same conditions have yielded the same results independently? This is in fact very implausible. Vernacular histories on ancient subject matter that include what are in effect glossed versions of classic texts are not simply the order of the day. The fact that two sets of editors separated by several decades should both do this same extraordinary thing is at the very least a striking coincidence. If we discount certain offshoots of the *Fet,* there are no other texts like our two that fall in those years. We should stress the obvious: the influence of arts and authors, of the old curriculum on vernacular literatures of the twelfth and thirteenth centuries was very sporadic and unsystematic. In this sense it was quite unlike the humanism of a later time. Arts, grammar, and *auctores* were a Latin language institution, with no vested interest in the vulgar tongues: there was no necessary and fixed relationship between what was written in Latin and what was written in another language. For this reason it would have been impossible to predict what the influence of arts on vernacular letters was to be. There is, therefore, nothing inevitable about the solution hit upon by our two sets of compilers. Using the pattern in a piece of vernacular history would represent a notable initiative at any time, and it is hard to believe that the two sets of editors made this initiative separately. It is the simpler hypothesis all around to suppose that the Alfonsine committee knew the *Fet* and learned in principle from it how to incorporate glossed ancient texts into historical works.

We remark finally that the glossed text of the *Crónica,* the *Estoria,* and the *Fet* is distinctive in another sense: it contrasts with other literary phenomena. On one hand there are other ways of doing translations from the Latin. There exist such, for example, which are very strict and close to their originals: the *Fet*'s own translation of Caesar is one case among many. On the other hand there are at this time other ways of writing ancient history. The *Orose en français* (called *Histoire ancienne*

9. Rico 1972, 137, 143–49.

jusqu'à César by P. Meyer) has generally little in common with the *Fet* and certainly has nothing in it that looks much like our pattern. The *Orose,* for example, shares a feature with certain parts of the *Crónica*. There are long stretches of both works that are largely amplified and medievalized versions of a mixture of Orosius and Eutropius, a mode of narrative with little to remind us of the *Fet* and of the *Crónica*'s Lucan passages.[10] Once again, there is little in the order of things to compel the Alfonsine compilers to follow the lead of the *Fet.* Yet they did, and it seems not implausible that they did it knowingly.

If this striking coincidence between our two texts still seems too diffuse and general, we may turn to our second formal feature shared by them, which is smaller, in some ways more peripheral, but by the same token more specific and thus even more eloquent as evidence. It is a formal pattern, a detail of style, and it is quite distinctive; as far as I know, it belongs exclusively to the two histories and some of their offshoots. It is a device that segregates generalities, moralizing observations, sententious matter, and other comments from the narrative properly speaking. The formula is simple. The nonnarrative element is attributed to an authority; the *sententia* or other comment is prefaced by a formula something like "como dize Orosio" [as Orosius says] or "como cuentan las estorias" [as the histories tell]. But these clichés must not be misunderstood. If the *sententia* is attributed to Orosius, this does not mean that it was imported for the occasion. Normally the whole passage, narrative and all, is from the author mentioned; the *sententia* or comment is already there in the Latin, and the formula merely points it out, calls attention to it. Thus in a largely Orosian passage on the Pyrrhic victory of Pompey over Sertorius, the *Crónica* has: "diz Paulo Orosio que era esta pequenna gloria pora los romanos" (Orosius 5:23) [Paulus Orosius says that it was small glory for the Romans] (Alfonso 1955, 56a). The Latin for this is simply part of Orosius's text. Similarly, as Pompey triumphs easily over Mithridates, we read "et uencieron los sin todo trabaio assi cuemo cuenta Paulo Orosio" (6:2) [and they conquered them without any effort, as Paulus Orosius tells] (60a), a belittling remark by the historian. In the *Pharsalia-Fet* account of the thirst of the beseiged Pompeians at Lerida, we have: "Cil qui burent le venim que Hannibal le rois d'Aufrique mist es fontaines quant li Romain le

10. I am acquainted with the *Orose* through the copy in the Morgan Library, No. M212. See also Meyer 1885.

chacerent furent boeneüreux a la comparaison de ces, ce dist Lucains"
(*Fet* 429) [Those who drank the poison that Hannibal, King of Africa,
put into the fountains of Rome were fortunate compared to these; so
says Lucan] (Lucan 4:319–20).[11] Other simulated quotations in both
works are simply legion.[12] The use of the device could, once again, be
seen as an inheritance from liberal artists of another day. The formula
simulates more or less a rhetorical device recommended by handbooks
from antiquity on, in which the student is taught to decorate his composition with *sententiae* taken from elsewhere; he often adds some sort of
introductory formula, sometimes an attribution. This procedure is familiar and needs no special comment here. The *simulated* ingrafting is quite
another matter. This singular pattern is an important and highly original
stylistic device; it plays, in fact, a large part in the great changes our
ancient texts undergo in the editors' hands. Different they assuredly are,
and the modest formula "como dize Orosio" does much to work the
transformation. Thus, the totally moralized historiography of the *Seven
Books of the Histories,* in which nearly every sentence trails off into a
moral judgment, inevitably has a different look after the nonnarrative
matter has been labeled and marked off. To segregate the moralizations,
as Alfonso does, not only highlights them but also saves the purely
factual and informative character of the narrative proper. Once one
draws the boundary around the moralizations, once they have been
segregated, the reader/listener can perceive fully the independence and
autonomy of the rest of the text, that is, the narration of events, the pure
information. One could add that the emphasis on the informative is a
considerable element in the makeup of certain species of medieval historical narratives: rarely does it monopolize a text, but as one important
order of discourse among several, it is something students of these texts
can hardly neglect. In any case the simulated ingrafting, with its effects,
is no monopoly of the *Crónica*'s Orosian passages. It has quite the same
impact on our two Lucan texts as it does on the single Orosian one. The

---

11. Lucan refers to Hannibal simply as "hostis" [enemy]; *Fet*'s identification of this
person with Hannibal also occurs in an important commentary on Lucan, that of Arnulf of
Orléans (Arnulf of Orléans 1958, 223).
12. Other examples among many in the *Crónica* (Alfonso 1955) are on p. 56b, lines 44
ff.; p. 61b, lines 12 ff. and 30 ff.; p. 62a, lines 11 ff.; p. 64b, lines 51 ff. Examples in the *Fet*
are very numerous. In addition to the case cited from *Pharsalia* 4 in the verses also used by
the *Crónica,* we can find instances at *Fet* 1: 424 and 431; elsewhere in the Lucan passages
they are legion.

naive reader may find it hard to think of the *Pharsalia* as a body of information about the civil war, and yet that is the way many medieval scholars regarded it.[13] The efforts of our two sets of editors were aimed precisely at giving their Lucan passages the look of such a body of information. The poetic text, so to speak—the one full of figurative language, of poetic fictions, of myths, of melodrama, *and* of moralizations—was not of interest to them, but the narrative and informative one was. To salvage the latter, all manner of surgery had to take place, and not the least important phase of this labor was the clear labeling of *sententiae* and other matter as Lucan's. I repeat that the whole pattern of the simulated ingrafting, systematically applied, is absolutely distinctive; I have been completely unable to find vernacular historical or chronistic texts other than the *Fet* and the *Crónica* and their derivatives in which anything like this occurs. To my mind the only sensible conclusion is that the Alfonsine compilers knew the French work very well, and that their use of the device was a conscious imitation.

The survival of our curious usage in the *Crónica* is interesting as a light on the methods and outlook of its editors: in an odd way it is a testimony to their originality. The segregation and labeling of sententious matter in the *Fet* is, as far as we can judge, pure formula. Whenever a *sententia* or bit of moralization occurs in Sallust or Lucan the editors apply the cliché. To some extent the same is true of the *Crónica*. But at times one suspects that the Alfonsine compilers understood the logic of the pattern better than their predecessors. The fact is that they employ the pattern in more kinds of settings than do the editors of the *Fet*. Figurative language unidentified could pose as great a threat to sober informative narrative as *sententiae,* generalities, and other comment. Their response is to treat figures exactly the same way as they do sententious matter: they attribute them in context to their authors. Here is an example: "E dize aqui Lucano que andaua alli Julio Cesar como el leon contral caçador, que desque se assanna non dubda en ninguna cosa de meterse por ell arma" [And here Lucan says that Julius Caesar carried on here like a lion before the hunter, who when he becomes enraged does not hesitate to go in the range of the hunter's weapons] (Alfonso 1955, 67b). The attribution keeps a proper distance between

---

13. See Crossland 1930. Ms. Crossland deals in general with Lucan's status as a historian in the Middle Ages.

the figurative language and its opposite, and so the rational and factual character of the narrative is highlighted. A second instance is more complicated. Lucan gives the following on Caesar at the Rubicon:

> ut ventum est parvi Rubiconis ad undas, ingens visa duci patriae trepidantis imago . . . adstare. (1.185–89)

> [When he reached the little river Rubicon, the general saw a vision of his distressed country.] (trans. Duff)

In Spanish this becomes:

> E llegando a la ribera daquel rio Rubicon, mientre andauan las compannas catando uado, paresciol alli en uision una ymagen. E segund lo que dend dize aqui Lucano, mostros le en figura de muger, et que era aquello cuemo en semciança de la magestad del imperio de Roma. (Alfonso 1955, 67a)

> [When he reached the bank of that river Rubicon, while his troops were looking for a place to ford, there appeared to him an image in a vision. And according to what Lucan says about the matter, it (the image) appeared to him in the form of a woman, and all of this was, as it were, a likeness of the majesty of the empire of Rome.]

In an odd sense the attribution and the amplification do the same work. What happens in the latter is that Lucan's poetic fiction—Rome appearing to Caesar—is reduced to history. The *Crónica,* by speaking of a *vision,* turns the anecdote into something medievals thought could happen. The entirely new "figura de muger" sustains the vision idea along conventional lines: female personifications often inhabit visions. The effect of all this is to remove the threat figurative language poses to a factual narrative: we can see here that the compilers did think that figures in their nature were an encumbrance to their narrative, since they are at such pains in this case to rationalize and practically devirtualize this one. The attribution itself in this setting counts for very little; it is there, as I would suggest, simply because Lucan's language is figurative. But the generous amplification, such as it is, shows why the compilers chose in principle to join metaphors and such to an attribution: because figures left to themselves obscure the plain, factual design of narrative.

Our last example is even more complex. The intent of the compilers here was not to segregate the figurative language—and still less to reduce it to history, to simple narrative—but to force it into conformity with the surrounding narrative, so that its reference *as* figure is identical with the narrative itself. The passage from Orosius compares the rise and fall of the sea to the changing fortunes of Rome:

> Igitur Romani status agitur semper alterna mutatio et velut forma Oceani maris, quae omni die dispar nunc succiduis per vii dies attollitur incrementis nunc insequentibus totidem diebus naturali damno et defecta interiore subducitur. (Orosius 1882, bk. 6, chap. 14)

> [Therefore the condition of Rome always undergoes an alternating change, like the level of the ocean which over seven days rises by progressively smaller increments, and in as many days falls from natural shrinkage and internal absorption.]

This meager text yields the following extensive paragraph in the *Crónica:*

> Sobreste cresçer e minguar dell imperio de Roma departe la estoria de Orosio en este logar e diz assi: que ell estado dell imperio de Roma la forma troxo de la grand mar, que numqua queda de crecer e minguar, e que assi fizo ell imperio de Roma que siempre crecio e mingo, e numqua souo en un estado. E desto da Orosio estos exiemplos e diz assi: que quando tomo Ponpeyo las Espannas, e el consul Lucollo e este Ponpeyo a Asia, e Julio Cesar las Francias, que crecio ell imperio de Roma fasta los cabos de los terminos de la tierra, que muy pocol ende finco que no fue todo del so sennorio. Del minguar dize otrosi que mingo mucho ell imperio de Roma quando mataron a Marco Crasso en Torquia, echandol por la garganta ell oro retido, e diziendol: «doro as set, e oro beue»; e otrosi quando se fizieron las lides de Julio e de Ponpeyo e las de los otros cibdadanos depues daquellas en que se perdieron tantas yentes que no ouieron cuenta, e murio por ello Ponpeyo que era princep de tan alta guisa, e otros principes e omnes onrados de Roma e dotras muchas tierras del so sennorio. E desta guisa crecio

e mingo ell imperio de Roma fasta que es uenido el so estado a
aquello en que oy esta. (Alfonso 1955, 66a)

[Concerning the rising and falling of the Roman Empire, Orosius's
history comments and says the following: that the estate of the
Roman Empire had the form of a great sea that never ceased to
rise and fall, and that that was the way the Roman Empire was,
always rising and falling and never in the same state. And Orosius
gives examples and says as follows: that when Pompey held Spain,
and when the consul Lucullus and this same Pompey held Asia and
Julius Caesar held France, the Roman Empire spread to the very
ends of the earth, and little was left of it that was not under its
(Roman) rule. Concerning the falling, however, he said that the
Roman Empire fell a great deal when they killed Marcus Crassus
in Turkey—forcing melted gold down his throat and saying, "You
thirst for gold; gold you must drink"—and also when all the battles
took place between Julius and Pompey, and the ones between
(Roman) citizens, in which so many people were lost that they
could not be counted; and Pompey died as a result (of the conflict),
he who was a prince of such high estate, and so did other princes
and honorable men of Rome and of other lands under its control.
And in this way the Roman Empire rose and fell, until it came to
the state in which it is today.]

The sense is entirely different, to say the least. Orosius, typically, calls
attention to the instability of what one might think most stable: Rome.
But the compilers, in an astonishing amplification, make it refer to
something else: Rome as it is fortunate when power is unified and unfor-
tunate when it is not. In other words, this simile, amplified, explained,
becomes the story in little of the civil war itself as conceived by the
Alfonsine committee. The rivalry of Caesar and Pompey, the envy of
Caesar in particular, spells doom for the Roman commonwealth; civil
discord and especially the division of power promises no good. Even the
mention of Crassus in our text is not in vain. If one reads a page or so
further in the *Crónica,* one discovers that his death, along with that of
Pompey's wife Julia, is the event that signals the declaration of hostilities
between the two great leaders, an enmity kept secret until that point.
The explained figure thus becomes a very visible signpost for the reader,
calling the reader's attention to what the editors think significant and

important in their story. The attribution has the function of heightening the relief, of fixing attention on a critical moment in the text. The tale, the story, the succession of events—that is the thing. The same jealousy for its integrity that elsewhere moves them to draw boundaries between it and other matter makes them here recast a figurative passage so as to sharpen the focus on the pure narrative.

In a sense, these final examples could be read as an index to the relationship between the *Crónica* and the *Fet* and to the one between their respective creators. The *Fet,* admirable as it is, is a much more cautious enterprise than the Roman sections of the *Crónica;* the compilers of the latter are a more inventive and adventuresome lot by far. If they knew the *Fet* and tried to copy it, in general or in detail, it seems likely that they saw it simply as a starting point: their aim was to produce not an analog but an outgrowth, an original variation on a theme.

Our two formal devices—the translation, which includes both original text and its gloss, and the simulated quotation or segregated comment— as they appear in the *Crónica,* suggest to us that its creators may have known the *Fet.* But from one point of view, at least, these patterns could be regarded as peripheral: their presence in the two works does not necessarily enforce on them any great likeness otherwise. But are there in fact any broader similarities, any other strains, thematic or structural, that could make us regard the two works as belonging to a single species? Once again, the answer is problematic; it depends on our standard of comparison. In gross terms the unlikeness of the two works is of course obvious. Most points of difference are hardly worth mentioning: we would only point out that while the *Fet* is made up in large part of long segments of single Latin authors in turn, the Roman section of the *Crónica* is an olla podrida of short pieces of old texts, so mixed and so modified as to bear few traces of any one of them. This by itself might suggest that structurally the two works were miles apart. And yet, oddly enough, the *Fet* and the *Crónica,* its Roman portion at least, show a kinship on several grounds—in their general scope and function, in their enunciation of certain Christian themes, and in their conception of antiquity. These are perhaps worth exploring. The *Fet* is, as we know, a life of Julius Caesar, compiled largely out of Sallust, Caesar himself, Lucan, and Suetonius. The *Crónica,* for its part, is an account of all the peoples that ruled Spain. The lengthy passage devoted to the Romans, though not the longest, is in some ways the most interesting; it is the one constructed with greatest care, the one that most nearly seems to answer to some sort of program. As we suggested, it is the section that reminds us most readily of the *Fet*. Not exactly in subject matter—the passage of the Spanish work covers a much longer period of history than does its predecessors—but in the ways we have mentioned.

The finality of the two histories cannot in any fundamental sense be called scientific: knowledge for its own sake plays at most a small part as a motive for their formation. Still less can they be conceived as belles lettres. One is not far wrong in placing them under the rubric *practical*. The notion of a literature designed to be useful—stressing not primarily moral or religious norms but rather practical rules for those who govern, ways of disposing things here below for the best in war and peace—is more widespread in the Middle Ages than one likes to think.[14] Both the *Fet* and the *Crónica* are in a significant and distinctive way secular histories. Though by no means devoid of Christian themes, both the *Fet* and the Roman section of the *Crónica* are this-worldly in emphasis: they focus on the prince's worldly and temporal concerns. The point is not trivial. They form a sort of species in sharp contrast to a contemporary form of historical narrative of those years, the Latin churchly and monastic chronicle, of very different style. This genre, curiously consistent throughout Europe regardless of the local origin of the author, or even of the degree of his talent, is designed to be morally and spiritually edifying, meant to excite astonishment at the works of God as they touch human affairs. The main point of these writings is the assimilation of all history—in particular the event being narrated—to sacred history. The New Israel in these chronicles at times is Christendom at large but more frequently is simply the local kingdom. Just as God is an agent among others in the affairs of the Old Israel, meting out justice, giving blessings and withholding them, so also do kings and their subjects in the New fare well or ill as He is kindly or angry. History is a spectacle, a theater, in which the wise will see the ways of God as they direct and shape the doings of men. I remark only that although the genre I have described is a sort of ideal type, it is striking how closely many chronicle texts really do conform to it.

---

14. Cf. Castro 1954, 79–80, 357, 463, and elsewhere in passages about Alfonso. Castro regards pragmatism as a mark of Alfonso's literary output as a whole. He is to my mind mistaken when he views this pragmatism as distinctively Spanish or as a part of Alfonso's Muslim inheritance.

The pattern, history as spectacle, as pageant, is completely alien to the narrative of the *Fet* and the early portions of the *Crónica*. Here instead of history as spectacle we are offered history as *example*. The example in question need not be moral example; as we suggested, it may be in a broad sense practical. Thus, in the *Crónica* Scipio is presented as an exemplary conqueror who keeps his newly won land at peace through love and goodwill. His successors in Spain appear as his opposite, men whose more violent ways lose them the goodwill of their subjects, and who simply cannot keep the peace. The civil war episode for its part illustrates the dangers that overtake the commonwealth when not one but two great men exercise power. Caesar's envy is the destructive impulse that the equality in power of the two men engenders. Then, Augustus's military power makes him feared throughout the empire, and by commanding fear and by promulgating laws he maintains universal peace; he is on this basis the exemplary prince. The list goes on. One should stress that all these dispositions of the narrative in the *Crónica* are entirely the doing of the compilers; the most cursory reading of their sources makes it clear how little of these thematic strains can be found there. Different Latin texts are combined, details added, changes made, and at times schemes of motivation supplied, all to create virtually new narratives that yield these various emphases, these patterns of exemplarity.[15] Now, curiously, the simpler and more cautious *Fet,* which is much more faithful to its source texts, has a general aspect not totally unlike that of the Roman portion of the *Crónica*. It is also a gallery of examples: Caesar in peace, Caesar at war, and others. Sallust's narrative has a logic of a sophistication undreamed of by the Alfonsine editors, even in the denuded form the *Bellum Catilinae* takes in the French work, but that logic is not really different in kind from that of the *Crónica* narratives. Analogous things could be said of the French Lucan. As concerns exemplarity specifically, we would have to admit that though this factor is very real in the *Fet,* indeed fundamental, it is much more general and diffuse there. Whereas the *Crónica*'s accounts of the lives of its heroes are strongly differentiated—one illustrating the fruits of benevolence, another of envy, and so on—most of the admired characters in the *Fet* seem to embody one thing more or less: knightly virtue. The pairs of lines in the prologue are a genuine index to what is to follow:

---

15. See the first essay in this book, "Sancho II: Epic and Chronicle."

Por ce escrivrons les gestes as Romains qui par lor sens et par lor
force et par lor proesce conquistrent meint terre; car en lor fez
puet en trover assez connoissance de bien fer et de mal eschiver.
(*Li fet des romains* 1938, 1:2)

[This is why we write about the deeds of the Romans, who by their
intelligence, their strength, and their prowess conquered many
lands, for in their deeds one may find the knowledge of how to do
good and avoid evil.]

The thinned-out versions of Sallust and Lucan leave little of the distinctive moral substance of each: not much is left that is not courage, skill in
arms, the capacity to lead men, and, occasionally and faintly, respect for
the common good, the interests of the "commun de Rome." Eloquence
on a smaller scale also survives as an ideal in the Sallust text. But the
impoverishment under one or two aspects of the very complex *Bellum
Catilinae* is most instructive. The *Fet*, for example, drops the lengthy
section recounting the decay in Rome's morals as her wealth and power
increases. Then too there are odd sorts of translation; Sallust's "bella
intestina" and "discordia civilis" (both in *Bellum Catilinae,* 5) are turned
to the vaguer "mauvese euvres" [evil deeds] and "meslees et toutes
descordes" [brawls and all kinds of dissension] (1:21).[16] These changes
and others like them are symptomatic. In one way or another the *public*
and *civil* emphasis of Sallust is seriously weakened. The *Fet*'s account of
the Catiline episode is simply of a rebellion led by a courageous, but
lustful and otherwise vicious, noble and is put down largely as a result of
the eloquence of a few wise men. Significantly, however, Catiline's heroic last stand on the field of battle is preserved entire. These two
elements, eloquence and manliness in defeat, are plainly supposed to
coincide with the wit and strength the "sens" and "force" recommended
in the prologue. All told, the *Fet* offers a much simpler *Bellum Catilinae*
than Sallust's. The same "force" and "sens" is what we are invited to see
in Caesar in the Lucan passages. The editors cannot, and perhaps do
not, wish to alter totally the largely unfavorable portrait the ancient poet
draws of him, but it is a striking and fundamental aspect of their presentation, as is noted by the modern commentator, that many of the lines in
the *Pharsalia* that refer to Caesar's vices—his pride, his envy, his impetu-

---

16. See *Fet,* commentary, 2:69.

ousness, his blood lust—are dropped.[17] If we combine this with the fact
that the medieval reader and writer bring a rather different sensibility to
the matter of violence and bloodshed, most of the point in Lucan's
account of Caesar is lost. What we have left is in great part simply an
exemplary warrior, shrewd and courageous, and a great leader of men.
None of these procedures of simplification, needless to say, makes the
exemplarity of the *Fet* of a different kind from that of the *Crónica*. On
the contrary, however divergent routes they follow, the goal is practically the same, both formally and materially. The scope, or function, of
the two works is in large part to show the great of this world the practical
art of leadership, in peace and especially in war.

Obviously this is an oversimple account. There is indeed a coun-
terstrain in the *Fet* and the *Crónica,* one that stresses poverty, the vanity
of greatness, and virtues other than military. We will deal with this
secondary current presently. As a final word on the *utility* of the two
works we may mention something very obvious: they both contain a
great deal of military lore. I am not thinking of the *Fet*'s interpolated
battle scenes, a species that is close to medieval epic and courtly narrative and that raises special problems we prefer not to deal with. Instead,
I have in mind battle episodes, from the source texts, that are actually
instructive, that picture military situations from which a great noble
could actually learn. Caesar's *Commentaries,* used by the *Fet,* is eminently full of such, but so also is the *Pharsalia:* Honorius Augustodanus,
after all, defines tragedy by citing the warlike Lucan: "tragediae quae
bella tractant, ut Lucanus" [tragedies, which deal with wars, as for example, Lucan].[18] Even Orosius, so important in the makeup of the first part
of the *Crónica,* preserves in some detail a number of battle scenes in his
sources. One can imagine the attention a professed knight would bring
to Lucan's account, in both vernacular histories, of how Caesarians and
Pompeians race each other to capture the eminences that command the
valley of the Segre.[19] Contemporary warfare must have been full of
similar situations. Or who would not have noted Caesar's resourceful-
ness, the building of sluices and the like, when the Segre overflows its
banks,[20] or the hazards of night fighting, illustrated in one dramatic

---

17. See *Fet,* commentary, 2:147–209 passim.
18. Quoted in Crossland 1930, 35.
19. Lucan 4.130 ff.; Alfonso 1955, 72a; *Fet* 1:425.
20. Lucan 4.157 ff.; Alfonso 1955, 71b; *Fet* 1:425.

battle sequence in Orosius?[21] The reader's life situation must have accorded such passages great importance.

Secular, this-worldly, pragmatic, realist, even utilitarian our two histories assuredly are. This certainly does not mean nonmoral or anti-
Christian. We have already spoken of certain emphases in both works
one could not call chivalric or military. Both the *Fet* and the early portions of the *Crónica* indeed have passages that are plainly and explicitly
Christian. Even the very process of adapting old texts to thirteenth-
century audiences implies a degree of Christianization. But it is one
strain above all in the two works, an order of discourse at odds with
some of their other lines of argument, that constitutes the Christian
dimension in largely secular histories. This is a series of details that
express precisely the limitations of a purely human greatness. The formula is simple and well known: it is the fall through pride. We should
explain that this, our second parallelism, is not between general qualities
in the two works. We are concerned not with a broad similarity in scope
or function but rather with a kind of formal pattern, expressive of a
theme that is sounded occasionally, sometimes with great emphasis, in
our French and Spanish texts. Thus, the compilers of the *Crónica* accept
from their sources at least two accounts of men whose very greatness
was in some way the occasion of their downfall. The tragic figures of
Theodoric, Ostrogothic king of Italy, and 'Abd al-Rahman, emir of
Cordoba, come entire to the *Crónica* from two separate works of the
learned archbishop of Toledo Rodrigo Ximénez de Rada.[22] More important, the editors themselves take the initiative and construct a fall narrative of their own, the very life of Julius Caesar himself, by their foresight
laid out on the order of a medieval tragedy.[23] Their account of his
character is a complex one. On one hand, they make him proud, envious, greedy, ambitious, and a lover of war and bloodshed. In all these
ways he is contrasted with the rational and moderate Pompey. But on
the other hand, they cannot deny Caesar statesmanship or great capacity
as a military leader. This portrait of Caesar as a man of mixed qualities
keeps his rise believable but also prepares us for his eventual fall: on this

21. Orosius 1882, bk. 6, chap. 4; Alfonso 1955, 60a.
22. For Rodrigo's Theodoric see Rodrigo Toledano 1793, 224–27; for 'Abd al-
Rahman, pp. 255–56. In the *Crónica* (Alfonso 1955) the two are on pp. 242–51 and 331–
33, respectively.
23. See the first essay in this book, "Sancho II: Epic and Chronicle."

basis alone one would see the assassination in the Capitol as the exemplary punishment of a great man gone wrong. But our text is in fact more specific. Caesar's pride, which is mentioned often, is in effect played against another theme, the limitations of power in a larger world. The victories one might wish to attribute to him—which, by implication, at least, he attributed to himself—are really the work of larger circumstance, fortune, or God Himself. The theme is sounded in two bits of moralizing commentary. The first is about his easy conquest of Spain, due not to him but to fate:

> E diz la estoria en este logar que en tal fecho cuemo esta, entender deuien los cabdiellos dalli et los de las otras tierras, si lo mesurassen, que aquello los fados lo aduzien e lo apressurauan, et que por ellos uinie mas que por la fuerça de Julio Cesar. (Alfonso 1955, 70a)

> [And the history says in this place that military leaders from there and from other lands should understand that a (successful) military action like this, if they should think about it, was brought about and hastened by the fates, and that it came about more because of them than by the power of Julius Caesar.]

The second comment is about a victory really due to chance; in the long run it is God who gives victories:

> E contecio esto no tanto por las armas de Julio Cesar cuemo por la buena uentura et mala de los otros; ca bien assi cuemo oyestes que se uio Julio Cesar con Ponpeyo el grand en ora que, si Ponpeyo en la batalla de Duracio sopiesse cuemo estaua Julio Cesar quando se uencio et en pos el ouiese ido, alli fuera Julio Cesar desfecho et perdudo por siempre; mas ni lo sopo Ponpeyo ni lo fizo, ni cayo otrossi Julio Cesar en aquel quebranto; et otrossi en esta batalla de Espanna, si los Ponpeyos fijos de Ponpeyo el grand et sos cabdiellos ouiessen sabudo ell estado a que fue aducho Julio Cesar en esta batalla, uencieran ellos et fuera Julio Cesar uençudo, et desfecho en Espanna el so poder pora siempre. Mas lo que es ordenado por el poder de Dios, no lo puede desfazer si no El quando quisiere. (91b–92a)

[And this came to pass not so much because of the arms of Julius Caesar but by (his) good fortune and the bad fortune of the others; for as you have surely heard, Julius Caesar met Pompey the Great at a moment when, if in the battle of Dyrrhachium Pompey had known the condition Caesar was in when he was defeated, and if he (Pompey) had followed in pursuit, there Julius Caesar would have been undone and lost forever; but Pompey neither knew (how things stood), nor did he do it (pursue Caesar), nor did Julius Caesar fall in that struggle; and also, if in the battle of Spain the sons of Pompey and their generals had known the state that Julius Caesar was in as a result of the battle, they would have won and Julius Caesar would have been defeated, and his power in Spain would have been undone for good. But what is disposed by the power of God only He can undo when He wishes.]

In a word, Caesar is an overreacher, a fortunate man, ignorant of his limitations, and his death is a punishment due such a man. It should again be stressed that the pivotal features of the Caesar narrative are entirely the invention of the *Crónica*'s editors. One will search in vain, for example, among the sources for anything like the texts just quoted: the first barely passes muster as a paraphrase of Lucan, while the second is entirely original.

The *Fet* presents Caesar in much the same light as does the *Crónica*. It is no accident that one of the Italian offshoots of the older work takes the form of a warning that overreachers come to bad ends: "li vincitori sono rimasi vinti" [the conquerors are conquered].[24] The very sequence of texts in the *Fet* gives it the look of a fall narrative. First comes Sallust, very favorable to Caesar, then the equally favorable *Commentaries* of Caesar himself, then the largely unfavorable Lucan—the French text softens the portrait of its hero only in part—and finally the very severe Suetonius. One can imagine, for example, what a totally different work it would have been if Caesar's own account of the civil war had taken the place of the *Pharsalia*. The *Fet* taken as a whole is a single mammoth fall narrative. This may seem an overtidy account of a very miscellaneous book. But there is a detail that makes it clear that the compiler regarded his work as a narration of an exemplary fall. One chapter title that accompanies the passage from Suetonius speaks of Caesar's pride: "Dou

---

24. *I fatti di Cesare* 1863, 1.

grant orgoill ou Cesar chaï" [the great pride into which Caesar fell] (735). But it is significant that Suetonius's text does not really sustain this theme, that Caesar's *arrogantia* before the senate, for example, is simply one motive among several in Suetonius. The sense of the rubric and its bearing on the *Fet* as a whole are the more evident: the great Caesar fell through pride. The fall pattern in the *Fet* is also very visible in another set of details. In the sections translated from Sallust and Caesar there is a group of characters plainly designed by the editors as overreachers who come to ruin. The raw material of these narratives is, of course, the original text; indeed, most of the detail of the French narrative comes from these Latin texts, as one might expect. But the French has certain twists of language that in the light of our problem are very suggestive. Twice in the translation of Sallust we come upon an expression something like "monter en hauteçe" [to rise to high estate]. Speaking of some of the young men who followed Catiline, the *Fet* has: "se tenoient a Catiline non pas por poverte, mes por covoitise a monter en hautece" [they adhered to Catiline not out of poverty but out of a desire to rise to high estate] (*Fet* 1938, 21). The last part of this line translates *Bellum Catilinae* 17: "quos magis dominationis spes hortabatur quam inopia aut alia necessitudo"; the French gives a blurry rendering, one might say. A little later in the *Fet,* in the middle of the translation of *Bellum,* we read of the same young men, "Mes cil greignor . . . li suivoient por achoison de monter en dignitez et en hauteces" [but the greater part . . . followed him for the chance to rise to dignity and to high estate] (22); this is an addition and has no analog in the Latin. The aspiration not to power, as Sallust has it, but to high place generically is plainly something the editors of the *Fet* want to emphasize. We could add that though Sallust and the *Fet* alike are severe with the followers of Catiline, both give them high marks for courage as they make their last stand: they are not totally vicious. But according to the *Fet* they fell because they tried to rise too high. Language something like the above occurs in one other moment in our text. Caesar's words about Orgetorix, "regni cupiditate inductus coniurationem nobilitatis fecit" (Caesar 1961, 1:2), become "il fist une conjuroison de noble jovente par covoitis(e), d'avoir regne et seignorie" [he formed a conspiracy of young nobles out of a strong desire for kingdom and lordship] (*Fet* 1938, 81). This is an accurate translation, but its similarity to the other passages we have just quoted is striking. The "jovente" is the editor's deduction; it is not in Caesar. The expression calls to mind the young men who followed Catiline:

"jovente" is, in fact, the word the *Fet* uses to refer to them; it follows Sallust, who uses "juventus" at this point. "Covoitise" is a good rendering of Caesar's "cupiditate" but is rather too strong for Sallust's "spes" of our first quotation: the push to uniformity goes backward in this case. This assimilation of language suggests that the editors of the *Fet* wished us to see Orgetorix as of a piece with Catiline's men; he is an overreacher like them. This odd set of details, the two translated bits of Sallust and the one, perhaps, of Caesar, make it clear that the compilers of the *Fet* indeed wished to include in their work a strain running in counterpoint to that of greatness and heroism, a line of argument showing the limitations of that greatness within a larger world.

Once again I warn the reader against dismissing these parallelisms between the *Fet* and the *Crónica* as trivial. The idea of the fall from greatness is so familiar to us, we are so persuaded that it is medieval, that we become convinced that it can be found everywhere. But in reality it is no small matter to find fully developed historical and biographical narratives that tell of great men, gifted, accomplished, powerful as the world judges, who are brought low by the decree of fate or Providence. The history of this pattern is in fact rather obscure, and it is no small thing to find literary texts from the period before Boccaccio that exemplify it as tidily as do the *Fet* and the *Primera crónica*. Speaking more generally, I would point out that the combination of ingredients, predominant secularity of the sort we have described joined occasionally to the Christian theme of the vanity of greatness, is not a universal pattern. Historical narratives of little sacral import decorated with occasional exemplary falls are not simply the order of the day. The *Fet* and the *Crónica* are like each other, and not many other works of their time are very much like either. Under this circumstance it is surely not unreasonable to think possible some general influence—in plan, theme, scope—of the older work on the newer, that the French work was itself a sort of example for the compilers of the Spanish.

Our last parallelism is of a lower order. It is in a sense our weakest and most diffuse. Rather than show a similarity, we will attempt to prove that one palpable difference between the *Fet* and the *Crónica* is less important than it seems. The gap between them is considerable. The *Primera crónica* as a whole is national history, while the *Fet* is entirely antique. But in fact in medieval perspective the *Fet* veers dangerously close to national history. In the first place, Julius Caesar is the conqueror of Gaul, significantly called "France" in the *Fet*. But also, quite as important, he became emperor, so medievals thought, and Charlemagne is thus his remote successor; the kings of France, in turn, represent one line of the succession from Charlemagne. We could add that had the original plan for the *Fet* been carried out, the imperial heritage of France would have been stressed the more; the work was to have been a heavily amplified version of the whole of Suetonius, through all twelve of his Caesars. Assuredly the *Fet* does not proclaim itself national history: the Roman heritage of the French king is not spoken of explicitly. But it is, as it were, common knowledge. It is alluded to in the *Grandes chroniques de France*. It is, indeed, mentioned in the *Primera crónica;* the Roman succession is always referred to in the chronologies, first the emperors themselves, the emperors of East and West, those of the East alone, and finally Charlemagne, who, as the text says, has heirs on both the German throne and the French.[25] Then, too, in a kind of mirror relationship to the *Fet,* the *Crónica* is more Roman than it might seem. The whole work, if completed, would have ended with the reign of Alfonso himself, who regarded himself for a time as legitimate Roman emperor. Alfonso's Roman heritage would in the completed chronicle have been prepared and supported by three elements: the bulk and general prominence of the Roman section, the favorable treatment of Charlemagne, and the chronologies we have spoken of, which on the German side would have ended with Alfonso.

This whole question is, to my mind, weighty enough to deserve treatment in a separate study, but for the moment we may make the following observations. The Roman section of the *Crónica,* so labeled, is divided into two parts. The first of these is in great part a history of Rome in Spain. It does not pretend to offer us a continuous narrative of events in Rome; Spain is its excuse for being, and one can scarcely doubt why it was included in a general history of Spain. Not so the second part. Although the chapters from 115 on are full of allusions to Spain, it is primarily and essentially imperial history and gives an account of every emperor of East and West within the period it covers. What is more, as the *Crónica* passes first into the section on the lesser German peoples

---

25. At the end of chap. 614 of the *Crónica* we read: "E daqui adelant dexa la estoria el cuento por los emperadores de Constantinopla e trael por los reys de Ffrancia que regnaron en Alemanna et en Ffrancia" [And from here on this history will abandon the reckoning (in the chronologies) by the Emperors of Constantinople and will continue it by the kings of France who reigned in Germany and France] (Alfonso 1955, 349a). Charles's German successors are, incidentally, called "emperador de Roma" from this point on. I am assuming with Catalán that our *Crónica* is fundamentally Alfonsine to chap. 896 (Catalán 1963a, 195–214).

and then into that of the Goths, the imperial history is continued, drop-ping the Western line when that is appropriate, carrying on the Eastern, until the narrative comes to the coronation of Charlemagne, whom medi-evals held to be Roman in a full and literal sense. Thereafter the *Crónica* gives information about each of the German successors of Charlemagne almost as far as the original Alfonsine project was realized, into the reign of Fernando I of León. In these later sections also, events in the reigns of the Gothic kings and their Christian successors are dated by the years in the reigns of contemporary Roman and German emperors. Absolutely none of this makes any sense within the *Crónica* as it now stands, and it is explainable only if the great work was to end with some allusion to Alfonso X's imperial status. A declared history of Spain in principle could not reasonably accommodate such extraneous matter unless the two strands of narrative, the Spanish and the Roman-German, were to merge at a decisive moment, in the reign of Alfonso the Learned.

On this premise too we could dissolve another anomaly of the *Crónica* in its present state, the extensive and favorable treatment of Charle-magne. Spanish historiography up to the time of Alfonso is uniformly severe with Charles. It is so for two reasons. The first is the general one that Spaniards resent his reputation as a reconqueror, an honor more properly theirs than his; the second, more specific one is that Spaniards find the projected vassaldom of Alfonso the Chaste to Charlemagne humiliating. In spite of this strong tradition, unfriendly to Charles, in-deed in the face of the fact that much of this older text is actually in the *Crónica,* its compilers attempt to balance the record. They do so in a series of passages: a group of curiously translated, very laudatory frag-ments from Sigebert; and most important of all, the prosified epic song celebrating the youthful exploits of Charles, the well-known *Mainet.* This effort to speak well of Charles is purely and simply a glorification of Alfonso X's illustrious imperial predecessor, and as an added benefit these passages call attention to Charles as an all-important link in an unbroken succession of emperors from Julius Caesar to Alfonso.

The *Crónica* therefore is not only a Spanish book but also an imperial book. In a strange way the parallelism between the French and Spanish works emerges. One is a national history; the other seems not to be but perhaps is. One is entirely Roman; the other, partially Roman, is actu-ally more so than one might guess. In both cases the Roman matter casts long shadows: it is there in both texts to enhance the prestige of a reigning monarch.

Alfonso X, the Empire and the
Primera crónica

There is a kind of fatalism that sometimes overtakes readers of medieval literature, a sort of resignation that says, in effect, this text really does not make total sense and it is pointless to try to imagine it more intelligible than it is. We put up with anomalies with scarcely a complaint. This is eminently the case with the *Primera crónica general:* though it is assuredly not a tidy book, we are not willing to admit that it may be tidier than it looks. I can think of three anomalies, two large and one small, that first and last critics have never tried to resolve. The small, least problematic of these is the fact that chronologies in the later chapters often include the year in the reign of the "Roman" emperor, be he Byzantine or German, and that readers are frequently tuned in to events in their realms. It is hard to see what this strain contributes to the work as a whole, with its largely "Gothic" emphasis. Much more serious difficulties are the extent and character of the Roman section of the *Crónica* and the favorable portrait of Charlemagne, the latter at odds with the more usual, unfriendly account in older Spanish historiography. All of these features seem gratuitous and unnecessary even in a very lengthy history of Spain, and although all have in one way or another been taken note of by scholars, their simple presence in the *Crónica* has never been explained, either singly or as a block. There they are, hovering over us, obscure, apparently arbitrary; no one wants to shoot them down.

As we have pointed out, the features have not gone unnoticed. In a remarkable book on Alfonso the Learned, Professor Francisco Rico does take a close look at some of them and does try to fit them into a context. The length of the Roman section in particular, he says, is best accounted for by referring to the influence of universal history. Up to Alfonso's time and past it historical works on local and national subjects frequently played their scenes against the backdrop of the whole history of humans, or of great parts of it. So also the *Crónica:* the Roman section, with its heavy dependence on Eusebius-Jerome, is just such an allusion to the larger human scene. Rico even suggests that the unmanageability of the local-universal combination may have been one of the reasons why Alfonso eventually abandoned the *Crónica*.[1] This whole account is indeed very convincing, but it leaves untouched the paradoxes presented by the very text, the very makeup of the *Crónica*. Why, for example, was the Roman matter allowed to get out of hand in the first place? Why does the disproportion exist? I believe that views can be framed that go further to resolve these paradoxes. Alfonso's motives throughout may not have been entirely literary, as Rico thinks. Menéndez Pidal is a help here. His diffuse account of some of these features does cast hints that are an aid in reducing the huge history to greater system and intelligibility. He speaks often of the "universalist spirit of the great king," Alfonso X; but according to don Ramón this ecumenical spirit shows itself in the *Crónica* only in the first part, which is more learned, with its emphasis on Rome. In the essay of 1916 he explains the restriction by declaring that the second part comes entirely from the time of Sancho IV, a king of more provincial outlook. In the study of 1955, by which time Pidal was convinced that Alfonso had a hand in the second part as well, the great scholar attributed the difference to the king's diminishing interest in his project and to his growing preoccupation with the *General estoria*.[2] We shall have more to say about the latter point presently. Under either hypothesis Pidal presents the first part as more manifestly Alfonsine, in great part because it is more Roman. The particulars of Pidal's argument are not my concern at the moment. What is striking is that he treats the supposed universalism of the Learned King as a known quantity, a psychological given that could in principle explain many of his attitudes and activities, among others his influence in the design of the first part of the *Crónica,* Roman

---

1. Rico 1972, 38–39.
2. The older study "La Crónica General de España que mandó componer Alfonso el Sabio" is included in the volume *Estudios literarios* (Menéndez Pidal 1946); the remarks to which we are alluding are on pp. 89–90. The latter essay is the introduction to the edition of the *Primera Crónica General* (Alfonso 1955); the pertinent passage is in vol. 1, pp. xxxiv–xxxv. Henceforth all page references to the *Crónica* will be to this edition.

in emphasis, redolent with learning. The whole notion, of course, valid or not, hovers very close to an important truth. We should be much less inclined to speak of Alfonso's ecumenism, so to speak, were it not for a certain very large project of his reign, his attempt to secure for himself the imperial crown. This is indeed the eminent and fundamental instance of his look beyond Spain, to Europe, to Christendom at large, and in particular to Rome. He regarded himself as Roman and universal emperor, simply, and that he should under these circumstances leave a very visible Roman stamp on his history of Spain is hardly surprising.

But the matter does not end there. As we shall see, pace Menéndez Pidal, the Alfonsine seal is on the second part as well as on the first and in the same sense: it too has quasi-Roman features. Medievals, as we know, thought Charlemagne and his German successors Roman emperors in the full and literal sense, and so there cannot be the least doubt that all three features of the *Crónica* we have spoken of—not just the bulk of the Roman matter in the first part, but the highlighting of Charlemagne and the allusions, chronological and otherwise, to later German emperors in the second—belong to the same series. All three are references to a single great empire extending over centuries ruled first by Julius Caesar and most lately by none other than Alfonso himself. Our features all answer to the same logic. It could be objected that although the imperial aspirations of the Learned King do explain why our three features are *in* the *Crónica*, though they do supply a motive for putting them there, they do not dissolve their anomalous character; they do not explain away their plain inappropriateness in context. But this problem disappears, if we reflect that the *Crónica,* if completed, would certainly have ended with the reign of Alfonso, and that its account of that reign would inevitably have spoken of his imperial status. We must recall that the extant *Primera crónica* in itself, patchwork that it is, gives little hint of how the original project would have ended. It has been shown that the work is in a significant way Alfonsine only to the middle of chapter 896.[3] The rest, of a later date, stops at the end of the reign of Fernando III. The circumstances that produced this ending are complicated and are of little interest to us here, except to remark that they tell us absolutely nothing about how Alfonso and his scribes would have rounded off the work.[4] And on the positive

---

3. The matter is a complicated one, and I am simplifying greatly: see Catalán 1963a, 195–215, 291–306.

4. Catalán 1962, 80–86.

side we may point out that two of the Alfonsines' most important sources and models, the histories of Lucas of Tuy and Rodrigo of Toledo, do run well into the time of the reigning monarch. Given especially the high prestige of the latter work for the *Crónica*'s compilers, one would guess that they meant to do likewise and include Alfonso in their narrative. Equally significant, the theme of the imperial succession is sounded loud elsewhere in Alfonso's historical writings. A text in the first part of the *General estoria* speaks of Jupiter, king of Crete, as ancestor through Aeneas of all the Caesars and emperors, to Frederick Barbarossa and to his grandson Frederick of Sicily.[5] The latter is at once Alfonso's uncle and his immediate predecessor on the imperial throne. It is therefore hard not to see in the passage at the very least an allusion to the Learned King's imperial aspirations. Given the way those arguments tended to go, it could even be read as an apology for those aspirations. In any event, on this other very important occasion the Alfonsine editors thought of using a historical text to affirm Alfonso's place in the imperial line, and this makes it the more likely that they meant to do the same in the *Crónica*. A fortiori, this would of course suppose that Alfonso appeared there. It is therefore more than plausible that the *Crónica* would have ended with the reign of its author. In such a case the whole long work would in effect have sustained two parallel narratives, the first a history of Spain from Hercules on, the second a genuine imperial history, running from Pompey and Julius Caesar through Charlemagne and on. The two strands would, of course, have come together in Alfonso, the latest figure in both series.

The coherence of the *Crónica* is in this respect saved, and the anomalies disappear. It remains to us only to comment in detail on each of the three features and to show as exactly as we can how each supports what I suppose to be the program of the work as a whole. First, let us consider the nature and bulk of the Roman section. The plan of Alfonso's great history is of course distinctive. Taking a cue, perhaps from the whole corpus of historical writings of Rodrigo of Toledo—who wrote a history of the Goths in Spain, of the Romans in Spain (largely so), of the Arabs in Spain and so on—the compilers of the *Crónica* give an account, in order, of the peoples who at one time ruled Spain: Hercules and his successors, the "almujuces," the Carthaginians, the Romans, various Germanic peoples, and finally the Goths. In every case but one the

---

5. Alfonso 1930, 200–201; see Rico 1972, 113–15.

matter in each of these histories is pretty much restricted to the doings of
the nation in question within Spain. The exception is, of course, Rome.
In a remarkable stretch of 344 chapters we are served up a great deal of
information that has very little bearing on Spain. We must make distinctions: not all of this long section is un-Spanish. A large portion of it is
well within the range of the plan we have described. Menéndez Pidal has
pointed out an important boundary in the *Crónica,* one that comes after
chapter 108; he has shown, for example, that the language of the chronicle up to that point has characteristics that differentiate it from that of
the rest of the first part.[6] One could remark that at about the same point
the predominant sources change, and that the technique of compilation
is of a different sort, even though we are still reading Roman history.
This watershed is also most significant from our point of view. If we
suppose that we are reading a history of Spain, we have, as it were, no
difficulties through the first 108 chapters, but afterward we find ourselves at a loss. We pick up Roman history early. The Carthaginian
section, so labeled, tells of that people's invasion of Spain, a set of
events that, as we know, is a prelude to the Second Punic War. There
follows a fair account of that war, divided between the Carthaginian and
Roman sections. The war in fact has a great bearing on Spain, much of it
is fought there, but even beyond this, one could say that the emphasis in
this part of the *Crónica* is decently Spanish. Then we have in succession
the troubled times in Spain after the departure of Scipio Africanus, the
uprising led by Viriatus, and the battle before Numantia. Then, oddly,
we are given a lengthy history of Carthage, an amplified and extended
version of Justin's well-known narrative. Thereupon, after a few miscellaneous events we plunge into the career of Pompey and into the civil
war. It is immediately after this very important episode that the boundary that we have spoken of occurs. Two observations about this section
must be made. First, impressive quantities of Roman history have been
left out. Second, there are only two portions that are not largely Spanish
in emphasis, the digression on Carthage and the civil war episode. But
even at that, the latter has an important Spanish portion. In any case this
passage, the masterpiece of the *Crónica,* answers to a very special logic
within the whole work. It is an exemplary narrative, so labeled by the
compilers, meant to illustrate the evils that overtake the commonwealth

---

6. Alfonso 1955, Pidal's introduction, 1:xxiii–xxiv.

when the fullness of power is held by more than one man. The episode is in great part a political object lesson, is abstract, and does not depend on its setting or its subject matter to convey its message. It has its place whether it is Spanish or Roman or neither. We recall that the prologue of the *Crónica* speaks of the ills that overtook Spain when the kingdom was divided, and that a lengthy series of chapters on the division of his lands by Fernando I and its aftermath tells in detail precisely this story.[7] The superb civil war episode plainly belongs to this series and emphasizes a theme with significant echoes elsewhere in the *Crónica*.

As we suggested, there is little in the Roman chapters up through 108 that does not fall within the manifest plan of the *Crónica* as a whole: it is one of the several sections on events in Spain under one of the peoples ruling it. But afterward everything changes. First we have a series of chapters full of general information about Rome, the origin of the name, its institutions, lists of kings and consuls and finally emperors, then the etymology of the name Caesar and of the word *emperor*. All of this is a fitting overture to what follows, which is a continuous history of the empire from Julius Caesar, through its division into two, East and West, down to the reigns of Theodosius and Honorius, in the middle of which the Roman section ends. Every emperor is treated. There are no chronological gaps in the story as there are in the earlier chapters. Spain is mentioned where this is appropriate, but references to it are by no means central or in any sense the excuse for the narrative as a whole. What we have is in every way an imperial history, autonomous and sufficient. It could stand separately: there is not much that binds it to the rest of the *Crónica*.

But our story does not stop here. As the Alfonsine work moves on through the rules of the lesser German peoples and finally of the Goths, the imperial narrative is sustained. This whole scheme of continuous narration of imperial affairs runs nearly as far as the Alfonsine project was realized, through the reign of Fernando I. We must repeat that for medievals Charlemagne and his successors were Roman emperors in every sense. So it is that at the appropriate moment the *Crónica*, following Sigibert, its main source for these imperial matters, abandons the line of Eastern emperors to pick up the Frankish: "E daqui adelant dexa la estoria el cuento por los emperadores de Constantinopla et

---

7. See the first essay in this book, "Sancho II: Epic and Chronicle."

trael por los reys de Ffrancia que regnaron en Alemanna et en Ffrancia" [From here on the history abandons the reckoning by the emperors of Constantinople and picks it up by the kings of France who ruled in Germany and France] (349a). And so we do not lack for emperors even as late as the eleventh century. Now the perfect gratu-itousness of all this imperial matter in the *Crónica* in any of the forms that we know it is patent: there is nothing in its general plan that justifies it, no thematic strand elsewhere in the text that explains it. We must think especially of the drift of the narrative in its later portions. It is a chronicle of the greatness of the Goths in war and in peace, and after the Moorish invasion it becomes in great part a celebration of the Reconquest. It is hard to see how in any way these elements are supported by anecdotes about Byzantine and German emperors. At times, as we will see, the interests of the two narratives actually clash and work at cross-purposes. But all of this starts to make sense, if we recall that the *Crónica* should have ended with Alfonso X, at once king of Castile and emperor of Rome.

We turn to our second problem. We are brought up once again to the questions raised by Charlemagne, the treatment he gets in the *Crónica*, the extent and character of passages devoted to him. The figure of Charles is anomalous in the work as it stands. Assuredly, Charlemagne *must* figure in a history of Spain and the Reconquest. The existence of the Spanish March cannot be lost sight of: events narrated in the *Song of Roland* are not forgotten. But the *Crónica*'s normal sources cover most of this material: the compilers would not have had to reach out further, as they did. Rodrigo of Toledo and Lucas of Tuy give them much of the detail a decent history of Spain requires. The former even has a line or so on Charles's youthful exploits in Spain in the service of the Moorish king of Toledo. Both histories preserve parts of the legend of Bernardo del Carpio, which in turn preserves important bits of Charlemagne lore, though it does not present that monarch in very kindly terms. But all of this is not enough. The most extensive passage about Charles is made up by the prosification of the epic song, the *Mainet,* which fills up most of three chapters. This work, composed, as Menéndez Pidal thinks, by a French poet residing in Toledo,[8] tells of Charles's youthful exile in

---

8. Menéndez Pidal 1941, 88–90.

Toledo; of how he covers himself with glory fighting one of the rivals of
the king; of how the latter's daughter falls in love with the Frankish
prince, is converted to Christianity, escapes with him to Paris, and marries him. There is nothing else quite like this in the *Crónica:* it has, for
example, little in common with the Castilian epic poems the compilers
so often laid hands on. Its availability and its Spanish setting may have
been the reasons it got included, but these cannot be the only ones. The
intent plainly is to enhance the glory of Charles. In a sense, any version
of the *Mainet* would do this: all and any would have to tell of his valor
and strength in the service of the king of Toledo. But the version in the
Crónica, perhaps the soberest and most beautiful, is distinctive in at
least one other respect: it is the most sacral. There is one feature in the
narrative that, as far as I know, does not figure in any other *Mainet*. In
the *Crónica* version Providence intervenes at a critical moment to save
Charles's life. He is fighting hand to hand with Bramant, the enemy of
the king of Toledo. Bramant delivers him a blow that should have been
mortal, but by God's will it was not:

> Bramant metio luego mano a la espada que dizien Durendart, et
> fuel dar un colpe tan grand por somo dell yelmo, que ge le taio a
> bueltas con una grand cosa de los cabellos de la cabeça, et aun
> grand partida de las otras armas; mas non quiso Dios quel prisiesse
> en carne. Deste colpe fue Maynet mucho espantado, et llamo a
> Sancta Maria en su ayuda. (341b)

> [Bramant laid hand on his sword, which is called Durandarte, and
> gave him such a great blow on the top of his helmet that he
> (Bramant) cut it to pieces along with a good part of the hairs on his
> (Charles's) head and moreover a great part of his other arms, but
> God did not will that the sword should touch his living flesh.
> Mainet was greatly frightened by that blow, and he called out to
> Holy Mary to come to his aid.]

This detail of the narrative, especially the Marian reference, is prepared
by an earlier one:

> Aquell escudero que uos ueedes es omne de mui alta sangre, et
> desde su ninnez nunqua ouo en costumbre de omillarse a ninguna

mugier que sea, sinon a Sancta Maria tan solamientre quandol faze
su oracion. (340b)

[That squire that you see is a man of very noble blood, and since
his childhood he never has had the habit of bowing to any woman
whatever, except to Holy Mary when he was at prayer.]

Note also Charles's speech to his men:

Esforçar, amigos, non ayades que temer. ¿Non sabedes que diz la
escriptura que quando Dios quier que los pocos uencen a los
muchos?' (340b)

[Courage, friends, you have nothing to fear. Do you not know that
Scripture says that when God wills, the few can conquer the many?]

As I suggested, none of these features appears, as far as I know, in any
other *Mainet*. There is no mistaking the sense of these lines: the future
king of France and emperor is preserved for that high and sacred function not by his own strength (something he has a great plenty of) but by
God Himself. This little cluster of lines, then, is meant to surround
Charles with an aura, with a color of lofty and holy destiny. One could,
of course, object that all of this was simply the text that the compilers
inherited—it is unlikely, after all, that they could have picked and
chosen among versions—and that they could neither add, subtract, nor
alter. But the argument does not stand. The least glance at any of the
known sources of the *Crónica* shows in a moment the immense freedom
they enjoy in preparing their texts: these scribes can suppress what they
like, preserve what they like, add what they like. We say further that
details of the kind we mention are precisely of the sort that is likely to
get blurred in the prosification of an epic poem. For an example, the
Cid's vision of St. Gabriel as told in the *Crónica* is rather unlike the same
detail in the *Poema*. The prehistory of the *Crónica* text of the *Mainet* is
unknown to us, but it is in fact quite as possible that the divine interven-
tion we speak of is the invention or deduction of the compilers, as it is
possible that they inherited it. In any case, if it appears in our text, it is
clearly meant to be there.

The prosified *Mainet* is, as we point out, the great Charlemagne text
in the *Crónica*. Its presence there is the more remarkable because
its drift is totally at odds with the predominant tradition of Spanish

historiography. From the *Historia silense* right up to other texts in the *Crónica* itself, Spanish historical and chronistic literature speaks almost in one voice expressing hostility to Charlemagne. This hostility centers on two issues: Charles's unmerited reputation as a reconqueror of Spain, and the project of the aged Alfonso II of becoming a vassal of the Frank in exchange for aid and comfort in the struggle against the Moors. The first theme is first sounded in the *Historia silense:* none but Spaniards ever undid the humiliation of Moorish conquest, least of all Charles "quem infra Pirineos montes quasdam civitates a manibus paganorum eripuisse Franci falso asserunt" [of whom the Franks say falsely that he took from the hands of the pagans certain cities this side of the Pyrenees].[9] The topic takes its most eloquent form in Rodrigo Toledano, who documents the general thesis of the modesty of Charles's Spanish conquests by listing at length cities taken from the Moors by others— Tarragona by Bernard, archbishop of Toledo; Toledo by Alfonso VI; and so on for nearly a page.[10] Rodrigo, the *Crónica*'s most trusted source, uniformly vehement against Charlemagne, is the one to articulate most fully the second theme. All the information about Alfonso's projected vassaldom is already in Lucas of Tuy's bland text, but the moral outrage comes from Rodrigo. When Charles makes war on Alfonso after he has withdrawn his offer, Rodrigo berates the Frank for shedding Christian blood rather than Muslim. Most vehemently of all, the narrator stresses the determination of Alfonso's nobles to die rather than submit to the Frank: "malebant enim mori liberi quam in Francorum degere seruitute" [they preferred to die free than live in servitude under the Franks] (Rodrigo Toledano 1987, 83). One must stress that this whole strain is living matter to the compilers of the *Crónica;* Alfonso's work preserves nearly all of the anti-Charlemagne texts in Rodrigo. He, for example, supplies much of the basis for the very savory and dramatic narrative in chapter 619 of the *Crónica,* which is climaxed by the story of the defeat and slaughter of Charles's forces at Roncevaux at the hands (partly) of Alfonso's men, and of the emperor's definitive retreat to his own lands. It is only natural that these texts, with their strong emphasis on the Gothic inheritance of the Christian kings of Spain and on the Reconquest, should look unkindly on Charlemagne on many scores. The *Crónica*'s compilers could in a sense do nothing else.

9. *Historia silensis* 1959, 124.
10. Rodrigo Toledano 1987, 128–30.

In effect, the plain incompatibility, as it were, between pro- and anti-Charlemagne passages surely proves that the presence of the former represents fully conscious initiative on the part of the compilers. Lest we think the *Mainet* an isolated case, we will cite another passage in the *Crónica* also very favorable to Charles. At the end of a chapter given over otherwise to the building activities of Alfonso II we read the following:

> Esse anno otrossi cobro Erena, la emperadriz, por su sabiduria ell imperio que su fijo Costantin le auie tomado; et priso a ell et sacol los oios, et echol de tierra, et murio en desterramiento. Et regno ella sola tres annos. Mas el papa Leo quando esto uio, enuio por Carlos, rey de Ffrancia, e alçol por emperador de Roma. E esto fizo el papa con conseio de los romanos, ca se tenien por desonrrados et maltrechos de assennorearlos mugier que tan mal fecho fiziera en cegar assi a su fijo. E por ende loaron ellos mucho los fechos de Carlos, et dizien que merescie bien de seer emperador. E pues que ell ouo ell imperio recebido, mantouol bien et en paz, et mato todos los malfechores del regno, et enderesço todas las cosas dell imperio, et llamaronle todos Carlos et augusto; e aun touieron por bien los romanos de dar el regno de Italia a su fijo Pepino (348b–349a)

> [That year also the Empress Irene, by her shrewdness, recovered the empire that her son Constantine had taken from her; and she took him prisoner and took out his eyes and cast him out of the land, and he died in exile. And she ruled only three years. But when Pope Leo saw this, he sent for Charles, king of France, and elevated him to be emperor of Rome. And the Pope did this with the counsel and consent of the Romans, who felt dishonored and ill-treated to be ruled by a woman who had done such an evil thing as to so blind her son. And for this reason they much praised the deeds of Charles and said that he indeed deserved to be emperor. And when he had received the empire, he maintained it in justice and peace, killed all the evildoers, and put in order all the affairs of the empire, and everyone called him Charles and Augustus; and the Romans even thought it fitting to give the kingdom of Italy to his son Pepin.]

All this comes from Sigebert, the sense of the source having been slightly changed, as Menéndez Pidal comments (Alfonso 1955, Pidal's index of

sources, 2:cxlv). The alteration of the meaning is, for a fact, very revealing. The fulsome piece in the Spanish is made out of exceedingly modest
and colorless raw materials. They consist of two separate entries in the
Chronographia. The first is from the year 798: "Hyrene imperatrix super
erepto sibi imperio foemineo dolore abusa Constantinum filium suum
oculis et imperio privat." The other piece occurs several lines further on,
under the year 801:

> Romani, qui ab imperatore Constantinopolitano iamdiu animo
> desciverant, nunc accepta occasionis opportunitate, quia mulier
> excecato imperatore Constantino filio suo imperabat, uno omnium
> consense Karolo regi imperatorias laudes acclamant, eumque per
> manum Leonis papae coronant; Pipinum vero, filium eius regem
> Italiae ordinatum collaudant.[11]

> [The Romans, who had in their hearts long since withdrawn alle-
> giance from the emperor at Constantinople, now seized the oppor-
> tunity, for a woman ruled who had put out the eyes of her son the
> emperor Constantine, and they of one mind acclaimed Charles the
> king as emperor and had him crowned by the hand of Pope Leo;
> they also acclaimed Pippin his son as the king of Italy.]

The most obvious changes the compilers of the *Crónica* make are to
push more responsibility onto the Pope, a matter of no concern to us
here, and to tell of the excellences of Charles's reign—maintaining
peace and order as well as putting down evildoers, something plainly
very important. But that is not all. The acclamation by the Roman
people, the "laudes imperatorias," represent for Sigebert (and for us) a
legal formula that declares and confirms Charles as emperor, but the
Alfonsine editors turn them into genuine praise, a simple judgment of
value: the people saw his deeds, took counsel, and awarded him the
crown he deserved. Likewise the concession of the titles Caesar and
Augustus has a new meaning in the Spanish text: the interpolation of the
clause beginning "pues que ell ouo ell imperio recbido" makes it appear
that the titles are a reward for doing good rather than merely something
that goes with the office. The passage in the *Crónica,* taken as a whole,
is, of course, primarily intended to tell of the "translatio imperii" from

---

11. Sigebert 1844, 336.

East to West, but as it stands it is a pair of contrasting portraits, of the totally hateful Irene and of the totally admirable Charles. It is as if the editors saw that by adding glamour to the picture of Charles they would gain for him at no cost the further luster of the contrast with his Byzantine predecessor. How deliberate and malicious are all these changes? Did the compilers intend to distort the meaning or not? The question is perhaps unanswerable. But we really do not need to know what the Alfonsine committee thought Sigebert meant. What is manifest and there for everyone to see is that the *Crónica* text is a celebration of Charles's greatness and that its original is not: the good words for the emperor are in any case the compilers' own.

The incompatibility of the two sets of texts, favorable to Charlemagne and unfavorable, is, in a word, not simply the unintended result of a compilation process more mechanical than rational. There perhaps are such incompatibilities in the *Crónica,* but this is not one of them. One could say of the anti-Charles strain that it is somehow traditional and that it comes in large part from Rodrigo, the source its compilers respect most: one could attribute it to a sort of inertia. But that is really not enough. On the one hand, the belittling of Charles supports an important theme, the notion that the Reconquest is a Spanish and "Gothic" enterprise; to fail to attack him would be to blur the picture. And on the other hand, the very least that can be said for the pro-Charles emphasis is that it is fully deliberate, as we have shown. There is simply no ducking the contradiction. Once again, the only motive I can think of for the compilers to introduce the jarring matter with full consciousness is that they intended to sustain a series built on an imperial theme, that the *Crónica* was to have ended sounding loudly the note of Alfonso's Roman and imperial heritage.

The imperial theme in the *Crónica* is there, if we will only look at it; it comes at us in the text from several quarters, as we have seen. But there is also something about the external history of the work that suggests to us that imperial matters there were to figure very large. This is the simple fact that the project was abandoned precisely at the time that it was. Professor Catalán, identifies the work as Alfonsine up to the famous "laguna cidiana" [the Cidian lacuna] and to that point the imperial references are frequent. But there the original text apparently breaks off, at some distance from any conceivable ending. As we also know, work on the *Crónica* was deliberately put to one side, and the writing of the *General estoria,* itself abandoned for some years, was taken up again. Work on the latter began this second time about 1280, and, again according to Catalán, the latest portion of the *Crónica* was written no later than 1274.[12] Menéndez Pidal, who assuredly holds rather different views about how the *Crónica* was composed, attributes Alfonso's shift in interest to reasons of taste: the fair field of universal history pleased him more than the history of Spain. But there is one possibility that has been overlooked. The year 1275, a date within a small range of time of the dropping of the *Crónica* and of the resumption of the *Estoria,* is the year Alfonso abandons his claim on the imperial throne. Is it not possible that the imperial theme in his Spanish chronicle was in his mind so fundamental that when he lost the empire, he also lost interest in his book? His sense of the incongruity of the imperial matter in the *Crónica* may have been something like ours: once he knew his narrative could not end with his double rôle, his history became a monster, with more members than it needed. An important structural feature of the project was permanently gutted, and so he could see no point in carrying it on. And so we return to our original theme. The *Crónica* looks miscellaneous, patchy, as though put together with scissors and paste. But if one is unwilling to look for logic one is not going to find it. What our coincidence of dates may show is that the logic in the *Crónica* was such an issue for Alfonso that the impairment of the logic made the completion of the work impossible.

I conclude with a word about texts. My quotations from the *Crónica* are, of course, from Menéndez Pidal's edition, the version that, so to speak, fills up the page. Variants appear in his footnotes. My choice was made for simplicity's sake, for my own convenience and for that of the reader. Pidal, as we know, chose to transcribe the so-called "versión regia," done in the time of Sancho IV, fulsome, free in its adaptation of Latin texts: this version is not strictly speaking Alfonsine. However, every feature of the *Crónica* that I have pointed out to support my argument does assuredly date from the time of the Learned King. A scrutiny of the variants presented by the two representatives of the older "versión vulgar" shows that this text is not significantly different from the newer version in any feature that affects our case. The passages dealing with Charlemagne are virtually identical in Pidal's version and in "T," first representative of the older text (Alfonso 1955, 1:lx). The

12. Catalán 1962, 26.

chronologies and references to the empire, so far as I can discover, are virtually the same in Pidal's text and in both "T" and "F," the other Alfonsine text (p. lix), which takes over from "T" at the beginning of the reign of Fernando I. One can indeed find a case or two in which the actual numbers in the chronologies differ, but what concerns us is the fact that they are there at all, and that they are where they are.

PART 3

The last three essays in this collection are about the ideas expressed in the *General estoria* on what could broadly be called philosophy and culture. Two of these essays are on that work's concept of natural theology. The third is on a subject that may seem unrelated, but that in the editor's argument is closely connected; it is on the Alfonsines' ideas about the growth of material culture. In all these essays, I allude to what is by any standards an extraordinary string of chapters in the *Estoria*, a sort of essay on the history of religion and on its growth and passage from the most servile worship of creatures to that of one God. What is distinctive about this account is that in it progress in religion is linked to the discovery of more and more general laws of nature. As the *Estoria* tells the story, humans first worshiped stones and animals, but, at a certain moment, some realized that all the variety of nature was to be explained by the interplay of the four elements; these then became the objects of cult. At a later stage it was further discovered that the very things that were made up of the elements were governed by the motions of stars in their spheres; these beings then became the imagined gods of those later days. But in the end these too gave way and came to be regarded as mere creatures; the patriarch Abraham taught his contemporaries and humankind at large that the stars were powerless to carry out their mission without the governance of a still higher being, God Himself. One should add that in this remarkable account advances in religion are equated with progress generally; in the same chapters we are told how the first humans lived in caves and lacked even the simplest practical arts, but that at later stages they learned husbandry and weaving, and that centuries later this process had its term in high civilization of the sort known to Alfonso himself, with sophisticated architecture, very specialized crafts, the production of luxury items—this as well as letters and learning (Alfonso 1930, 61–68).

Speaking of the purely religious and philosophical side of this exposition, I have observed that its narrative, which is ostensibly historical, dealing successively with different groups of people, could also be read as about the mind's progress in knowledge and devotion, as it contemplated more and more general causes in nature: elements, stars, God. Echoing Bonaventure I went so far as to speak of an Alfonsine *itinerarium mentis in Deum*. This allusion to the great Franciscan schoolman should not be misread. I certainly did not mean that Alfonso and his associates in any fashion borrowed from Bonaventure or that his theory and theirs were similar in any but the most general way. In Bonaventure's conception, broadly speaking, the soul finds God as it withdraws from sensible things, whereas, in the Alfonsines' view, the mind comes to understand the very order and hierarchy of visible nature and of visible beings and comes to see them as the handiwork of the unseen God.

At the heart of this whole outlook is the conviction that astrology is the master science, that it is edifying, and that it inspires faith in God. This view is expressed everywhere in the *General estoria*; some of its most important characters are devout astrologers—Adam, Seth and his line (Alfonso 1930, 21), and, as we have seen, Abraham. Astrological piety, if we may use such a term, is a rare species. It is a mistake to suppose that everywhere in medieval Christendom there were men and women who found God by contemplating the stars. It has been my conclusion that Alfonso acquired the view that astrology was edifying from sources that could be called Hermetic or were somehow associated with Hermeticism. This line of influence is the theme of two of the essays that follow. Hermeticism is a very long subject, and there is no need to try to sum up here all the variety of doctrines and practices that fall under that rubric. Hermeticism was originally a salvation religion that flourished in the early centuries of our era. Its supposed founder is none other than the god Hermes, who figures in the cultic texts as at once the eminent spiritual teacher and the bringer of civilization. It is dangerous to generalize, but it is probably safe to say that on its philosophical side Hermeticism is roughly Platonic, and that many of its doctrines are close to those of the *Timaeus* (Yates 1964, 2–3). The texts, as one should note, present themselves and their teaching as dating from a very early time and as among the first to speak of God and of the origin of the cosmos. At various times in history elements of Hermeticism were accepted and even revered by scholars and members of the biblical religions, especially Christianity and Islam. The two factors that make this absorption possible are the supposed antiquity of the Hermetic texts and the admission of Hermes himself into the Judeo-Christian-Islamic pantheon; incredibly, the god gets identified with several figures in sacred history—most frequently, though not exclusively, with Enoch, who is the son of Jared and whom Muslims call Idris.[1]

It is in its Islamic form that Hermeticism comes to the Learned King and his court. It is of course well known that Alfonso patronized a large body of translations from the Arabic, and it is also beyond doubt that many of these Spanished texts are full of allusions to things Hermetic (Kahane 1969). It is, therefore, hardly incautious to suggest that certain strains in the Alfonsine historical writings might also be Hermetic. In my essays to date I have tried to make a case for Hermeticism in the *General estoria* using a broad approach, pointing to striking parallels between Alfonsine texts and Islamic ones, dwelling on remarkable coincidences between the two groups. In this short introduction I would like to make a stronger case, concentrated on a single Arabic work of decidedly Hermeticist coloring, the one known in Western Europe as *Picatrix* (1962). This text is well within the Alfonsines' range, was translated in their circle (Kahane 1969, 449–52), and was therefore probably accessible to the compilers of the *Estoria*. The older work's great interest is that it gives utterance to certain Hermetic themes that are very important in the system of ideas expressed in Alfonso's history. The *Picatrix*, or *Goal of the Sage*, is primarily a text on sympathetic magic. It does, however, include material on other subjects, eminently astrology and Neoplatonic philosophy. The large proportion of the work given over to astrology should surprise no one: discussions of magic would make little sense without generous allusions to that science. Philosophy too has its part to play. Its place in the *Picatrix* is perhaps harder to define, but it is not therefore less fundamental. It supplies the large frame: the many chapters on the governance of the cosmos serve to explain and justify to the reader, sometimes directly and sometimes less so, the very practice of

---

1. See the references cited in the essays that follow. In brief, for the early Christian acceptance of Hermeticism, see Yates 1964, 6–9; for the Christian identification of Hermes with Enoch, p. 48. The *General estoria* itself identifies Hermes with Enoch (Alfonso 1957–61, 1:34–39). For the equation Hermes-Idris and for a view of the place of Hermeticism in Islam generally, see Plessner 1954. We should understand that for ancients and medievals alike there were three Hermes; it is of course the first of the three that is identified wth Enoch.

magic. The philosophical part of the *Picatrix* depends heavily for its ideas, and at times for its very words, on the *Rasa'il*, the scripture encyclopedia of the Islamic group known as the Brethren of Purity—in Arabic, Ikwan al-Safa (*Picatrix* 1962, Plessner and Ritter's introduction, lix–lxi). We will return to this text. I will consider the parallels between the *Picatrix* and the *General estoria* under three headings: the alliance between knowledge and piety, the antiquity of philosophy, and the association between Hermes and material culture.

The first of these themes, the godliness of philosophy, is expressed everywhere in the *Picatrix*, in some places explicitly, elsewhere as an unspoken premise. The plainest utterance on the subject is in the very first chapter of the first part (1962, 4–6), where we are told that the aim of philosophy is to raise the mind to God, Unique Being and First Cause. Elsewhere the *Picatrix* tells us in detail what is involved in the upward journey. One passage, for example, gives us the Neoplatonic ladder of being. The cosmos is a hierarchy: God, intellect, the world soul, the heavenly spheres, and finally the sublunary world. All but the last are causes; each is the cause of the entity below it. The calling of the wise man, resident on earth, is to complete the cycle; the mind returns to God by climbing up, as it were, the ladder of causes, comprehending the astral system first, then the soul, then intellect itself, and finally, in some fashion, the First Cause (1962, 51–52). My paraphrase here is simplifying matters brutally. As we have seen, the link between knowledge or philosophy and the mind's approach to God, expounded as it is in the *Picatrix*, is also a theme in the *General estoria*; Adam, Seth and his descendents, and Abraham are all men of learning and science who are also godly. And, as I have pointed out, in the case of Abraham the connection between philosophy and piety is made very explicit: it is his study of the stars, precisely, that obliges him to confess the one true God. The only difference between the way the philosophical life is presented in the *Estoria* and its presentation in the *Picatrix* is that the former carries us up only one rung of the cosmic ladder; Alfonso and his collaborators apparently do not wish to guide us up the rest of the way, beyond the study of astronomy.

Now, for the theme of the antiquity of philosophy and scientific knowledge, we may turn to a passage in the *Picatrix* that refers plainly to Idris, who, as we recall, is the Koranic equivalent of Enoch and is identified with the first Hermes. The wise men of old achieved their mastery over nature by their knowledge of the great astral system, of the sphere of the fixed stars, called the Throne of God, of the planets and of the special nature of each, of the zodiac and of the special power and personality of each sign. All this lore is written in the books of the great masters of astrology:

> This knowledge the first sage . . . has in mind when he says: "I am he who was lifted above the seven spheres"; for with the expression "was lifted" he alludes to scientific understanding by means of thought. The same is also hinted at in the word of God which says: "We lifted him to a lofty place." (*Picatrix* 1962, 10–11; the translation is in Kahane 1969, 451)

As the editors of the *Picatrix* point out (1962, 11 n), the "first sage" is the prophet Idris himself, that is, Hermes and Enoch. The *Rasa'il*, the collected writings of the Brethren of Purity, has a passage that parallels this one and that clarifies it considerably. It tells how Hermes-Idris was carried up to the sphere of Saturn, spent thirty years observing all its operation, and then returned to earth to teach humans the science of astrology (*Rasa'il* 3.24, quoted in *Picatrix* 1962, 11–12 n). A modern commentator says of this utterance, "The study of the heavens has, therefore, an aspect of revealed truth and is of a sacred nature" (Nasr 1993, 76). The point is clear: the *Rasa'il* related philosophy to the first revelation, not to the final—that is, to that of Idris-Enoch-Hermes, not to that of Mohammed. Thus, when we reflect about the thought of the Brethren of Purity and of the *Picatrix,* we have to set aside familiar ideas about the relationships between reason and revelation, the terms in which we generally tend to think about Jewish, Muslim, and Christian philosophical speculation. Philosophy in our texts, especially natural philosophy, astrology, is simply revelation—not a product of human ingenuity, but a direct concession by God. The bearing of all this on the views about knowledge in the *General estoria* is obvious. Its doctrine, so to speak, is not identical to that of *Rasa'il* or *Picatrix*, but the notion is present in Alfonso that liberal knowledge, especially knowledge of the stars, is a divine gift, a possession of Seth and his offspring, inherited by them from Adam, who received it from God (Alfonso 1930, 21).

The third strain common to the *Picatrix* and *General estoria*, in the connection of Hermes with material culture, is easily disposed of. The passages in Alfonso that actually mention Hermes seem to reflect Hermetic writings that link all three Hermes—including the first, identified with Enoch and Idris—with the invention of certain practical arts, that is, architecture, city planning, and medicine. The *Picatrix* is acquainted with this current. Hermes, the first of the three, as the text specifies, is credited at the dawn of history with the building of a city and a temple to the sun and with creating pictures with magical qualities (1962, 322–23).

Abraham in the *General estoria*

In this essay I wish to discuss three subjects. The first is a piece of mistranslation, a passage of the *General estoria* the Alfonsines take from Flavius Josephus and get all wrong. I will try to show that when the compilers chose this particular bit of Josephus for its particular place in the *General estoria*, they had the original meaning in mind and not the one in the mistranslation. I am led to my views in this matter by what seems to me to be the pattern of themes in that portion of the text. Second, I will say something about the conception the Alfonsines had of the patriarch Abraham as a civilizing hero. Finally, I will make some observations about the archaism particularly evident in the work's treatment of Abraham.

The *Antiquities of the Jews* by Flavius Josephus tells us that the patriarch Abraham was the first monotheist. The Abraham narrative there begins by presenting him as an astronomer and natural philosopher who uses his knowledge to prove (for the first time) that God is one. The Latin version of the text, known to the Alfonsine editors of the *General estoria*, presents the following argument (the translation and italics are mine):

> He [Abraham] was the first who had the courage to declare that God, creator of all things, was one; he also affirmed that each of those separate things that further our well-being receives its power from the giver of all, and that they do not subsist of their own power. He [Abraham] formed these judgments by *observing* the motions of land and sea, what happens to the sun and moon, and what is always taking place in the heavens. He taught that there was a certain power that disposed all these things, and that by their

own power, without His guidance, we would possess none of the
things we needed.[1]

It is important to stress that the "separate things that further our well-
being," the "ad felicitatem tendentia . . . singula" of our text, are meant
to be the stars, simply: the Greek original, as we should note, is wholly
explicit on this point, and at least one old translation of the Latin, that of
Thomas Lodge,[2] reads the text in this way. The orderly movement of the
spheres and their benign influence on humans, mediated through nature, are the subject matter of this page. Josephus is putting into the
mouth of Abraham an argument for the unity of God drawn from design
in the universe. The *Antiquities of the Jews* is, as we know, one of the
principal sources of the *General estoria*, and the passage I have quoted
figures large there, at the beginning of its own Abraham story. But the
sense of its Latin original is wrecked in Alfonso. Everything goes awry.
Cosmology and the cosmological argument for monotheism are forgotten. The "ad felicitatem tendentia . . . singula" become not astral beings, but "cosas temporales," and instead of saying that the stars, without divine guidance, cannot help humans, the text tells us that men
themselves are helpless without God. Devout reflection replaces natural
philosophy. Observations about the stars, the order of the heavens, and
their influence on humans give way to the bland reminder that all good
things come from God. Here are some of the pertinent passages in the
Castilian:

> Ca el fue el primero que se atreuio a dezir, ante que todos, que uno
> era el Dios que criara todas las cosas; e delas otras cosas tempo-
> rales les dizie otrossi *sus* razones, *e* eran estas: que las cosas tempo-

---

1. Josephus 1958, 143–44. The Latin text has the following: ". . . primus itaque
praesumpsit praenuntiare deum creatorem unum esse cunctorum. reliqua vero licet ad
felicitatem tendentia per praeceptum praebentis singula quaeque dari et non propria sub-
sistere virtute confessus est. haec vero coniciebat per terrae passionem et maris, et ea quae
continguent circa solem et lunam, et ex omnibus quae circa caelum semper eveniunt.
virtute enim eis praesente et providentia ordinationis eorum cuncta disponi docebat,
quibus quicumque privarentur manifesti fierent, quia neque ea quae ad utilitatem nobis
necessaria sunt sua potestate poterunt possidere, quae scilicet secundum iubentis
fortitudinem ministrantur, ..."
2. For the Greek, see Josephus 1956, iv; this volume was the beginning of the *Antiquities*, and the book and chapter I cite is of that work. For Lodge, see Josephus 1602, 12. The
passage in question is obviously a rendering of the Latin.

rales, que maguer que aduzien a bien andança alos om*n*es, qui
dellas bien usauan, que pero por el mandado dAquel que cria
todas las cosas eran dadas todas a todos . . . aquellos a quien las
cosas del mundo non uinien tan bien como ellos querien *e* les eran
tolludas quelas non auien, que manifiestos uiniessen de otorgar
que nin aun aquellas cosas que eran mester, sin que ellos se non
podrien mantener, quelas non pueden auer por el su poder dellos;
e son estas aquellas mismas que aquel Dios solo criador dio poral
seruicio delos om*n*es, segund la fortaleza *e* el poder del su
mandado.[3]

[He was the first who dared to say that the God who created all
things was one, and again, concerning temporal things he (Abraham) had his own explanation, and this is what it was: that although temporal things bring about the well-being of those men
who make good use of them, it is nevertheless by the command of
Him who makes all things that all (these temporal goods) are given
to all. . . . Those persons to whom the things of the world did not
come as they would have wished, and from whom some things
were (even) taken away, should grant it as obvious that even those
things that are necessary, without which they (humans) could not
exist, they may not have by their own power, and those are the
very things that God, who is the only Creator, gave for the good of
men, by His power and His command.]

We observe a drastic change of meaning, a change not for the best. The
fact is that the large context in the *General estoria*, the greater text,
would have gained had the sense of the translation of this passage been
left as it was in the Latin and made to refer to cosmology and the stars,
not to the frailty of man. It has been observed that natural philosophy
plays a great role in the argument of the work, in particular the notion
that the study of creatures is a kind of theology.[4] Astronomy and the
quadrivial arts generally figure large in this scheme because they lay
bare the secrets first of nature and ultimately of nature's God. On the
one hand, the Latin Josephus translated correctly would have added one

---

3. Alfonso 1930, 88. This passage is from book 4, chap. 8. Page references will henceforth be to this edition. For the second part, see Alfonso 1957–61.
4. Rico 1972, 123 ff. Rico devotes a section to the arts beginning on p. 142.

more unit to this important series. And on the other hand, the inaccurate *Estoria* text as it stands, the devotional one, adds very little to the substance and structure of the work at large. This in itself is an exceptional circumstance. We must emphasize as strongly as we can that in similarly altered passages in the two Alfonsine histories this is not the case. Typically, when an Alfonsine translated text differs from its source, it is for good reason. The context gains: something is afoot in the large text. We will cite at least one instance of such a happy alteration in the course of this essay, but for the present a simple example will do, one from the *Estoria de Espanna*. In some lines adapted from Orosius we are told that Orgetorix orders the Gauls to burn their villages and their lands before facing Julius Caesar in battle. Caesar prevails, however, and sends them back home: "Enuioles a sus tierras, que auien ellos mismos destroidas, *que las poblassen e que fuessen del sennorio de Roma*"[5] [He sent them back to their lands, which they themselves had destroyed, to (re)populate them, and to submit to the power of Rome]. The words I have italicized are not in Orosius and are part of the editors' attempt to brighten up the dark picture of Caesar they inherit from Orosius and Lucan. We are plainly supposed to admire the great general's act for both reasons, the rebuilding of the town and the extending of Rome's power. The point is that Caesar, Roman emperor in the Alfonsines' view, is a predecessor of the Learned King himself, and that the empire in all its forms constitutes an important theme in the *Estoria de Espanna*. But in the Josephus piece about the astrologer Abraham in the version of the *General estoria,* the change of subject, from stars to temporal good, works no miracles: it does not bring a new focus, does not mark out a new path in the text. It does not light up the surrounding territory. The inevitable question arises: what went wrong? Is all this simply a mistake? Is it in any way possible that the compilers originally meant the natural-astrological reading to be the definitive one? Is it unreasonable to judge that their original plans called for a text of Josephus closer to the Latin? The answer is closer at hand than one might guess. There is another, earlier passage in the *General estoria* about Abraham, one completely independent of the Abraham narrative proper, which tells us part of the story. Some men, says the *Estoria*, worshiped the stars,

---

5. Alfonso 1955, 1:62. For the corresponding passage in Orosius, see Orosius 1882, bk. 6, chap. 7.

because they knew that astral bodies determined the way the elements combine and separate; the text goes on:

> Pero entre estos ouo y algunos om*n*es letrados *e* sabios, que, por su razon *e* por su saber, entendieron que non eran muchos dioses nin podie seer mas de uno Aquel que da fuerça *e* uirtud a todas las cosas *e* ninguna otra cosa non da poder a El; *e* dixieron que no conuinie orar a otri si non Aquel solo; *e* ensennaron que aquellas ymagenes *e* oraciones que fazien alos çielos *e* alas estrellas que de creaturas eran *e* fechas a creaturas; *e* que meior era de fazer las a Aquel quelas criara a todas. E entre todos aquestos, el que nos fallamos que meior lo entendio *e* lo mostro enel su tie*m*po fue Abraha*m* . . . &c. (68)

> [But among these, there were some learned men and wise who on the basis of their reason and knowledge understood that there were not many gods, and that the Being who gave power and virtue to all things could not be more than one, and that no other thing (being) gives power to Him; and they said that it was not fitting to pray to anyone but Him, and that all the charms and prayers that humans make to influence the heavens and the stars were creatures and were addressed to creatures, and that it was better to address them to Him who made every creature. And among the men of that time we judge that the one who best understood these matters was Abraham.]

This picture of Abraham's convictions is, oddly enough, closer to the sense of the Latin underlying book 4, chapter 8, than is the actual translation of that very Latin. In the passage we just cited he is plainly made to teach that the stars that shape and move things in the sublunary world would not have this power were it not given them by a still greater power. In other words, the association of this whole view with the belief and preaching of Abraham is already in the *Estoria*, and it is therefore believable that the compilers originally intended to have the Josephus passage speak in these terms.

The issue is not a trivial one: it has a bearing on the technique the Alfonsine editors used in composing the two histories. The prevalent view, as we know, has this composition take place more or less in three stages. First, the source texts are translated or prosified entire. Then the sewing-together process is carried out: the editors determine the exact place in their text that this piece of Orosius or that bit of Lucas is to occupy. Finally the product of the second stage is polished: the style is smoothed out, certain incompatibilities between source texts are reconciled, and the whole generally is put into order.[6]

But if, indeed, something has gone astray in our Josephus passage, if the sense of the original is really more appropriate in its setting than the final version, then we must focus our special attention on the second moment. This stage, the sewing together, must have been the great theater of the invention of the Alfonsine compilers. Large thematic considerations must have been before their minds as well as the humbler tasks of storytelling. On this basis one would guess that the Josephus passage as it reads in the Latin was admitted to the text of the *General estoria* in the company of other passages that either bore the same message or somehow supported or confirmed it. Then, at a later moment, the original plan must have been lost sight of, enough that our Josephus passage was deformed and made incapable of doing its original job. The matter is, as I would judge, serious enough to merit further treatment.

As is obvious, the question of the setting, or context, of our passage is here capitally important. It is above all the context of ideas that demands, as it were, a version of Josephus closer to the Latin than the extant one. But at this point the context we have in mind is not the diffuse one Rico speaks of. The many references in the *Estoria* to natural philosophy and the value of learning are of course very important from our point of view, but what we need in this case is something much more specific and local. The paragraph in the speculations of the patriarch Abraham is in fact part of a very determinate pattern of exposition in the *Estoria*. Our passage is, in the first place, a part of the whole Abraham narrative in the *Estoria:* it fits in especially with certain of the later chapters in the story, the ones based on Islamic sources. These too, like the Josephus passage, give us an astronomer and a zealous preacher of monotheism. Thus the picture of a natural philosopher at the beginning of the Abraham narrative would have dovetailed nicely with the matter that followed. The whole conception of the patriarch as we have

---

6. A sort of common doctrine: my presentation is simple and bypasses difficulties. See Menéndez Pidal's introduction to the 1955 edition of the *Primera crónica* (Alfonso 1955), xvi and xxix; and Catalán 1963b, 354–75, and 1962, 27.

spoken of it is confirmed even more strongly by a text that precedes these chapters on the life of Abraham. This is a passage with visible links to our lines from Josephus, one that has the greatest bearing on how the latter should have read. This is the long development in book 3 on the history of religion (62–68). This section is remarkable in that it is at once on cult and the objects of men's worship and on the material and cultural progress of the race. In an extraordinary series of chapters we are given one account of early humans in hardly any way like the story of the race told elsewhere in the *Estoria*. The passage is in narrative form but deals in genera and species: *humans* first worshiped stones, *humans* farmed at such and such a stage. The advances in the mechanical arts and in religion go hand in hand: *humans* first gathered fruits and kept flocks, then wove cloth and tilled the soil, first worshiped stones, then animals, and so on. The heart of the treatise is the notion that humans in the early days worshiped successively more excellent beings. Most notable, the series of the four elements and the stars are supposed to have been cult objects: humans paid reverence to earth first, then to water, then to air and fire, and finally to the stars. This whole conception is entirely distinctive to the *General estoria*. Here, incidentally, we have an eminent case of a text that has been tampered with. Literally speaking, the source is the *Chronicon mundi* of Lucas of Tuy, which does speak of the worship of the elements and of the stars.[7] But in Lucas these cults are contemporary: at one and the same time *some* humans worshiped earth, some water, and so forth. To adapt this material to their program the Alfonsine compilers made the cults successive: humans first worshiped earth, *then* water, and so forth. The progressive element is new. The editors also enlarged the list of cult objects to make a broader sweep: before humans worshiped elements, they worshiped stones, then trees and plants, then land animals, then fish. The last step in this elaboration of the treatise in the *General estoria* was perhaps the most daring. To serve notice that the succession really was progress and improvement, the pieces about the advances in the mechanical arts were sandwiched in

---

7. Lucas of Tuy 1608 (ed. Schottus), 7: "alii colebãt ignẽ, alii aqua, alii solẽ & sic de aliis elementis." *Solem* seems to be out of place in this list; one would guess that we should have *solum*, "earth," instead: "some worshiped fire, some water, some earth, and so on for the other elements." A text like Schottus's would, however, supply the notion that the elements were cult objects to the Alfonsines and could also on the basis of *solem* have suggested to them that men worshiped the stars. My friend Professor Bernard Reilly of Villanova University tells me that the *Chronicon mundi* is long since ripe for reediting.

between the various stages in the history of cult. The term of the whole process is of course the worship of a single, omnipotent God: in a passage I have already quoted we are told that some humans saw that the stars, however powerful, were not gods, that their power would have been nothing without that of the one true God. The hero of this moment in history is, of course, Abraham.

This history of religion, by now quite independent of its modest source—Lucas—has itself a well-defined architecture: it is no mere catalog. The objects of worship fall into three classes: natural objects (mineral, vegetable, and animal), the four elements, and then the stars. All these are arranged so as to represent more and more general causes in the universe. The beings at one level govern those of the lower level but are governed in turn by those of the higher. The history of religion is thus a climb up the ladder of causes. Why worship animals, for instance, if the interplay of the elements brings about their existence, and if the elements themselves outlast them? Elements therefore are more worthy of worship than animals; the passage that expresses this notion is very precise:

> *E* estos metieron mientes a todas las cosas que orauan los dantes dellos, *e* uieron que aquellas cosas que los *sus* antigos que aoraran, que todas eran creaturas que se leuantaron delos elementos *e* enellos se criauan *e* se mantienen, *e* non durauan luengo tie*m*po; *e* mesuraron como durauan much*o* los elementos, como nascien dellos todas las otras creaturas *e* animalias de la tierra *e* del aer, *e* ellos las gastauan en cabo, . . . &c. (64)

> [They reflected on all the things the people who lived before them had prayed to and saw that those things that the ancients adored were creatures, that they arose from the elements, that they were made out of them and sustained by them, and that they did not last a long time; and these (later humans) calculated that the elements did last long, since all creatures and animals were engendered out of earth and air, and that these (elements) outlived them in the long run.]

By the same token interaction between elements finds its fullest explanation in the stars; therefore they are yet more excellent beings to worship:

mas ualie aorar alos cielos *e* alas estrellas, dond uinie la fuerça alos elementos, que non alos elementos mismos nin a las cosas que dellos se fazien en que ellos creyen. (68)

[it was better to worship the stars and the heavens, from which the power of the elements came, rather than the elements themselves or the things that were made out of them, in which they (deceived humans) had believed.]

The compilers of the *General estoria*, like many of their contemporaries, thought the cosmos governed by a hierarchy of causes, and with an optimism typical of Alfonsine culture, they pictured mankind in its early stages climbing up the ladder of being in search of an object of worship.

What, then, does the cult treatise tell us about the passage about Abraham in book 4? It tells us that it should have offered us the figure of an astrologer, a natural philosopher who read the designs of God in the stars and in the sublunary beings they influence. How could one conclude otherwise when the very Latin text the compilers used and mistranslated gives us precisely this figure or when the content of the Latin actually appears elsewhere in the *Estoria*? Abraham completes our great series, not the merely devout hero of our Castilian text, but the speculative one of its Latin original. He is the last term. Men's worship passes from natural objects to elements, thence to the stars, until finally Abraham teaches men to worship not nature but nature's God. Most significant of all, we have a parallelism, a symmetry: men thought elements a more general cause than natural objects, stars an even more general cause, and God the most general cause of all. Each step in the reasoning is like the last. All of this compactness of argument is sustained if we have an accurate Castilian Josephus and a speculative Abraham; it is in great part lost if we do not. The context, the philosophical argument, if we could call it that, demands a reading of Josephus more faithful to the Latin; such a reading manifestly gives us a more coherent and significant text. We may, therefore, conclude that something may have gone awry in disposing the extant version of book 4, chapter 8, and that it should have read otherwise.

We are speaking, then, of an invisible manuscript, something that might have been produced, under circumstances we can only guess at. No one has ever seen a Josephus text in Castilian more accurate than the one we have; the variants given by Solalinde give us no hint that any such version ever existed.[8] But even this lack of direct evidence is less telling than it seems. If there ever was a recurring note in Alfonsine studies, it is this: in successive versions of a translated text the latest is the least accurate. It makes little difference whether we are speaking of the recensions of the *Estoria de Espanna* or of the drafts of the *Kalilah* or of Lucan.[9] There is always a gap between the polished version the Alfonsine committee may have thought definitive and the *borradores*, the more literal rough drafts of translations. And if the studies of the species of Catalán's admirable "El taller historiográfico alfonsí"[10] have any value at all, we might well guess that a *borrador* of Josephus, close to the Latin, must have existed and is now lost. We are not treading on air. Not only did some of the compilers read Latin well; the second stage in the compilation, the sewing together of the bits and pieces, might well have been done using a Castilian text of Josephus that said more or less what the Latin did. And if this version stressed cosmology, as it must have, a variant of the *General estoria* more or less like the one we have imagined might actually have been written down.

Our two pieces, on the religion of early mankind and on the young Abraham, separated locally in the text, are in fact one single thing, an undivided whole. Not the least important job this unit does is to present the reader a picture of Abraham as a civilizing hero. We must begin with a summing up. First of all, our unit sets forth some very distinctive notions of culture, religion, and the relationship between the two. In our famous treatise in book 3 progress in religion goes hand in hand with progress in the mechanical arts: as we have seen, the text moves back and forth, telling of successive steps in both series. The conclusion must be that we are meant to see monotheism as the fulfillment of culture taken large and Abraham as the hero of that culture. Humankind takes steps forward on more than one front, and in the short run, at least, Abraham is the term of that process. Monotheism is a cultural boon and he is a civilizing hero. It is, of course, a capitally important part of this

---

8. Alfonso 1930, 776.

9. For Lucan, see Herrero Llorente 1959. For *Kalilah*, see G. Menéndez Pidal 1951, 378. The *borrador* "draft" of the *Estoria de Espanna* does not correspond to a text finished in Alfonso's time; nevertheless it is closer to the Latin sources than is the text reproduced in Menéndez Pidal's edition: this is well known, pointed out by, among others, Catalán 1962, 178.

10. See n. 6.

whole conception that he is a teacher and a dispenser of culture. The *translatio studii* theme, pointed out by Rico,[11] depends heavily on the figure of Abraham: he is the one who teaches the quadrivial arts to the Egyptians, who in turn pass them on to the Greeks and, through them, to humanity generally. It should be stressed that the idea of the culture hero is in no sense alien to the world of the *General estoria*. Narratives about extraordinary human figures who bring the blessings of civilization to all of mankind or to some part of it are not rare in the work. Thus the euhemerized Prometheus of Eusebius comes to the *Estoria* virtually unaltered.[12] The "real" Prometheus did not create men; he wrought their humanity, so to speak, by leading them out of barbarism and teaching them sciences:

> departen sobrello Eusebio *e* Jh*e*ronimo *e* los otros sabios que dend fablan, *e* dizen que esta razon quiere seer que tanto era este Prometheo sabio *e* ensennaua bien los saberes alos om*n*es, que delos nescios *e* sin todo saber, que eran fascas como muertos o bestias en los entendimientos, fazie sabios *e* ensennados tanto quelos sacaua dela muerte dela nesciedad *e* los tornaua a uida de saber. *E* por esta semeiança *e* esplanamiento sale de fabliella esta razon. (261)

> [Eusebius and Jerome and the other wise men who speak of him (Prometheus) have this to say, that Prometheus was wise and learned, and that he taught sciences and disciplines in such a way that he turned ignorant and foolish men, who indeed were virtually dead or were brutes as far as their understanding was concerned, into wise and intelligent persons; in effect, then, he brought them back from the death of foolishness (and ignorance) to the life of knowledge. And through this comparison and explanation we may draw the above account out of the fable (that Prometheus created men).]

Prometheus becomes an exemplary bringer of civilization. So also, eminently, does the euhemerized Jupiter of the *General estoria*. This purely human figure brings learning, law, and wise government to a humanity ignorant of all. Ceres teaches humans the agricultural arts. And so,

---

11. Rico 1972, 160.
12. Eusebius 1923, 47.

there are many more teachers. The monotheist Abraham in Alfonso is thus one of a large company. We would observe, incidentally, that the figure of Jupiter is, like that of Abraham, in its whole scope an invention of the Alfonsine compilers. The slimmest of texts from Godfrey of Viterbo's *Pantheon* supplies the basis for a long treatise on the demythologized god,[13] for Alfonso and Godfrey alike a purely human king of Crete. This imposing monarch as presented in the *Estoria* establishes in Athens a *studium* for the liberal arts; promulgates the first written legal code, basis for subsequent laws; and becomes the first universal emperor. Most significant of all, this triad of activities is played against another theme, the general barbarism of men of his time. We would stress that the passage on the bad state of humankind is wholly independent of Godfrey: the odd compost of Cicero and Ovid is quite new (198– 99). The point is not a small one. The trinity teacher-lawgiver-ruler *opposed* to the barbarism of men of the time is as a whole a conception distinctive to the *Estoria*. The presence of the civilizing hero in the work would be striking even if his biography came entire from another text, but here, in typical Alfonsine style, the combination of texts, the very act of compiling, creates a figure that was not in any single source text.

Prometheus, Jupiter, and Abraham do not exhaust the list of civilizing heroes in the *General estoria*. The matter could well be the subject of a separate study.

The great unit that is the subject of this study, the story of Abraham and his predecessors, yields up one other very weighty message, a message hardly usual in a universal history. Our cluster gives an original and distinctive expression to the concept of the *itinerarium mentis in Deum:* the compilers project onto the history of early man an account of the mind's ascent to God through the hierarchy of creatures. The story of how our ancestors came to know the one true God is here simply a dramatized version of the liberal artist's own long journey to ever higher levels of understanding. Professor Rico, once again, speaks of the twelfth-century flavor of many of the conceptions of the *General estoria*.[14] Here we have a remarkable case in point. We need only to

---

13. Godfrey of Viterbo 1726, 78.

14. Rico 1972, 155–56. He is speaking specifically of the continued prestige of the liberal arts in Alfonso and, in particular, of arts not only as *organon* but, in the case of the quadrivium, as divisions of knowledge about real things. My own text, therefore, draws a generality and makes an analogy.

think about the Platonism of the school of Chartres,[15] of the great prestige in that day of the *Timaeus*, with its picture of a hierarchical universe. This dialogue, with its commentary by Chalcidius, was, as no other, the basic text of the time,[16] and it put before a generation the notion of God as the last rung on the ladder of being, and of the philosopher's life as a climb up that ladder. This enormous subject we have broached is well beyond the range of our study. Archaism is obviously something other than exact copy, and 150 years of history do make a difference. But we can affirm this: the somewhat old-fashioned cosmos of liberal arts that to Rico's mind is so present in the *General estoria*— one of natural philosophy and natural theology—is eminently so in our series of chapters on material culture, on religion, and on Abraham.

---

15 For the Chartrians, see Parent 1938, 24–43.

16. Gregory 1958 traces the evolution of twelfth-century Platonism in terms of a gradual change in the way the *Timaeus* was read.

A Hermetic Theme in the *General estoria*

The *General estoria* says notable things about Seth and his descendents: not least, it tells us that these men were the first to have knowledge of the liberal arts, eminently of astrology.[1] This bit of information comes to the work from Josephus's *Antiquities of the Jews*; the Alfonsines do scarcely more than expand Josephus's astrology to cover all seven liberal arts and theology.[2] The statement in the *Estoria* is followed by a curious explanation: the Sethites' knowledge of heavenly things may be attributed to two causes, to the teaching of Seth's parents (Adam and Eve), or to their own righteousness, which gave their minds a special disposition, a unique subtlety (Alfonso 1930, 21). Lines later, it is explained that Adam's knowledge, in this case something like the twelfth-century curriculum—seven arts, especially astrology, plus physics and theology—came to him directly from God (21). Earlier we are told that Seth's wisdom, in this case the rules of righteous living, was taught him by his father Adam, who in turn received it from God during the former's sleep at the creation of Eve (20). This Alfonsine initiative, the tracing of Seth's knowledge back to Adam and ultimately to God, may be an innocent addition, the kind of plausible etiology that so frequently decorates the pages of the two Alfonsine histories. It may, however, be something more. The effect of all these additions is, of course, to enhance the standing of astrology and of learning generally.

---

1. Alfonso 1930, 20. References to this portion of the *Estoria* will be to this edition; references to the second part will be to Alfonso 1957–61.

2. Josephus 1958, 132. References to the Latin version of the *Antiquities* will henceforth be to this edition.

Josephus's history, with its Stoic bias, introduces the lore of the stars early in his narrative—he attributes this science to Seth and his offspring—but the Alfonsine committee pushes it back one generation to the very beginning of the race and ultimately to God Himself. All of this could be entirely deliberate. Less than two decades ago, Francisco Rico devoted pages in his study of the *Estoria* to the large and important place of astrology and natural philosophy in its world. He points to many passages where the mammoth compilation welcomes texts that treat astrology as one of the greatest human accomplishments.[3] It should be made quite clear that this focus on stars and natural philosophy does not depend exclusively on the editors' skills as compilers. In at least two passages these scribes strike out on their own and make points about astrology that are nowhere in their sources. The first of the pair has to do with the famous "pillars of wisdom." Adam foresees the twofold destruction of the world by water and fire, and the Sethites, fearing that their precious star-lore will be lost, construct two pillars— one of brick to withstand the fire, and the other of stone to survive the water—and on both they inscribe the fruit of their learning. This is Josephus's account (1958, 132). The Alfonsines do not leave this story as they find it. They take over, largely from Josephus once again (1958, 131), a long account of the mechanical arts and of material culture generally. Cain invents boundaries and weights and measures and builds the first cities, Tubal invents metallurgy, Jabel invents tents and hus- bandry, and so on (Alfonso 1930, 11–15). Now, in Josephus, this whole development carries a negative sign. Material progress is tainted by the wickedness of its inventors, the Cainites, and in any case, to the semi- Stoic Josephus this set of inventions represents a departure from the simple life in harmony with nature and is therefore essentially perverse. The Alfonsines do little to soften this picture, but they make a very important addition. In their version all this practical knowledge is also inscribed on the two pillars, along with the liberal (Alfonso 1930, 14). The writing on the pillars, therefore, is made up of two contrasting texts, one worldly, touched by sin, and the other holy, the fruit of righteousness. This dramatic pairing is, as I say, entirely the doing of the Alfonsines: Josephus knows nothing about the inscription of the Cainite lore, and Petrus Comestor, curiously, limits the writing on the pillars to

---

3. Rico 1972, 123–56.

Jubal's art of music (Petrus Comestor, column 1079). The rhetorical effect of this little expansion is, of course, to emphasize by contrast the essential holiness of the Sethite enterprise. This in turn puts even greater stress on the knowledge-piety pair already in Josephus but augmented and amplified in the *Estoria*.

This common element is distinctive. The harmonies do not end here. Our second original text also develops a pro-astrology strain alien to the *Estoria*'s sources. Alfonso inherits from Josephus a remarkable motif, the idea that the patriarch Abraham was the first monotheist, in effect, the first natural theologian: a student of the stars, of their motions, and of their effects on the world below, he was the first to show that the spheres could not impart their blessings to humans unless they were guided, and indeed had been created, by a superior being (Josephus 1958, 143–44). The compilers bolster this theme by virtually inventing its prehistory: they effectively create a narrative that tells of the slow progress of the race toward a true conception of divinity.[4] First, humans worshiped stones, then animate beings; first plants and then animals; land dwellers first and afterward fish. But realizing that the interplay of the elements underlay all this generation of species, they turned the elements themselves into objects of cult, earth first and then, in order, water, air, and fire. But the dance of the elements, producing all the variety of the world, was not itself a sufficient explanation of this splendid show; only the stars and their influence could account fully for the way earth, water, and the rest combined to make our world what it was. These heavenly beings, then, became the gods of our ancestors. It is only at this point in the story that Abraham appears, bringing the history of religion to its term: for him only did the stars speak directly of the one true God. This passage, almost entirely new, also harmonizes with our little etiology about the Sethites and their science: not only do both texts glorify star-lore, but both also maintain the thematic bond between astrology and piety. The Sethites' holiness disposes them to a knowledge of the heavens and their Creator, while Abraham completes the generations-long search for the only genuine divinity and teaches humans henceforth to see always the hand of God in the motions of the heavens. One could add that the knowledge-piety pair in the history of religion may be more closely allied than it seems. The narrative is in

---

4. Alfonso 1930, 62–68 passim. I point out that this development, virtually original, is an extensive and daring expansion of the source, Lucas of Tuy 1608, 21.

reality a systematic *itinerarium mentis in Deum:* as I once tried to point out, the text could be read as an ascent of the mind to God through a hierarchy of ever more general and powerful causes.[5]

The brief amplification in the narrative about Seth might, therefore, have a rhetorical function, the highlighting of a theme that is to be important later in the *Estoria*. But there are puzzling features in our cluster of passages. The single bit of information that Seth's knowledge comes from Adam, or, in effect, that Adam is the true father of science, poses problems. The motif is assuredly not in any of the history's better-known sources for its biblical history: it is in neither Josephus nor Petrus Comestor—the Eusebius-Jerome chronologies do not cover the beginning of the race. What is the origin of this element? This is simply not an easy question. The Alfonsines' information about Adam and Seth is certainly not unique, but the pathway to their text is obscure. Late antiquity knew that learning and science begin with Adam and that he was the first astrologer; this theme was widespread in the Renaissance, as was the notion that his knowledge came from God.[6] But aside from the *Estoria*, the only Western Christian medieval text known to me that floats either concept is the *Parzival* of Wolfram of Eschenbach: the possibility that this work influenced the editors of our text is of course very slim. Wolfram says simply that our father Adam knew of the motions of the spheres and of their powers over the things of earth.[7] But as I say, the *Parzival* does not do great things for our cause. A hint as to what might be brewing in Alfonso's history could be lurking in an important Renaissance text, one that seems to recover many themes of interest to Alfonso the Learned and his circle. Paracelsus's *The Aurora of the Philosophers* appears to echo many of the motifs of our history. Adam is the inventor of arts and sciences. His lore is preserved for the postdiluvians in hieroglyphics inscribed on the two pillars: these were found by Noah on Mount Ararat after the Flood. Abraham, astrologer and mathematician, carried his secret lore from Canaan to Egypt, whence it was passed on to the rest of the world.[8] The significant detail

---

5. See the essay immediately preceding this one in this book, "Abraham in the *General estoria.*"

6. For the Hermetic view of Adam's knowledge in antiquity, see Festugière 1944, 268, in a quotation from Zosimus, and 334–35. For the theme of Adam the astrologer in the Renaissance, see Allen 1941, 34, 67, 85, 134, and 136.

7. Wolfram von Eschenbach 1974, 518, 1–8.

8. Paracelsus 1894, 45–50, cited in Shumaker 1972, 182.

here is the hieroglyphics: this motif inevitably connotes things Egyptian and Hermetic. And indeed, Paracelsus's text elsewhere does speak at length of the Thrice Great Hermes. We might therefore ask if the tracing of liberal knowledge back to Adam has some sort of connection to Hermeticism itself. We know that the Hermetic myth always claims great antiquity for its sacred doctrine and its first teacher, and we also know that Hermes was at times identified with the biblical Enoch, son of Jared, and with the Koranic Idris. But did medieval Jews, Muslims, and Christians of Hermetic bias ever push things back to the beginning of the race? The answer is that they did. A late Muslim thinker, Sadi al-Din Shirazi, declares that "wisdom originally began with Adam and his progeny, Seth and Hermes, i.e. Idris, and Noah, because the world is never deprived of a person upon whom the science of unity and eschatology rests." A modern commentator identifies this author as "the greatest of the later Muslim sages."[9] I know little about Islam, but it seems incredible to me that the mention of Adam here has no sanction in the tradition. And indeed, at least one Islamic text that antedates the *Estoria* also speaks of Adam as the first to study the heavens. Abu Ma'shar, in the ninth century, tells us that Hermes/Enoch/Idris learned from Adam the hours of the day and night, and that the latter was versed in the ways of the heavens.[10] We should note that Henry and Renée Kahane, who in their study of Wolfram's *Parzival* propose for its whole argument a background of Islamic Hermeticism, point to the text by Abu Ma'shar precisely to explain, more or less, the association Wolfram makes between Adam and star-lore.[11] I would add that the information in Abu Ma'shar may in turn have come to him from late antiquity: certain early texts do connect astrology with Adam, as we have seen, and some actually equate him with Hermes.[12] The notion, then, that the father of the race is also the father of science is ancient and, at the very least, is not alien to Islamic literature of Hermetic tendency. It may be, there-

9. Nasr 1981, 106, has the quotation from Sadi al-Din Shirazi and identifies him as "the greatest of the later Muslim sages."

10. The lines from Abu Ma'shar are from the *'Uyun al-anba'* of Ibn Abi Usaibi'a. The passage is quoted in English in Plessner 1954, 51, quoted in turn by Kahane, Kahane, and Pietrangeli 1984, 119.

11. Kahane, Kahane, and Pietrangeli 1984, 119–20.

12. See page references to Festugière in n. 6: the text from Zosimus equates Adam himself with Hermes, and Festugière in the other citation mentions texts in which Adam teaches astrology to Seth or to Enoch.

fore, not implausible that the text of Abu Ma'shar, or one like it, might be the source of the motif in the *Estoria,* and that this element in Alfonso's work might be in some sense Hermetic. We must not be put off by the fact that in the *Estoria* the beneficiary of Adam's teaching was not Enoch but Seth. The text attributing star-lore to him is indeed Josephan, but there are for a fact Islamic Hermeticist writings that make Seth the first astronomer and that also identify him with Hermes.[13] We should note that in Alfonso, Enoch himself poses a certain difficulty: in the first part he is in no way singled out for his science (Alfonso 1930, 21–22). It is hard to judge exactly what is going on in this passage, but we should remember that Alfonso and his fellow historians were not in the habit of leaving things as they were: their hand may be heavy in just this episode.

Can we carry this matter of Hermeticism further? Is this strain in any way a factor in the formation of the *General estoria* and its conceptions generally, or at least beyond the details we have considered? The information that Adam instructed Seth in the ways of the heavens may open up just this possibility. So also, as I would add, may the notion that Adam acquired his lore directly from God. If there is a recurring theme in the Hermetic texts, it is that their great doctrine is not simply one philosophy more but a gift of Heaven.[14] But the general question of whether Hermeticism has some large or small part in the makeup of the *Estoria* and the themes and ideas it sets forth may seem an unmanageable one. On one hand, the large body of ostensibly Hermetic texts from many different periods and milieus sets forth doctrines and teachings of a variety that is genuinely chaotic. On the other, the possibility of a Hermetic strain in the *Estoria* challenges much of what we know about the sources of the work. We would have to conclude either that the Hermetic material came from "authorities" as yet unidentified or that the influence of Hermeticism was diffuse, not easily linked to any particular sources. The essence of our first difficulty is the question of definition: "What is Hermeticism?" The only honest answer is not an encouraging one. Hermeticism is a phantom, something reducible to a hundred special cases, a loosely connected set of topics on dozens of questions, practical, alchemical, magical, astrological, philosophical, and religious. I am not suggesting that the very genuine question of what

---

13. Massignon 1944, 390.
14. Fowden 1986, 32: "The Hermetica are presented as revelations of divine truth, not as the products of human reason."

thematic elements in the *General estoria* might be called Hermetic is meaningless. There is, in any case, a shortcut. In a way, the defining element in Hermetic literature, the one factor that makes it definitively Hermetic, is not at all doctrinal or thematic but narrative and formal.[15] In the Hermetic text, the fount of wisdom, the ageless teacher, who may actually make his appearance in the narrative, is the Thrice Great One himself, Hermes Trismegistus. Less essential characters are the ones who surround the sage, his disciple Asclepius, the godlike Poimandres, and Tat, who is sometimes Hermes himself, sometimes his son, and sometimes merely a disciple. It is really this narrative apparatus that defines the Hermetic discourse, content regardless. In Jewish, Christian, and Muslim Hermetic literature, as we have seen, there is one further element, the identification of Hermes with personages in the Bible, normally Enoch, at times Seth, or the Koranic Idris. Where then does the *Estoria* stand with respect to this mythology? The answer, as I think, is a complicated one, in great part because the *Estoria* itself is difficult to read. In the first part the mythology is gutted almost completely, as we have seen. Discounting Adam, the great source of liberal knowledge is not Enoch but Seth. Seth is indeed sometimes equated with Hermes, as we have seen, but the Alfonsines do not tell us this directly or otherwise: they say not a word about Hermes at this point, and in fact, the privileged place of Seth in the *Estoria* comes to it from the very un-Hermetic Josephus. One should add that the editors of the chronicle present Enoch, son of Jared, much as the Bible does, as a holy man whom God removes from the human scene: nothing whatever is said about his science. At the very best, the Hermetic element in these early chapters is very weak. The figure of Seth is indeed a kind of Hermes substitute: his cosmological wisdom does come ultimately from God, and this factor is not wholly negligible. But this is thin broth: some of the substance of the Hermetic message may be present, but the narrative, the mythology, has all but disappeared.

But the second part of the *Estoria* brings us a complete turnabout. Hermes, Tat, and Asclepius are out in force, and the connection with Enoch is made explicit. The text, following Eusebius, begins by distinguishing three Hermes: first, Trismegistus, identified with the "god" Mercury; second, his son, also known as Tat; and third, one of whom we

---

15. Fowden 1986, 32. For the survival of these patterns in Islamic Hermeticism, see Nasr 1981, 106 and passim, 107–16.

hear nothing (Alfonso 1957–61, 1:34–35). Most significantly, our text assigns the first Hermes to the time of Joshua. Pages later, indeed, this Hermes is identified with Enoch: we will consider this equivalence presently. Once our main character is presented, a strange narrative gets under way, one very unlike those of the writings in the ancient *Corpus hermeticum*. Asclepius, unidentified, has come into possession of a book by Hermes written in characters he cannot read. In time he finds an interpreter, an old woman who claims to be of the race of the giants and, not least, a niece to Nimrod. The letters, she says, are those of the giants, her own people. Asclepius, learned in biblical history, needs clarification. There were many generations of giants: with which was the alphabet associated? Her pregnant answer follows. It was a generation notable for three things: for its great public works, its roads, canals, and castles; for its domination over other peoples; and for being the first to have knowledge of the stars and their motions. Her account then moves on to Hermes Trismegistus himself. Hermes, also called Enoch, was not himself a giant but was kin to them; he was the father of philosophers. He of all men was the one with the greatest desire and the greatest capacity to learn about the things of earth and the secrets of the heavens. It is said of him that he spent more than thirty years *de suso*, "aloft," perfecting this latter knowledge (35–37). This last motif of course echoes a very ancient theme in the tradition. Hermes, thanks to his status as god, was thought to be able to comprehend the heavens and its mysteries and, having done so, to have transmitted this divine knowledge to humans. More significantly, perhaps, an Arab legend has it that Hermes/Idris was taken up into the celestial spheres and then carried back to earth to teach astronomy to his fellow beings.[16] We could add that the *Estoria*'s account of Hermes/Enoch gives us what we might consider a solid lead in our search for the possible Hermeticism of the work. The rest of the old woman's account does not interest us. The critical moment in the story comes when Asclepius asks her to explain the strange characters that appear in his book. Her answer is remarkable. They are not, apparently, ordinary letters. In a complicated way we need not consider, they represent the seven planets, the twelve signs of the zodiac, and the twenty-four hours of the day. She makes a great

---

16. See the Stobaean fragments of the treatise *Kore kosmon*, in *Corpus hermeticum* 1954, 1–3; Festugière is the editor of this particular text; Kahane, Kahane, and Pietrangeli 1969, 451.

claim for these strange marks. All the past and all the future is ciphered in them, just as they are in the heavens themselves. She emphasizes that the power of these figures rests in the fact that they actually resemble the patterns made by the stars in the sky (39). We will return to this remarkable book presently.

This is not the place to comment on all the difficulties posed by the Hermes narrative in the *General estoria*. Suffice it to say that neither of the two Alfonsine histories is a seamless garment. The chronology here is strange. Enoch appears late. There is no suggestion that our Enoch/ Hermes is not the one in Genesis or in the first part, but here he is placed in the time of Joshua. Beyond that, the text equates Hermes with the first of the three Mercurys, who is, in turn, the son of the euhemerized Jupiter, in the *Estoria* a contemporary of the patriarch Jacob, well after the Flood (Alfonso 1930, 179 ff.). Finally, we could point to a further anomaly, the fact that the account of Enoch in the first part in no way anticipates the passage about him in the second. My suspicion is that the source text—unknown to me and apparently also to Solalinde, the great authority in these matters[17]—made the standard equation between Hermes and Enoch, but that the Alfonsines, having linked him to the euhemerized Mercury, were forced to put him into an inappropriate time slot. Whatever the explanation, the resulting text is assuredly not tidy.

But in all this confusion one thing is certain: Hermes Trismegistus is a character in the *General estoria*, and his name is associated, at least vaguely, with a certain significant teaching. Let us consider the latter point. The passage in part 2 includes two very powerful texts that bear on our problem: the lines describing Enoch-Hermes and his lore, and the account of Asclepius's wonderful book. In the first place, we are presented with no one less than the father of philosophers, "el padre de todos los philosophos" (Alfonso 1957–61, 1:37), a man who strove for and achieved the fullest knowledge of the things of the heavens and of those of earth. It is suggested that his access to the truth was somehow privileged in that he spent some thirty years aloft, close to his celestial subject. For the Alfonsines, *Philosopher* almost certainly means "liberal

---

17. I have in my possession a mimeographed index of the sources of the *General estoria* given me by a former graduate student at the University of Wisconsin (Dr. John Ginzler), a text supposedly put together by Solalinde. The entry "Hermes" sends us to the passage I am speaking of but states that its source has not been found.

artist."[18] If so, the air is cleared considerably; things click as we recall the repertory of arts and sciences of the Sethites, seven arts plus physics and theology. This is weighty stuff indeed, which makes especially good sense to old readers of our history. The Hermes of the *Estoria*, along with Abraham, the euhemerized Prometheus and Atlas, and many others, is one of the typical "philosophers," liberal artists and heroes of the life of the mind, that decorate the pages of the great Alfonsine text. The teachings of the Thrice Great are those we have encountered before, connected precisely with some of these persons—astrology and its dependent science, natural philosophy. With respect to our other passage we can say that Hermes is associated there with what we could call the total book: the mysterious symbols that make it up refer to virtually everything in heaven and earth, the motions of the spheres and all things human—past, present, and future—that depend on them. Hermes, the author of the text, becomes, perhaps more than any other character in the *Estoria*, the bearer of total knowledge. These elements should be seen in context: the high value of the seven arts, especially astronomy/astrology, and the close alliance of the latter with natural theology and the knowledge of God are matters the editors of the *Estoria* hardly neglect, and in this setting it is plain that they meant our two motifs in the Hermes story to be important moments in this scene and in their whole narrative. One should add in particular that the mysterious nature of Hermes's knowledge and the prodigious, indeed, preternatural, character of his book harmonize in some way with the proposition in part 1 that Adam's astrological lore was the product of divine inspiration: the two elements do not quite mesh as far as narrative detail is concerned, but they are surely akin thematically.

The close link the *Estoria* forges between cosmic knowledge and piety is, as I believe, the main inheritance the Alfonsines received from Hermeticism. Aside from the bits of evidence we have come upon to date, there are, as I think, two solid reasons for making the connection. The first is the prominence of the astrology/piety theme in Hermetic literature, and the second is the feebleness of certain other hypotheses. On the first score, we may assert that the linking of the science of the heavens to the search for God is virtually omnipresent in philosophical Hermeticism. The all-important *Asclepius*, for example, ancient and

---

18. Huygens 1970, passim. One should add that Muslims also call Hermes the father of philosophers (Nasr 1981, 100).

Greek, but in its Latin version widely copied in the Middle Ages,[19] is a
telling case in point. Its opening pages run more or less as follows. Once
preliminaries have been disposed of, Hermes gives a long account of the
unity in diversity in all things, and of the divine One that is its origin.
This cosmic vision has God, perhaps a sort of Platonic trinity, at its apex,
with undifferentiated matter at its other extreme. Divinity, apparently at
several removes, encounters matter, and the incalculable number of
species of earthly things is the result: these are in God first but end by
having a partially independent existence. The middle rung in this great
ladder of being is the heavens, which Hermes significantly calls the
"visible god" [sensibilis deus]. The heavens administer all bodily things,
presiding over their generation and corruption, their waxing and wan-
ing. But lurking behind this visible god is the creator himself, and the
former's working is simply the mediation of the greater god's power
(*Corpus hermeticum* 1945, 298–300). These ideas are in no way peculiar
to the *Asclepius*. A whole range of Hermetic texts repeats in various
forms these very notions. Crucial to many of these writings is the view
that knowledge of the heavens and of the things on earth that depend on
them is the eminent way to the understanding of the greater god or gods
that preside over the whole system. It should further be emphasized that
the *Asclepius* and writings like it are devout texts: the reflections they
propose about the cosmic order are supposed to awaken in the spirit a
longing for God and immortality. Obviously, none of this general doctrine is in any way alien to the message of the *General estoria:* Abraham,
Seth, and Hermes all represent much the same enterprise outlined in the
Asclepius, or in the philosophical Hermetica as a whole. Lest it be
thought that the *Asclepius*, in my paraphrase, is too narrow a base for
argument, we may consider a very different text, one actually translated
within the Alfonsine circle. The *Goal of the Sage*, also known under the
Latin title *Picatrix*, is an Arabic Hermetic treatise of the eleventh century: it is largely on astrological magic, but sections of it set forth philosophical and religious themes. In its terms, astrological lore is the

---

19. *Corpus hermeticum* 1945, 298–300, had the passage I have paraphrased. Nock, in
his introduction (*Corpus hermeticum* 1945, 259), and Fowden (1986, 6) tell us that the
Greek original was in existence by the early fourth century. Nock bases his edition on
seven manuscripts, all medieval; four are from the twelfth century, and the rest are more
recent (*Corpus hermeticum* 1945, 259–64).

knowledge the first sage . . . has in mind when he says: "I am he who was lifted up above the seven spheres"; for with the expression "was lifted" he alludes to scientific understanding by means of thought. The same is also hinted at in the word of God which says: "We lifted him to a lofty place." (Kahane's translation)

The modern editor does not hesitate to associate the passage and its message with Hermetic speculation.[20] The one "who was lifted" is, of course, Hermes/Idris, the first astronomer.

Professor Rico's reflections about the *Estoria* and its world of thought are relevant here. He speaks of the archaism of the work, the twelfth-century flavor of some of its conceptions: he mentions in particular the arts curriculum that keeps getting associated with certain characters in the book (as we have seen). These curricular schemes have more in them of twelfth-century Chartres than of thirteenth-century Paris. And more important, the notion that the study of the cosmos leads to a knowledge of God is surely one many twelfth-century masters made their own.[21] But what needs to be emphasized is that Hermeticism is a large ingredient in this whole mix: the *Asclepius*, once again, is one of the great texts for this age and this generation: the traces of the work in the writings of the time are widespread and conspicuous.[22] If indeed the Alfonsines took a great leap backward when they formed their ideas, it would be in no way remarkable if their repertory included certain Hermetic elements.

But is the knowledge-piety pair distinctively Hermetic? Is it so easy to eliminate other possibilities? Do we really need Abu Ma'shar and his sort to explain the presence of this great theme in the *Estoria*? I am not an authority on the forms of devotion in the Europe of Alfonso's time, but it is not my impression that spiritual writers of the time advised their readers to study the stars and the things below that depend on them, or that this was the sure way to the love of God. Scholasticism also is an unlikely choice for an influence on the editors of the *Estoria*. One could, of course, be tempted to look in this direction, since at least the earlier

---

20. *Picatrix* 1962; quoted in Kahane, Kahane, and Pietrangeli 1969, 451. Nasr 1993, 152, cites a text that speaks of the zodiac as the "face of the Beloved."

21. Rico 1972, 155–56.

22. See Nock, introduction to the *Corpus hermeticum* 1945, 266–68, and for Bernard Silvester in particular, see Stock 1972, 102–4 and passim.

scholastic theologians tended to accept planetary influences in some form: conceivably the Alfonsines could have picked up their cosmic piety from them. But the point is trivial: the notion that heavens and earth are linked is common to many philosophies and is not especially scholastic. History, in any case, is the great stumbling block: in the Castile of Alfonso's day scholasticism is not a large feature on the landscape. Not until the middle of the fourteenth century did a scholastic theologian actually teach in a Castilian university, and indeed, the university curriculum the Learned King sets forth in the *Siete partidas* is, with the all-important addition of law, much like the ones I have alluded to in this study and very unlike that of the universities in which scholastic theology was the main discipline.[23] One could of course say that scholasticism has little place in a vernacular chronicle, or that, certain famous exceptions aside, the impact of scholastic thought on vernacular literature was small. But this is not a pertinent argument. The *Estoria* is not at all shy speaking of God, of causes, or of the Great Chain of Being. Obviously, there is a large dose of natural philosophy in the work, but it so happens that this philosophy is not scholastic. I do not mean to oversimplify. The argument from design—the one that impresses the Alfonsines—is not very characteristic of scholastic theology. Bonaventure asserts that God is the first object in the human mind: in other words, he accepts a form of the ontological argument. Thomas has his Five Ways: humans know God through creatures and not through Himself. Henry of Ghent accepts the ontological argument. In a sense; so does Duns Scotus. He argues to God from contingency and necessity: one cannot think of one without the other.[24] None of this has much to do with the theology of the Alfonsine Abraham, Seth, or Hermes. And in conclusion one could perhaps say that Alfonso's great master and teacher may have been none of these theologians, not Thomas or Bonaventure, but a much more ancient one, the Thrice Great Hermes himself.

---

23. Nader 1979, 146–47.

24. All this information comes from a popular manual of medieval philosophy, Knowles 1962, 245–46 for Bonaventure, 261 for Thomas, 302 for Henry of Ghent, and 305 for Duns Scotus.

The *General estoria:* Material Culture and Hermeticism

Hermes the Thrice Great, depository of the secrets of God, mystagogue, inventor of arts and sciences, is no stranger to the Alfonsine *General estoria*. His appearance there is brief, but it is not unimportant (Alfonso 1957, 1:34–39). The editors of the chronicle tell us that he is nothing less than the father of philosophers, a resident of the heavens for thirty years and hence a privileged astrologer; they identify him with the biblical Enoch. They also declare him the author of a prodigious book, one that would exceed the imagination of even a Borges. Its scope is not modest: it is about human history entire, past, present, and future. Alas, this text is not accessible to ordinary readers, for it is written in cipher: essentially its characters represent the planets and the fixed stars in all of their possible positions. But its mystery is also its power: it contains the whole of astrology, obviously, and consequently can speak of the heavenly causes of every event in the sublunary world without exception.

This extraordinary volume appears in the *General estoria* as the innermost of a nest of boxes. As we read in Alfonso, Hermes' great opus, of which we get to see not a single line, is mentioned in a second book, by a certain Asclepius. In it this second author tells us of his discovery of the miraculous text. He informs us that a happy fortune put the volume of Hermes in his hands, all to his great joy, because he judged that the book contained ancient wisdom long forgotten. His first task, plainly, was to find an interpreter, since he was unable to understand a single word. After a long search he meets Gogligobon, a woman of great age, of the race of the giants, a niece of Nimrod, herself a person of prodigious wisdom and science. Asclepius becomes her disciple and so acquires great knowledge. In time, of course, he shows her the all-important book. She immediately recognizes its characters as those used in the writings of her own people and imparts its lore to her student. But as I have said, her teaching does not end there. Asclepius also learns from her of the extraordinary achievements of the giants themselves, in the liberal arts and in the mechanical. As the *Estoria* presents the matter, a great part of this second book, the one by Asclepius, is given over to the information about the giants conveyed to him by Gogligobon.

This memorable text is the second box in our nest. The third and outermost is the *Estoria* itself. Asclepius is for the Alfonsines a genuine *auctor,* a major source for the subject at hand, which is the life and career of Hermes, here also called Tat. But before we get to read in the book, the Thrice Great One must be introduced. Hermes-Tat belongs to the time of Joshua and is the last of a series of three to bear the name Hermes. This particular one is the son of the second of the trio. Of the first we hear nothing. This last, Tat or Hermes Trismegistus, is further identified with Mercury, whom the ancients worshiped as the god of commerce and of the trivium. His mastery of the three arts of grammar, dialectic, and rhetoric was what earned for him the name Trismegistus. All three Hermes were philosophers renowned for their wisdom and learning, but the third, Tat-Hermes-Mercury, was the wisest and greatest of the lot. More commentary follows in the *Estoria*, but in time the narrator turns to the Asclepius book and uses it to complete his story.

The whole Hermes passage is obscure. The linkage to Mercury is troublesome. Mercury, son of Jupiter, appears in part 1 of the *Estoria*, in the Genesis section, a contemporary of Abraham (Alfonso 1930, 160–62). For the editors to stretch out his life to reach the days of Joshua would imply prodigious age, like that of the patriarchs. It is of course possible that the editors really, or originally, meant to identify him not with the third Hermes but with the second, but that is not what the text says. The complications do not end here. Gogligobon, niece to Nimrod, of the race of the postdiluvian giants, identifies Hermes as their contemporary, though not one of them. But in virtually the same breath we are told that he is identical to Enoch, who of course lived well before the Flood. "Asclepius" also tells us that the great teacher spent thirty years in the heaven studying their motions. As we will see, this motif is borrowed, directly or otherwise, from an important Islamic text, but there it is presented as one of the prodigies not of the third Hermes or of the second, but of the first, identified with the Koranic Idris and the biblical Enoch. Finally, we must note that the fit between the Asclepius book and the matter that precedes it in the *Estoria* is not very close. Our text places Hermes in the time of Joshua, not at all in that of Nimrod or the mighty men. In general one would conclude that the hand of the compilers, very secure in other parts of the *Estoria*, was rather lax here, leaving more than one anomaly to bedevil us. It might not be far wrong to guess that the second-order book itself is not a seamless garment, that the editors did some of their careless sewing here as well.

Such, then, is the layout of the Tat-Hermes episode in the *General estoria*. Let us start by focusing still further on the weightiest part of the passage, the Asclepius book itself. What is its origin and history? It must be repeated, first of all, that Asclepius is a genuine Alfonsine *auctor*; for the compilers Hermes's own writings are a matter of report, a piece of history, but Asclepius is actually a source, quoted, or at least paraphrased. To be sure, its contradictions may be the sign of some sort of editorial tampering, but there is undoubtedly an independent text here, with a profile and personality of its own. As far as I know, the source of the Asclepius passage has not been found. I am witness that Solalinde, our great authority in the matter of Alfonsine sources, was at a loss here.[1] He could not, however, fail to see the Islamic coloring of these lines; indeed, it is hard to miss. In any case, even if we cannot locate the original Asclepius book, the history and background of the lines in Alfonso need not be completely obscure. As one might guess, an acquaintance with things Hermetic sheds a good deal of light here: the passage in the *Estoria* is not, after all, the only medieval text to speak of the Thrice Great One. What concept do the Alfonsines have of their hero? In this text he is linked to the giants. Our access to him is, of course, through Gogligobon, and in her account the accomplishments of both run parallel. Hermes, as we have seen, is not himself a giant but a contemporary of theirs, one who shares many interests with them. What is most significant about them all is that they all, Hermes and the mighty men alike, are founders; they are not simply adepts in astrology and natural philosophy but are actually inventors of these sciences.[2] The mysterious signs that make up the book of

---

1. I have in my possession a mimeographed index of the sources of the *General estoria* given me by Dr. John Ginzler, a former graduate student at the University of Wisconsin. This text was supposed to represent Solalinde's work. The entry "Hermes Trismegisto" refers to the passage I am discussing but declares that its source has not been found.

2. One should understand that the *General estoria* is not at all consistent in attributing inventions to its characters. Astrology, for example, here said to have been invented by Hermes and the giants, is elsewhere attributed to Seth or even to Adam (Alfonso 1930, 20–21).

Hermes are, after all, the common written language of the giants. We are also told separately that Hermes-Enoch is the father of philosophers, "el padre de todos los philosophos" (Alfonso 1957–61, 1:37). In medieval parlance, *Philosopher* means "liberal artist,"[3] and the queen of arts for the Alfonsines is, of course, astrology. He is, therefore, at the very beginnings of systematic knowledge. But in the *Estoria* account, the giants were themselves also the first to come to know the heavens and their motions and the nature of the four elements; in Gogligobon's words, "fueron los primeros omnes que mesuraron los cursos de las estrellas e los mouimientos de los cielos, e lo sopieron todo, et connoscieron el poder e las naturas de los quatro elementos" [They were the first humans who measured the course of the stars and the movements of the heavens, and they knew all this [astronomy], and they were acquainted with the power and the nature of the four elements] (36–37). But in her account the giants are pioneers in another sense: they were the founders of the arts of civilization, the inventors of material culture. The text gives two passages to this effect. In one we are given their collective accomplishments: their splendid buildings, unlike any then in existence; their roads, some of which opened up areas until then impassable; the clearing of wild places; their topographical science and skill at finding sites for their cities; and finally, their great metropolitan centers themselves (36). The second account is a list of seven great inventors among the giants, of the uses of fire, of letters and writing, of stonework and architecture, of ironwork, of silversmithing, of carpentry, and of work in ceramics (37–38). Material culture, in a word, is the creation of the mighty men.

Liberal knowledge, mechanical knowledge—is this linkage a Hermetic theme? This question is, more or less, the one we must ask if we wish to learn something about the race and lineage of the Asclepius book. Let us begin with Hermeticism itself. From the time the *Estoria* was composed back to antiquity the name Hermes has accumulated a wide range of associations; the range is wider than one would like, much wider, obviously, than we can deal with here. But as we descend to particulars the scope narrows. In a classic article, Henry and Renée

---

3. The information is well known. The equation between philosopher and liberal artist is assumed throughout the texts collected in Huygens 1970. It should be noted that Muslims also call Hermes the father of philosophers; see Nasr 1981, 100.

Kahane have already dealt with the very special question of Hermetic influence on Alfonso and his circle (Kahane, Kahane, and Pietrangeli 1969, 443–57). Without wishing to air all the ins and outs of their argument I would comment as follows. Their study examines mainly three Romance texts taken ultimately from Arabic originals: the *Bocados de oro*, known to the Alfonsines; and the *Picatrix* and the *Libro de las estrellas fixas*, both translated by them. In the Kahanes' presentation the moral philosophy and the spirituality of the *Bocados* is recognizably Hermetic, while the *Picatrix*, a work primarily on astrological magic, in some of its passages gives expression to a metaphysics and a cosmology of clearly Hermetic stamp. For its part the *Libro de las estrellas fixas* contains an allusion to the Krater, the Hermetic vessel of gnosis. Globally the Kahanes' message is that Hermeticism comes to Alfonso's Castile in Arabic and Muslim dress. This capitally important point is one I believe I can confirm with an observation of my own. As I have mentioned, the motif of Hermes's thirty-year residence in the heavens, a crucial element in the *Estoria*'s account, does appear also in an Islamic text. The *Rasa'il* of the Brethren of Purity, the Ikwan al-Safa, says of the sage:

> Hermes Trismegistus, that is, the prophet Idris, rose up to the sphere [of Saturn] and moved with it for thirty years until he had observed all its properties, and then he did the same with the other spheres, and finally he went down to earth [once again], where he instructed men in the knowledge of the stars. (Quoted in *Picatrix* 1962, 11 n; the translation from Plessner's German is mine)

Solalinde's suspicion that the Asclepius book is somehow Islamic is thus partially vindicated. More important since, as far as I know, the motif of Hermes's thirty-year stay in the heavens in uniquely Islamic (and, as I suspect, quite local), we can be fairly certain that the Alfonsine editors of the *Estoria* were acquainted with at least one Islamic text of Hermetic coloring. There is, let us note, no reason to exclude in principle the possibility of Latin Hermetic influence on the Alfonsines. The wake of the Antique *Latin Asclepius* (totally unrelated to our Asclepius book) in twelfth- and thirteenth-century European letters is very wide, and Latin translations and reworkings of Arabic Hermetic literature are also extensive.[4] But it is my impression that none of this material has very much bearing on the patently Hermetic portions of the *Estoria.*

Islamic Hermeticism has its own history and its own complexities. Its own range is for its part astonishing; it is hard to think of this literature as having any single focus. But for all of that, the two great themes of our Asclepius book, the beginnings of the liberal arts, astrology and natural philosophy, and the beginnings of material culture, are relatively easy to trace to their Hermetic roots. We must backtrack. Hermeticism is, of course, a religious and philosophical current with its origins in antiquity. The incorporation of this strain into Islam is undoubtedly one of the strangest episodes in the history of that religion. The details of the story do not concern us. What is significant for us is that Hermes, originally a pagan god and eventually the mystagogue figure in the body of writings now known as the *Corpus hermeticum,* gets identified with the Koranic prophet Idris (as well as with the biblical Enoch) and thus becomes a major actor and personage in Islamic sacred history. As I suggested, Islamic Hermetic literature could cover several provinces, but in this case I am not speaking of a theme scattered randomly over a few texts in that vast body of literature. The assimilation Hermes-Idris belongs to *hadith,* Koranic commentary, and thus to Islamic historiography of a fairly central sort (Lory 1988). Now a great deal of what we learn about Hermes-Idris in these writings is eminently pertinent to our theme. He figures there as the civilizing hero sent by God to impart the arts, liberal and mechanical, to primitive humanity. He has several missions. He teaches architecture—sacred and profane—the building of cities, mathematics, astrology, and medicine. This last is understood to include natural philosophy and even cosmology and has no small connection with sympathetic magic. He is sent by God. We must understand that architecture, medicine, and the rest are by no means his personal discoveries. They are a divine revelation, conveyed to him from the other world. We must also note that the speculative side of his teaching is essentially a theosophy: astrology and the rest are supposed to raise the mind of the adept to thoughts of divinity.

We can now make the comparison between the contents of the

---

4. For the influence of the *Latin Asclepius* on European letters, see Nock's introduction to that text in *Corpus hermeticum* 1945, 266–68. For the influence of both the *Asclepius* and of Muslim Hermeticism in Latin translation and paraphrase on Bernard Silvester, see Stock 1972, 102–5 passim.

Asclepius book and this Hermetic lore in some further detail. The doctrine of the three Hermes is, as we must note, a feature of the Arabic material. The first Hermes lived before the Flood, is called Idris in Arabic, and is identified by the Jews with Enoch. In one account, that of Abu Ma'shar,[5] this Hermes was the first to speak of the motions of the stars and was the inventor of medicine and of sacred architecture. He also invented clothing and the reading of books, the latter apparently created directly by God. Other accounts broaden this architecture to include secular structures and the building of cities; the Muslim authorities are here clearly confusing Enoch son of Jared with Enoch son of Cain. One of this first Hermes's gifts was his ability to read the future, and foreseeing the Flood, he inscribed all this learning on the walls of one of his temples. This theme echoes the one in Josephus about Seth and his offspring inscribing their astrological knowledge on pillars of stone and brick, to survive the Flood and the Conflagration, respectively. Abu Ma'shar's second Hermes was Babylonian and lived after the Flood. He revived the study of medicine, philosophy, and mathematics and was the teacher of Pythagoras. The third Hermes, Egyptian, was a great physician and alchemist and a surveyor who supervised the building of cities. He was also competent in the practical arts—ceramic work, glassblowing, and others. Asclepius was his disciple. All this information obviously sheds light on our Asclepius book and its frame. As we recall, the *Estoria*, like our Arabic texts, speaks of three Hermes. The very appearance in Alfonso of Asclepius is for its part significant. Even though his role in the Spanish text is not strictly the traditional one of Hermes's disciple, his prominence in the story is a clear allusion to the third Hermes in Abu Ma'shar's series. The identification with Tat seems to tell the same story. So also, surely, does the emphasis on mechanical arts and public works. Of course, the Alfonsines transfer these practical inventions from Hermes to the giants. But even this transgression is less than it seems. The giants are the kin of Nimrod, who built the tower of Babel; Gogligobon is his niece. In the medieval Christian tradition Babel is the same as Babylon, the equivalence is made in Josephus (cherished by Christians, virtually a Christian author), and the theme is

---

5. The passage from Abu Ma'shar is quoted in the *'Uyun al-anba'* by Ibn Abi Usaibi'a; the English version of these lines is included in Plessner 1954; the quotation from Abu Ma'shar is on 51–52. On 53, Plessner makes it clear that the account of Abu Ma'shar is but one variant of a widespread archetypical Hermes story.

preserved in the *Estoria* itself (Alfonso 1930, 43–44). As we know, one of the three Hermes—not the third, to be sure, but the second—is actually Babylonian. Finally, there is a series of references in the Asclepius book to the first Islamic Hermes. The text certainly says not a word about Idris, but it does equate the prophet with Enoch, who cannot in any way be connected to either of the postdiluvian Hermes. Making him the first astrologer assuredly ties him to the first Hermes of the three. And as we have already seen, the theme of Hermes-Enoch's thirty-year heavenly journey ties him closely to the Hermes-Idris of Islamic lore. One last observation should be made about the Islamic inheritance of the whole passage in the *Estoria*. I pointed out that for Islam Hermes-Idris is not only a civilizing hero, but a teacher of the ways of God, and that his astrology and natural philosophy were meant to awaken awe and piety in mortals. Ostensibly this strain is missing in the Hermes chapters in the *Estoria:* the references there to the astrology of its hero say nothing about its connection to spirituality and devotion. But in point of fact, the mention of it is unnecessary. From the very earliest chapters of the *Estoria* astrology and piety are linked. The pairing of interests is attributed explicitly there to Seth and his offspring, and it is hinted that it is not alien to Adam himself. The attributing of astrological piety to the father of the human race and to his son is, incidentally, a theme in the Hermetic tradition (see the preceding essay; I speak there of both the link between astrology and piety and Adam as the source of Seth's knowledge).

One could sum up this part of our investigation as follows. Although we are still in the dark about the original of the Asclepius book in the *Estoria*, we can be reasonably sure that most of its themes are traceable to some of those in Islamic Hermetic literature. We must not oversimplify. The match between the information in Alfonso and that in the text of Abu Ma'shar, for example, is far from complete. But the family resemblance is close enough; I do not think the point needs to be pushed further. What is to my mind striking about the parallelism is the emphasis on both sides on the growth of material culture in early human history. This focus is remarkable, I think, for two reasons. First, Christian literature generally does not link material progress as closely to the designs of God as our texts seem to. Occasionally a Western writer will speak of the mechanical arts as a divine remedy for the weakness of humans in their fallen state. More commonly, however, the discovery of one or another practical technique is simply relegated to secular history.

Our second reason is narrower in scope. Medieval universal histories more or less comparable to Alfonso's compilation do not treat material culture with the same focus and emphasis or under quite the same perspective as does the *General estoria*. I will have more to say about this matter presently. This focus and perspective are in any case authentically Alfonsine. The inclusion of the chapters on Hermes in the great Castilian text with its quotations and allusions to the Asclepius book is not a caprice. There are other passages in Alfonso's work in the same mode that also speak eloquently about how under God's blessing humans better their physical conditions and circumstances. What I am suggesting is that the Hermetic materials we have explored and others like it may have influenced the Alfonsine compilers very broadly. Hermes is from the first associated with the practical arts and with letters, and in his Muslim guise, equated with Idris, he is a prophet of the one true God and a bringer of culture. In his two subsequent incarnations the improvement of the race at his hands continues. In other words, the progress of humankind—material, intellectual, and spiritual—comes close to being a part of Islamic sacred history; I am not informed about the state of things nowadays, but at some periods surely, advances in culture were viewed in Islam as an important part of the divine-human story. Since, then, the *General estoria*, untypically for its time and tradition, sets forth similar views in passages other than the ones we have examined, and since we know that the editors knew something about Hermeticism in its Muslim phase, one might guess that the doctrine of progress presented there has generally some kind of Islamic Hermetic background.

I must emphasize that I am speaking here of a diffuse influence, of a broad communication of ideas. The two passages in the *Estoria* I have mentioned are not in any obvious sense Muslim: their known sources are mainly those familiar to Western Latinists of the day, and their flavor generally smacks of nothing particularly Islamic. My first example is notoriously un-Oriental. This bit involves a feather touch, the minimal altering of a source, so typical of the Alfonsines, which changes the sense and drift of the passage as a whole. The *Estoria* inherits from Josephus's *Antiquities of the Jews* the story of the two lines of descent from Adam; the bad, deriving from Cain; and the good, descending from Seth. In Josephus both groups are founders: Seth and his offspring are the first astrologers, while Cain and his descendents are the inventors of the practical arts. The Stoic bias of the *Antiquities* is evident in its treatment of both lines. The good Sethites' knowledge of the heavens is linked there to their love of God, whereas the inventions of the wicked Cain and his line are presented as departures from the simple life of humankind in harmony with nature. Their arts are perverse. Cain's inventions of boundaries and of weights and measures grow out of his greed and lust for power; Tubalcain's metallurgy is the product of his love of bodily pleasures. One should emphasize that Josephus's list of inventors is the biblical one, more or less: Jabal is associated with tents and husbandry, Jubal with music and musical instruments, and Cain and his son Enoch with the first city. Alfonso makes no significant changes in his version of this passage. The Sethites' astrology is of course expanded to all seven liberal arts plus medicine, but there is little else to report. The Pillars of Wisdom are another matter. Josephus tells us that the Sethites, recalling Adam's prediction of general destruction, built two pillars, one of stone, the other of brick, on which they inscribed all their learning, so that it would survive both the Flood and the Conflagration. The Alfonsines preserve all this material (Josephus 1958, 131–32; Alfonso 1930, 11, 14, 20–21) but add a chapter of summary in which all the liberal knowledge of the Sethites is repeated as well as the mechanical knowledge of the Cainites (Alfonso 1930, 20–21). The latter is listed, as it were, without prejudice: the wickedness of those inventions is not once recalled. The passage simply sums up the achievements of the human race, both liberal and mechanical, up to the time of the Flood. Then comes the decisive blow: the editors open up the possibility to their readers that the Cainite lore was written on the pillars as well as the Sethite (21).

One could, of course, take the view that Alfonso's circle of editors wished to be clear, or at least explicit. In their account liberal knowledge was there from the beginning. Seth is in a sense its founder, but his lore comes to him from his father Adam, who acquires it in turn from God Himself (21). Astrology and the other arts survive in modern times, and the pillars are the explanation: the writing on them assured posterity access to this knowledge. But where do the mechanical arts come from? The Bible attributes their invention to individuals who lived before the Flood. How could all their lore come down to us unless it too was inscribed on the pillars? Nature abhors a vacuum, and so do the Alfonsines. It does not need to be repeated that when explanations are lacking in their sources, they are more than eager to supply their own. But this is surely not a wholly satisfactory account of the matter. An impressionist reading of the Alfonsine text would tell us that this motif, the inscription of practical knowledge on the pillars, was a dramatic one, a good piece of *amplificatio*; it frames that body of information, canonizes it, highlights it. A soberer judgment would recall that, as Rico has told us, the transmission of knowledge is an important theme in the *General estoria* (Rico 1972, 159–62), and that on that basis the inclusion on the pillars of practical knowledge along with the liberal can only mean that the mechanical arts are part of official knowledge, just as are the liberal, and that civilization rests on both. I would observe that the initiative of the Alfonsine committee, which draws on absolutely no Islamic materials, nevertheless brings the passage closer in theme to our Hermes chapters in two senses: first because it presents the growth of material culture in a positive light, and second because it pairs off this progress with the parallel growth of astrological knowledge and piety. Both motives are striking not only because they are in some sense uncharacteristic within Western Christian literature but in particular because they contradict the plain sense of the Josephan source, even in the editors' vernacular version of it.

Our second *Estoria* passage about progress, material and other, is also mostly un-Islamic; it is so at least in the sense that no Muslim source is directly quoted or paraphrased. The text comes after the long account of the lineages of Shem, Ham, and Japheth and of the lands their people inhabited. The narrative here takes a strange turn. Proper names disappear, and the text begins speaking in terms of genera and species. "De las primeras costumbres de los omnes" [Concerning the first customs of men], runs one chapter heading, and the text itself begins, "Primera mente, los omnes non creyen en Dios" [At first, men did not believe in God] (Alfonso 1930, 61). The story itself (61–68) is an extraordinary one. It tells, on the one hand, of how successive generations of humans passed step by step from the most abject worship of creatures to that of the one true God and, on the other, of how the same generations in turn passed from a life of the purest savagery, unsupported even by the simplest arts, to one of great sophistication, on a level, shall we say, with that of Alfonso's own time. The text specifies that the subject of this narrative is the Gentiles, or, negatively, those outside the righteous *linna* (line), the forebears of Jesus Christ. The history that is more systematically told is that of religion. The objects of cult of early humans become progressively more noble. The race set out with no religion at all, but then men worshiped successively stones, plants, land animals, fish, and birds. Then, realizing that the play of the four elements was what produced all these other beings, some rendered cult to them, first earth, and then water, air, and fire. At that point comes what we could call the period of the Greco-Roman gods: extraordinary human beings—great rulers, culture heroes, and others—were thought to be divine, and temples were built in their honor. The penultimate stage of this history of religion is a crucial one, the worship of the stars. We should understand that this phase of the story represents entirely living matter to Alfonso and his group. One critical passage in the chapter on astral cults speaks especially of the art of making planetary influences take possession of gems and bits of gold and silver bearing certain magical images. This remarkable practice is, as we know, the subject of no less than two books translated under the Learned King's patronage, the *Picatrix* and the *Lapidario*, versions, significantly, of Arabic texts (*Picatrix* 1962 and Alfonso 1981). The last step in the evolution of religion is, needless to say, the passage from the worship of creatures to that of the Creator. At this point in the text we finally see a proper name: the hero of this moment in history is the patriarch Abraham.

This whole account is notable for its continuity and, I would insist, for its logic. The sequence that concerns us more, the passages on the growth of material culture, is spottier and less organized. The editors of the history seem to concern themselves more with the early parts of their story than with the later. We begin, as I have suggested, with the lack of practical arts of any kind. Humans eat the herbs and fruits that are at hand and clothe themselves, some in leaves, others in the skins of animals. They practice only the most elementary forms of animal husbandry. At the next stage weaving and the building of simple huts out of branches and leaves come on the scene; so does elementary farming and the eating of meat. It is unnecessary to give every stage of this account; cooking evolves, and so does the more artful building of houses. One should note that there are no culture heroes in this story, and that up to this point not a word is said about the higher arts of peace, medicine, the construction of large buildings, city planning, or the laying out of roads and canals. But we are nevertheless invited to believe that the growth of material culture goes the whole route and runs parallel to the prodigious evolution of religion. Thus, we are told that at an advanced stage of the latter, material life had also reached a high point, that temples were nothing but splendid, as were the accoutrements of royalty—crowns and the like. It is obvious that we are supposed to take this moment seriously: the same point in history is marked by its high learning and literary culture (Alfonso 1930, 67). Learning, higher religion, and a solid standard of material life all go hand in hand at this turn of time.

Several points should be made. The first bears on the all-important allusions to sympathetic magic, the induction of astral influences into bits of stone and metal. The lines that speak of this practice do not in any obvious sense have a source, but as I remarked, the lore they speak of is expounded in two books in the Alfonsine canon, both of them taken from Arabic originals, the *Picatrix* and the *Lapidario* (Kahane, Kahane, and Pietrangeli 1969, 449–52 and 456). In the latter the voice of authority, the master and wise man, is none other than Hermes Trismegistus, while the other, as the Kahanes have shown, is frankly Hermetic in much of its scope. One important detail in the long passage in the *Estoria* has, therefore, a plain connection to Islam and to Hermeticism. It is unique: the rest of the text has no such link. The sources, translated or paraphrased, have nothing exotic about them: the lines on the original barbarism of the race are from Cicero's *De inventione* (1.2), scarcely an unfamiliar text; and the passage on the worship of the four elements is a highly elaborated version of a page of Lucas of Tuy's *Chronicon mundi* (see my essay "Abraham in the *General estoria*" in this book, especially note 7). The chapter on the divinization of eminent humans draws on the repertory of any Latinist of Alfonso's time. However, the details about the beginnings of farming, weaving, and the building of houses have only the faintest likeness to the events narrated by the likes of Abu Ma'shar. With the one exception noted, therefore, the *Estoria*'s account of the growth of material life has all the look of an independent construction and owes nothing in detail to Islamic sources.

Our two Alfonsine initiatives, the report of the mechanical arts inscribed on the pillars and the unique account of the progress of the race, are both distinctive: they are deliberate departures on the part of the compilers and as such are meant to be significant. My control material, my term of contrast in this matter, is nothing as vague as the "Western tradition," or some general sense of things expressed broadly in European Christian literature. There is an identifiable body of contrasting texts that let us see clearly where our two passages stand apart. What makes these writings especially eloquent is that, unsystematic as they are, they do have certain things to say about the material culture of early humankind. I have in mind a group of historical works that in some ways are very similar to the *General estoria*. We must recall that Alfonso's great compilation, in many senses highly original, is first and foremost a universal chronicle, and thus it belongs to a well-defined literary genre. Other representatives of the class resemble Alfonso's work in many ways: they tell more or less the same story of the first days; draw on Josephus, Orosius, and Eusebius-Jerome for their information; make much the same mixture of biblical matter with other. Belus, Ninus, and Semiramis appear in all their glory, along with Nimrod and his crew. Euhemerized divinities—Prometheus, Ceres, and others—make their entrances. Quite simply, anyone familiar with the *General estoria* finds himself or herself entirely at home in the world of these other writings. A scrutiny of a few of these should convey to us clearly enough what the Alfonsines were up to in the passages that interest us.

My corpus of histories consists of the *Chronicon universale* of Ekkehard of Aura, the *Two Cities* of Otto of Freising, the *Historia scholastica* of Petrus Comestor, the *Pantheon* of Godfrey of Viterbo, and the *Speculum historiale* of Vincent of Beauvais. To these I can add the chronicle of Hélinand de Froidmont; the chapter headings and the marginalia identifying sources are now accessible in a recent edition (Paulmier-Foucart 1986). I hardly need add that my choice is arbitrary. It is not, therefore, irrational. These works are typical, and the likeness they bear to each other and to the *General estoria* makes the uniqueness of some details of the last all the more striking. What I propose to do first is simply to list some of the allusions in these non-Alfonsine works to the state of human culture after the Fall. I will include references to liberal knowledge and to practical and political without distinction. Ekkehard reports that Jubal invented music and Tubalcain metallurgy. A few lines later the text tells us that since the people of the day knew of Adam's prophecies, they built the two pillars on which they recorded their inventions (Ekkehard 1844, 35). The first detail comes from Isidore (Lucas 1608, 7 [Lucas's *Chronicon* includes Isidore's history]), the second generally from Josephus (Josephus 1958, 132), but the attribution of the pillars to the men of the day, "homines . . . illius temporis," alters somewhat Isidore's meaning. In his version the pillars are built under the direction of Tubalcain; he is the genuine architect, moved to his task by the prophecies of Adam about the coming destruction. Original with Ekkehard also is the thought that early generations had discovered arts and disciplines through God-given talent and intelligence, "per ingenium divinitius traditum per tot annorum vitae spacia diversarum artium et disciplinarum repertores erant" [thanks to the wit and intelligence given them by God, they were over the years of their lives the inventors of various arts and disciplines]. These latter details are not uninteresting. Less weighty, perhaps, are some of the chronicle's other short entries. Zoroaster was the first magician (Ekkehard 1844, 36). Phorneus, son of Inachus and Niobe, was the first to give laws to the Greeks. His sister Io invented the cultivation of barley (37). Prometheus, said to have made men out of the slime of the earth, did so in figure, in that his teaching turned them from brute beasts into humans in the full sense. His brother Atlas, sustainer of the world, was so only in metaphor: he was the first astrologer (38). All of this material comes from the chronologies of Eusebius-Jerome (Eusebius 1923, 35, 47, 51). Otto of Freising for his part preserves the motif of the two pillars, but in his version the writing on them bears not on arts, liberal and mechanical, but on the ceremonies used by the Sethites to honor the one true God (Otto 1912, bk. 1, chap. 2). The chronicle also borrows from Josephus the passage on the prodigious age of the patriarchs as facilitating the growth of arts and sciences (Josephus 1958, 136–37; Otto 1912, bk. 1, chap. 3). Otto mentions the backwardness of early humans to explain the extensive conquests of Ninus; their ignorance of the arts of war in particular makes them vulnerable to his violence and cruelty (1.6). The compiler underlines their uncivilized ways in a coupling of quotations that was to enjoy a certain currency. The first of the pair, from the *Historica ecclesiastica* of Eusebius (1.2.19), is about how men of early days were more bestial than human, lacking a life in common, laws, a moral sense, or arts and sciences. The second is the passage from Cicero's *De inventione* that plays such a crucial role in the *Estoria*'s chapter on human progress, the lines on the barbarism of early times—the irreligion, the lack of lawful wedlock, the poor care of children, the low level of material life (1.6). Otto, like his predecessor Ekkehard, borrows from Eusebius the information that Zoroaster invented magic (1.6); that Prometheus's teaching made his brutish contemporaries genuinely human, men, as it were, out of clay; that Atlas was the first astrologer; and that Atlas's grandson, Mercury, or Hermes Trismegistus, was a great philosopher (1.16). Otto observes in his own words that the Greeks imported agriculture, but that they invented laws on their own, and that they had laws and justice before they had bread (1.16). Finally, he preserves Josephus's proposition that Abraham was learned in the ways of the heavens (1.7).

Petrus Comestor's hand weighs heavily on later chronicles; as we know, he is one of Alfonso's most extensive sources. His version of the pillars episode is his own: in his account the only lore written there is Jubal's art of music. He also preserves the notion that Zoroaster is the inventor of magic, but he takes the further step of identifying him with Ham and, more important, of making him also the inventor of the seven liberal arts; these he inscribes not on two pillars but on fourteen, two for each art (Petrus, column 1090). Petrus also speaks of Abraham's knowledge of astrology (column 1092). All of these elements in Comestor apparently survive in the chronicle of Hélinand (3.113, and 4.87, in Paulmier-Foucart 1986). One chapter in the latter work is a mosaic of many sources, given over entirely to the growth of culture, "de humanibus operibus a diluvio usque ad Abraham" [of the works of humans from the Flood until Abraham] (4.89). The *Pantheon* of Godfrey of Viterbo preserves Petrus's identification of Zoroaster with Ham (Godfrey 1726, 66). Godfrey also includes Josephus's lines on the old age of the patriarchs as facilitating the growth of arts and knowledge (61). A passage on the many contributions to culture by Saturn is apparently of Godfrey's own making (73). So also is his chapter on Jupiter, at once teacher of the liberal arts and promulgator of laws (77). This last section, as we know, is the basis for a brilliant and lengthy sequence in the *Estoria*. Godfrey also coincides with Otto in joining together the bits of Eusebius and Cicero on the barbarism of early times (65). Vincent of Beauvais's treatment of human progress is wholly unlike any of the ones I have discussed to date. Early in his history of the world, he abandons narrative completely, to give us a long treatise on the pitiable condition of fallen man and on the divine remedies for his unhappy state. Vincent presents a series of triplets. The effects of the Fall are ignorance, concupiscence, and infirmity. The remedies for these generally are wisdom, virtue, and necessity. Each of these has a concrete form: wisdom gets embodied in theoretical knowledge, virtue in practical, and necessity in mechanical. Theory in turn breaks down into mathematics, medicine, and theology; practical knowledge into ethics, economics (household management), and politics; and mechanical knowledge into weaving, the making of arms, navigation, agriculture, medicine (*sic*), and theater (Vincent 1473, 4: bk. 2, chaps. 53–55).

So stand our terms of contrast. Further reading in the universal history of those years might bring some new shadings to our picture but hardly any major surprises. The first observation we must make is that much of this medley of information in all of these chronicles is already in the *General estoria:* what the Alfonsines give us in the crucial two passages is not an alternative to the matter in our other texts but, practically speaking, an addition. One might say further that the broad effect of these odds and ends as they appear in the non-Alfonsine texts—the bits about Prometheus, Atlas, and the rest—is less striking than the clear focus in Alfonso in his two passages. The details, in any case, can leave us in no doubt. What is written on the original two pillars? The several answers to this question, Alfonso's and the others, are revealing. In Otto the inscriptions are not about arts in any form, liberal or otherwise. Comestor's account, oddly enough, speaks only of music. Ekkehard's solution alone comes close to what the *Estoria* has to say; his version suggests that human achievements of all kinds are recorded on the pillars. But even here the gap is notable. Ekkehard is vague: it is not clear exactly what arts he is speaking of. If we assume, as we probably should, that they include the mechanical, their presence in the writing on the pillars is unproblematic: he conveys absolutely no sense of anomaly. But by contrast, the Alfonsines inherit and actually translate a text that draws a clear line between the perverse arts of the Cainites and the holy ones of the Sethites, and that insists that only the latter appear on the pillars. The editors, speaking in their own voice, begin by neutralizing this contrast, this in their brief chapter of summary. And they end by declaring their belief, also on their own, that the arts invented by Cain and his descendents were also preserved on the pillars. In other words, the lines in the *Estoria* on the antediluvian arts read like a correction, an emendation of a text they actually transcribe. Alfonso's whole message in this episode is thus made up of three motives: the value of the mechanical arts, the value of the liberal arts, and, finally, the value of piety. We must recall that in Josephus, as in Alfonso, the astrology of the Sethites is closely allied to their holiness and devotion to God. The triplet is, as I think, unique. As we have seen, universal chronicles by no means neglect those moments in history at which humans, individuals and groups, improve themselves and others by their discoveries, but this particular conjunction of themes, material and intellectual progress all linked to holiness, has, as far as I know, no parallel in comparable historical texts.

Our second passage, the string of chapters on the parallel growth of religion and material culture, is also entirely unlike anything we can read in Otto or Comestor. The only text I can recall that comes anywhere close to it is a section of Alfonso's own *Setenario*, his essay on false religion (Alfonso 1984b, 47–67), and even there the argument does not in any way suggest that there was a forward movement, that every new belief brought men closer to God. It certainly does not link different forms of religion to the stages of material life. What the *Estoria* text does have in common with some other chronicles is, of course, the quotation from the *De inventione* on the sorry state of humans in the early days. We recall that this text occurs in approximately the same place in the texts that quote it. In Alfonso the passage from Cicero heads the sequence about progress, but in Otto and Godfrey the fragment stands alone or, at best, is linked to a passage on a local and relatively trivial theme, Ninus's success in warfare. One could say that in a diffuse way the two fragments on primitivism give a sort of color or logic to later moments of the story as they tell it, the steps taken by some to establish civility and law, or the invention of various arts. But all of this taken together is nothing compared to the consistent, continuous, and almost completely abstract narrative that follows Cicero in the Alfonsine work. Needless to say, the explicit pairing of material progress with religion is totally alien to both the earlier histories in all of their parts, close to the Cicero quotation or far.

What, then, does our survey of universal chronicles tell us as we try to establish the place in the *Estoria* of our two passages? The message of the older histories is, I think, very simple. These works surely do not make the case for the advance of culture as eloquently as does Alfonso's compilation, and more important, with one exception we will consider presently, they do not associate the growth of material well-being to the designs and interests of God. This latter motive is, after all, our real quarry. In at least some of its versions Muslim sacred history does include it. It is also beyond doubt that parts of the Hermes sequence in the *General estoria* are based on Islamic material. Witness the motif of the thirty-year heavenly sojourn; the same passage does speak of the mechanical and liberal achievements of the giants in a narrative that seems scarcely biblical or even Christian. On all of these grounds it is credible, to put the matter as modestly as possible, that the themes in our two critical passages show the influence, however diffuse, of Islamic Hermetic literature. Assuredly their substance, line by line, owes little to Koran or Hadith, but their drift and their profile as definitive texts may well run parallel to the certainly Islamic material, not by chance, but thanks to the fully conscious design of the compilers.

I conclude with an anticlimax. The Christian text that comes closest in substance to our two Alfonsine passages is, of course, the section of Vincent of Beauvais's *Speculum historiale*. Theoretical knowledge, practical knowledge, and mechanical knowledge are God's gift to the race to compensate for its ignorance, concupiscence, and infirmity. Vincent in these thoughts might seem to breathe the same air as the Alfonsines; the parallels are obvious. Could the passage in the *Speculum* be the general inspiration for our two loci in the *Estoria*? Two factors in Vincent suggest the contrary. First of all, the set of chapters in the Latin work is not narrative. Its mode of presentation is general and abstract. It deals with the situation of fallen humankind as a whole: it does not touch on particular moments in the early history of the race. One could add incidentally, that in the strictly historical part of his text, Vincent shows no special interest in these moments. Thus, in a very exhaustive index of the *Speculum historiale*, a list made in the early fourteenth century, the only plain reference to arts generally is to this very passage, and the only names of early culture heroes that appear in the index are Prometheus and Atlas. Hermes Trismegistus is also included, but only as a great moral teacher (Hautfuney 1980–81, 2:81 and 3:92). In other words, Vincent, in his history, does not seem to put special emphasis on the growth of the arts; and globally, neither the narrative nor the abstract presentation reflects any unusual interest in this development, this unfolding in time. My second objection is more serious. Vincent speaks of the arts as one set of remedies for the Fall: redeemed humanity enjoys divine support for its intellectual and practical activities as well as for its moral and spiritual ones. As far as I know, nowhere in the *General estoria* do the Alfonsines suggest that the liberal and mechanical arts were meant to offset the effects of original sin.

References

Alfonso el Sabio. 1930. *General estoria*. Part 1. Ed. Antonio G. Solalinde. Madrid: José Molina.

———. 1955. *Primera crónica general de España*. Ed. Ramón Menéndez Pidal. 2 vols. Madrid: Gredos. The pagination over the two volumes is continuous.

———. 1957–61. *General estoria*. Part 2. Ed. Antonio G. Solalinde, Lloyd A. Kasten, and Víctor R. B. Oelschläger. 2 vols. Madrid: Consejo Superior de Investigaciones Científicas.

———. 1981. *Lapidario del rey don Alfonso X*. Edited with notes and vocabulary by Sagrario Rodríguez M. Montalvo, prologue by Rafael Lapesa. Madrid: Gredos.

———. 1984a. *General estoria* (antología). Ed. Milagros Villar Rubio. Barcelona: Plaza y Janés.

———. 1984b. *Setenario*. Edited with an introduction by Kenneth H. Vanderford, introductory study by Rafael Lapesa. Barcelona: Crítica.

Allen, Don Cameron. 1941. *The Star-Crossed Renaissance: The Quarrel about Astrology and Its Influence in England*. Durham: Duke University Press.

Arnulf of Orléans. 1958. *Arnvlfi Avrelianensis Glosvle svper Lvcanvm*. Ed. Berthe M. Marti. Rome: American Academy in Rome.

Ballesteros Gaibrois, M. 1936. *Don Rodrigo Jiménez de Rada*. Barcelona: Editorial Labor.

Billanovich, G. 1951. "Petrarch and the Textual Tradition of Livy." *Journal of the Warburg and Courtauld Institutes* 14:137–208.

Brandt, William J. 1966. *The Shape of Medieval History: Studies in Modes of Perception*. New Haven: Yale University Press.

Caesar, Julius. 1961. *Bellum gallicum*. Ed. Otto Seel. Leipzig: Teubner.

Cancionero de romances. 1550. Antwerp: Martín Nucio.

Castro, Américo. 1954. *La realidad histórica de España*. México: Porrúa.

Catalán, Diego. 1962. *De Alfonso X al conde de Barcelos*. Madrid: Gredos.

———. 1963a. "Crónicas generales y cantares de gesta: El *Mio Cid* de Alfonso X y el del pseudo Ben-Alfaray." *Hispanic Review* 31:195–215, 291–306.

———. 1963b. "El taller historiográfico alfonsí: Métodos y problemas en el trabajo compilatorio." *Romania* 84:354–75.

La chanson des quatre fils Aymon. 1909. Ed. Ferdinand Castets. Montpelier: Coulet et fils.

Cicero. 1913. *De officiis.* Trans. Walter Miller. Cambridge: Harvard University Press; London: William Heinemann.

———. 1949. *De inventione, De optimo genere oratorum, Topica.* With an English translation by H. M. Hubbell. Cambridge: Harvard University Press; London: William Heinemann.

Cole, A. T. 1967. *Democritus and the Sources of Greek Anthropology.* Cleveland: Press of Western Reserve University.

Corpus hermeticum. 1945 and 1954. Vols. 2 and 4. Ed. A.-J. Festugière and A. D. Nock. Paris: Société "Les Belles Lettres."

Crónica albeldense. 1932. In "Las primeras crónicas de la Reconquista: El ciclo de Alfonso III," ed. Manuel Gómez Moreno, *Boletín de la Real Academia de la Historia* 100:600–609.

Crónica del obispo don Pelayo. 1924. Ed. B. Sánchez Alonso. Madrid: Imprenta de los Sucesores de Hernando.

Crónica latina de los reyes de Castilla. 1964. Ed. María Desamparados Cabanes. Textos Medievales 11. Valencia: Nácher.

Crónica najerense. 1966. Introductory study, critical edition, and notes by Antonio Ubieto Arteta. Textos medievales 15. Valencia: Darío de Anúbar.

Crossland, Jessie. 1930. "Lucan in the Middle Ages with Special Reference to the Old French Epic." *Modern Language Review* 25:32–51.

Curtius, Ernst Robert. 1953. *European Literature and the Latin Middle Ages.* Trans. Willard R. Trask. New York: Pantheon.

Dante Alighieri. 1916. *De Monarchia, the Oxford Text.* Ed. E. Moore, with an introduction on the political theory of Dante by W. H. V. Reade. Oxford: Clarendon.

Deyermond, Alan. 1976. "Medieval Spanish Epic Cycles: Observations on Their Formation and Development." *Kentucky Romance Quarterly* 23:281–303.

Donald, Dorothy. 1943. "Suetonius in the *Primera crónica general* through the *Speculum historiale.*" *Hispanic Review* 11:95–115.

Drake, H. A. 1976. *In Praise of Constantine: A Historical Study and New Translation of Eusebius' Tricennial Orations.* University of California Publications: Classical Studies 15. Berkeley, Los Angeles, and London: University of California Press.

Ekkehard of Aura. 1844. *Chronicon universale.* Ed. G. H. Pertz. In *Monumenta Germaniae historica*, scriptorum vol. 6. Hannover: Hahniani.

Entwistle, William J. 1928. "On the *Carmen de morte Sanctii regis.*" *Bulletin hispanique* 30:204–19.

Eusebius. [1479?] *Historia ecclesiastica.* Translated into Latin by Rufinus of Aquileia. Mantua: Johannes Schallus.

———. 1923. *Evsebii Pamphili Chronici canones. . . .* Ed. John Knight Fotheringham. London: Humphrey Milford.

———. 1989. *The History of the Church from Christ to Constantine.* Trans. G. A. Williamson. Revised and edited with a new introduction by Andrew Louth. London: Penguin.

Eutropius. 1979. *Breviarium*. Ed. C. Santini. Stuttgart: Teubner.

I fatti di Cesare: Testo di lingua inedito del secolo XIV. 1863. Ed. L. Banchi. Bologna: Presso Gaetano Romagnoli.

Fernández-Ordóñez, Inés. 1992. *Las "estorias" de Alfonso el Sabio*. Madrid: Istmo.

Festugière, A.-J. 1944. *La révélation d'Hermès Trismégiste*. Vol. 1. Paris: Librairie Lecoffre, Gabalda et Cie.

Li fet des romains, compilé ensemble de Salluste, et de Suétoine et de Lucain. 1938. Ed. L.-F. Flutre and K. Sneyders de Vogel. 2 vols. Paris: Droz; Groningen: J. B. Wolters.

Fita, Fidel. 1884. "Dos libros (inéditos) de Gil de Zamora." *Boletín de la Real Academia de la Historia* 5:131–200.

Fowden, Garth. 1986. *The Egyptian Hermes: A Historical Approach to the Late Pagan Mind*. Cambridge: Cambridge University Press.

Fraker, Charles F. 1990. "How Original is the *Estoria de Espanna*? Problems of Translation and Others." *Romance Languages Annual* 2:395–99.

Fuero juzgo, en latín y castellano. 1815. Madrid: Ibarra, Imprenta de la cámara de S. M.

García Solalinde, A. 1941. "Una fuente de la *Primera crónica general*: Lucano." *Hispanic Review* 9:235–42.

Ghisalberti, Fausto. 1932. *Arnolfo d'Orléans, un cultore di Ovidio nel secolo XII*. Memorie del Reale Istituto Lombardo di Scienze e Lettere 24:157–234.

Ginzler, John. 1971. *The Role of Ovid's "Metamorphoses" in the "General estoria" of Alfonso el Sabio*. Ann Arbor: University Microfilms.

Girart de Roussillon, chanson de geste. 1953–55. Ed. W. Mary Hackett. Société des anciens textes français 96. Paris: A. Picard and J. Picard.

Girart de Vienne. 1977. Ed. Wolfgang Emden. Paris: Société des anciens textes français. Paris: A. Picard and J. Picard.

Godfrey of Viterbo. 1726. *Pantheon*. In *Rerum germanicarum scriptores*, ed. Johann Pistorius, 2:9–392. Ratisbonae: J. C. Peezii.

Gregory, Tullio. 1958. *Platonismo medievale: Studi e ricerche*. Istituto Storico Italiano per il Medio Evo: Studi storici, nos. 26–27. Rome: Nella Sede dell'Istituto.

Hart, Thomas R. 1962. "Hierarchical Patterns in the *Cantar de mio Cid*." *Romanic Review* 53:161–73.

Hautfuney, Jean. 1980–81. *Tabula super 'Speculum historiale' fratris Vincentii*. Spicae: cahiers de l'atelier Vincent de Beauvais, 2:19–263, and 3:11–185.

Herrero Llorente, V. J. 1959. "Influencia de Lucano en la obra de Alfonso el Sabio: Una traducción anónima e inédita." *Revista de Archivos, Bibliotecas y Museos* 67:697–715.

Historia hierosolymitana. 1876. In *Récueil des histoires des croisades: Histoires occidentales*, ed. H. W. and A. R., 3:314–585. Paris: Imprimerie Impériale.

Historia silensis. 1959. Critical edition and introduction by Justo Pérez de Urbel and Atilano González Ruiz-Zorrilla. Escuela de Estudios Medievales, textos vol. 30. Madrid: Consejo Superior de Investigaciones Científicas.

Horrent, Jules. 1961. "La jura de santa Gadea, Historia y poesía." In *Studia philologica: homenaje ofrecido a Dámaso Alonso por sus estudiantes*, 3 vols., 2:241–65. Madrid: Gredos.

Hunt, R. W. 1948. "The Introduction to the 'Artes.' " In *Studia mediaevalia in honorem R. P. Martin O. P.*, ed. B. L. Van Helmond O. P., 85–112. Bruges: De Temple.

Huygens, R. B. C. 1970. *Accessus ad auctores, Bernard d'Utrecht, Conrad d'Hirsau, Dialogus super auctores*. Leiden: E. J. Brill.

Jones, George Fenwick. 1963. *The Ethos of the "Song of Roland."* Baltimore: Johns Hopkins University Press.

Josephus, Flavius. 1602. *The Famous and Memorable Workes of Josephus . . . Faithfully Translated out of the Latin and French by Tho. Lodge*. London: G. Bishop, S. Waterson, P. Short.

———. 1956. *Josephus, with an English Translation*. Trans. H. St. John Thackery and Ralph Marcus. Vol. 1. Cambridge: Harvard University Press; London: William Heinemann.

———. 1958. *The Latin Josephus*. Introduction and text. *The Antiquities*, bks. 1–5, ed. Franz Blatt. Acta jutlandica: Publications of the University of Aarhus 31. Copenhagen: Universitetsforlaget I Aarhus.

Kahane, Henry, and Renée Kahane, in collaboration with Angelina Pietrangeli. 1984. *The Krater and the Grail: Hermetic Sources of the "Parzifal."* Illinois Studies in Languages and Literatures 56. Urbana: University of Illinois Press.

———. 1969. "Hermeticism in the Alfonsine Tradition." In *Mélanges offerts à Rita Lejeune*, 1:443–57. Genbloux: Duculot.

Kiddle, Lawrence B. 1936. "A Source of the *General estoria:* The French Prose Redaction of the *Roman de Thèbes*." *Hispanic Review* 4:264–71.

———. 1938. "The Prose *Thèbes* and the *General estoria:* An Illustration of the Alphonsine Method of Using Source Material." *Hispanic Review* 6:120–32.

Knowles, David. 1962. *The Evolution of Medieval Thought*. London: Longmans.

Lázaro Carreter, F. 1961. "El *modus interpretandi* alfonsí." *Ibérida* 6:97–114.

El Libro de Alexandre. 1934. Texts of the Paris and the Madrid Manuscripts, prepared with an introduction by Raymond S. Willis. Elliott Monographs 32. Princeton: Princeton University Press.

Lida de Malkiel, María Rosa. 1958. "La *General estoria:* notas literarias y filológicas." Part 1. *Romance Philology* 12:111–42.

Linehan, Peter. 1971. *The Spanish Church and the Papacy in the Thirteenth Century*. Cambridge: Cambridge University Press.

———. 1993. *History and the Historians of Medieval Spain*. Oxford: Clarendon.

Livy. 1948 and 1949. (*Ab urbe condita*). With an English translation by Frank Gardner Moore. Vols. 7 and 8. Cambridge: Harvard University Press; London: William Heinemann.

Lory, Pierre. 1988. "Hermès/Idris, prophète et sage dans la tradition islamique." In *Présence d'Hermès Trismégiste*, Cahiers de l'Hermétisme, 100–109. Paris: Albin Michel.

Lovejoy, Arthur O., and George Boas. 1935, reprinted 1965. *Primitivism and Related Ideas in Antiquity*. New York: Octagon Books.

Lucan. *The Civil War*. 1959. Trans. J. D. Duff. Cambridge: Harvard University Press; London: William Heinemann.

Lucas of Tuy. 1608. *Chronicon mundi*. In *Hispaniae illustratae . . . scriptores*, ed. Andreas Schottus, 4:1–116. Frankfurt: C. Marmiani et haeredes Ioannis Aubrii.

Manitius, Max. 1935 [1965]. *Handschriften antiker Autoren in mittelalterichen Bibliothekskatalogen*. Leipzig: Harrassowitz. Reprint, New York: Octagon Books.

Maravall, José Antonio. 1954. *El concepto de España en la edad media*. Madrid: Instituto de Estudios Políticos.

———. 1972. "Un tópico medieval sobre la división de los reinos." *Estudios de historia del pensamiento español*. Madrid: Ediciones Cultura Hispánica, 91–101.

Márquez Villanueva, Francisco. 1994. *El concepto cultural alfonsí*. Madrid: Mapfre.

Massignon, Louis. 1944. "Inventaire de la littérature hermétique arabe." In *La révélation d'Hermès Trismégiste*, ed. A.-J. Festugière, 1: app. 3, 384–400. Paris: Librarie Lecoffre, Gabalda et Cie.

Menéndez Pidal, Gonzalo. 1951. "Cómo trabajaron las escuelas alfonsíes." *Nueva revista de filología hispánica* 5:363–80.

Menéndez Pidal, Ramón. 1923. "Relatos poéticos en las crónicas medievales." *Revista de filología española* 10:329–72.

———. 1941. *Poesía árabe y poesía europea*. Buenos Aires: Espasa-Calpe Argentina.

———. 1946. *Estudios literarios*. Buenos Aires: Espasa-Calpe Argentina.

———. 1951. *Reliquias de la poesía épica española*. Madrid: Espasa-Calpe.

———. 1952. "Alfonso VI y su hermana la infanta Urraca." *Miscelánea histórico-literaria*. Madrid: Espasa-Calpe, 79–88.

———. 1953. *Romancero hispánico (hispano-portugués, americano y sefardí) teoría e historia*. 2 vols. Madrid: Espasa-Calpe.

———. 1955. *Castilla, la tradición, el idioma*. Madrid: Espasa-Calpe.

———. 1969. *La España del Cid*. séptima edición. 2 vols. Madrid: Espasa-Calpe.

———. 1976. *"Cantar de mio Cid": Texto, gramática y vocabulario*. 5th ed., 3 vols., Madrid: Espasa-Calpe.

Meyer, Paul. 1885. "Les premières compilations françaises d'histoire ancienne." *Romania* 14:37–81.

Moncayo, Ann G. 1993. *The Use of Rhetoric in Biographical Portraits of the Twelve Roman Emperors in Alfonso X's "Primera crónica general."* Ann Arbor: University Microfilms.

Nader, Helen. 1979. *The Mendoza Family in the Spanish Renaissance 1350 to 1550*. New Brunswick: Rutgers University Press.

Nasr, Seyyed Hossein. 1981. *Islamic Life and Thought*. Albany: State University of New York Press.

————. 1993. *An Introduction to Islamic Cosmological Doctrines*. Rev. ed. Albany: State University of New York Press.

O'Callaghan, Joseph F. 1975. *A History of Medieval Spain*. Ithaca and London: Cornell University Press.

Orose en français. Morgan Library ms. no. M212.

Orosius. 1882. *Pavli Orosii Historiarvm adversvm paganos libri VII*. Ed C. Zangemeister. Vindobonae: apud G. Geroldi filivm bibliopolam academiae.

Otto of Freising. 1912. *Ottonis episcopi frisingensis Chronicon, sive Historia de duabus civitatibus*. Second edition by Adolphus Hofmeier. Hannover and Leipzig: Hahniani.

Ovid. 1977a. *Heroides and Amores*. With an English translation by Grant Showerman. 2d ed., revised by G. P. Goold. Cambridge: Harvard University Press; London: William Heinemann.

————. 1977b. *Metamorphoses*. With an English translation by Frank Justus Miller. 3d ed., revised by G. P. Goold. 2 vols. Cambridge: Harvard University Press; London: William Heinemann.

Oxford Annotated Bible. 1962. Ed. Herbert G. May and Bruce M. Metzger. New York: Oxford University Press.

Paracelsus. 1894. *The Aurora of the Philosophers*. In *The Hermetic and Alchemical Writings of Aureolus Philippus Theophrastus Bombast, of Hohenheim*, trans. and ed. Arthur Edward Waite, 48–71. London: James Elliott and Company.

Parent, J. M. 1938. *La doctrine de la création dans l'école de Chartres*. Paris: J. Vrin.

Paul the Deacon. 1914. *Pauli Diaconi Historia romana*. Ed. A. Crivellucci. Rome: Tipografia del Senato.

Paulmier-Foucart, M. 1986. "Hélinand de Froidmont: Pour éclairer les dix-huit premiers livres inédits de sa chronique." *Spicae: cahiers de l'atelier Vincent de Beauvais* 4.

Petrus Comestor. 1855. *Historia scholastica*. In J. P. Migne, *Patrologia latina*, vol. 198, columns 1053–1722. Paris: J. P. Migne.

"Picatrix" Das Ziel des Weisen, von Pseudo Magriti. 1962. Translated into German from the Arabic by Helmut Ritter and Martin Plessner. London: Warburg Institute.

Plessner, Martin. 1954. "Hermes Trismegistus and Arab Science." *Studia Islamica* 2:45–59.

Poema de Fernán González. 1951. In *Reliquias de la poesía épica española*, by Ramón Menéndez Pidal, 34–153. Madrid: Espasa-Calpe.

Poema de mio Cid. 1972. Ed. Colin Smith. Oxford: Clarendon.

————. 1976. Ed. Ian Michael. Madrid: Castalia.

Powell, Brian. 1984. "The *Partición de los reinos* in the *Crónica de veinte reyes*." *Bulletin of Hispanic Studies* 61:459–71.

Prelog, Jan. 1980. *Die Chronik Alfons III*. Study and Critical Edition of the four redactions. Frankfurt, Bern, and Cirencester: Peter Lang.

Quinn, E. A. 1945. "The Medieval *Accessus ad auctores*." *Traditio* 3:215–64.

Quintilian. 1920–22. *Institutio oratoria*. With an English translation by H. E. Butler. Vols. 1–4. Cambridge: Harvard University Press; London: William Heinemann.

Raoul de Cambrai, chanson de geste du XIIe siècle. 1924. Ed. Paul Tuffau. Paris: L'Artisan du livre.

Rico, Francisco. 1972. *Alfonso el Sabio y la "General estoria": tres lecciones*. Barcelona: Ariel.

Riquer, Martín de. 1964. *Historia de la literatura catalana*. Vol. 1. Barcelona: Ariel.

———. 1968. *Les chansons de geste françaises*. French translation by Irénée Cluzel. Paris: Librairie Nizet.

Rodrigo Toledano. 1793. *PP. toletanorum quotquot extant opera, Tomus tertius: Roderici Ximenii de Rada, Toletanae eccclesiae praesulis, opera praecipua complectens*. Madrid: apud viduam Ioachimi Ibarra.

———. 1987. *Roderici Ximenii de Rada Historia de rebvs Hispaniae sive historia gothica*. Ed. Juan Fernández Valverde. *Corpvs Christianorvm, Continuatio Mediaeualis* 72. Turnhout: Brepols.

Russell, P. E. 1952. "Some Problems of Diplomatic in the *Cantar de mio Cid* and their Implications." *Modern Language Review* 47:340–49.

Sallust. 1931. *Sallust, with an English translation by J. C. Rolfe*. Cambridge, Mass.: Harvard University Press; London: William Heinemann Ltd.

Sánchez Albornoz, Claudio. 1945. *La sucesión al trono en los reinos de León y Castilla*. Buenos Aires: Academia Argentina de Letras.

Shumaker, Wayne. 1972. *The Occult Sciences in the Renaissance*. Berkeley, Los Angeles, and London: University of California Press.

Sigebert. 1844. *Sigeberti Gemblacensis Chronografia*. Ed. D. Ludowicus Conradus Bethmann. Monumenta Germaniae historica scriptores 6. Hannover: Hahniani.

Smalley, Beryl. 1952. *The Study of the Bible in the Middle Ages*. Oxford: Blackwell.

Smith, C. Colin. 1964. *Spanish Ballads*. Oxford: Pergamon Press.

———. 1971. "The Personages in the *Poema de mio Cid* and the Date of the Poem." *Modern Language Review* 66:580–98.

Sneyders de Vogel, K. 1933. "Recherches sur les *Faits des Romains*." *Romania* 59:41–72.

Statius. 1968. *The Medieval "Achilleid" of Statius*. Edited with introduction, variant readings, and glosses by Paul M. Clogan. Leiden: Brill.

Stock, Brian. 1972. *Myth and Science in the Twelfth Century: A Study of Bernard Silvester*. Princeton: Princeton University Press.

Suetonius. 1886. *C. Suetoni Tranquilli Quae Supersunt Omnia*. Ed. C. L. Roth. Leipzig: Teubner.

Thompson, James Westfall. 1942. *A History of Historical Writing*. Vol. 1. New York: Macmillan.

Usatges de Barcelona. 1933. Ed. J. Rovira i Ermengol. Barcelona: Editorial Barcino.

Vincent of Beauvais. 1473. *Speculum historiale*. 4 vols. Strassburg: Johann Mentelin.

The "Vulgate" Commentary on Ovid's "Metamorphoses": The Creation Myth and the Story of Orpheus. 1991. Ed. Frank T. Coulson. Toronto: Pontifical Institute of Mediaeval Studies.

Walafrid Strabo. 1879. *Glossa ordinaria*. Vol. 1. In J. P. Migne, *Patrologia latina*, vol. 113. Paris: J. P. Migne.

Wallace-Hadrill, D. S. 1960. *Eusebius of Caesarea*. London: A. R. Mowbray and Company.

Wolfram von Eschenbach. 1974. *Parzifal*. Ed. K. Leitzmann. Berlin: W. de Gruyter.

Yates, Frances A. 1964. *Giordano Bruno and the Hermetic Tradition*. New York: Vintage.

Index of Persons

I have omitted from this list references to Alfonso X of Castile. References to fictional characters and to certain obscure historical figures are accompanied by the names (in parentheses) of the works of literature in which they appear. Names of the most famous Romans are listed in their familiar English form, e.g., "Pompey" rather than "Gnaeus Pompeius Magnus."

Charles Fraker is Professor Emeritus of Romance Languages at the University of Michigan.